THE
PASTA
BIBLE

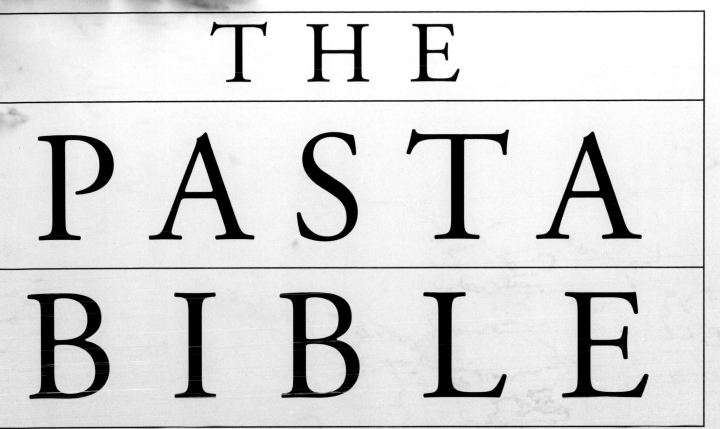

THE PASTA BIBLE

The Definitive Sourcebook, with over 1,000 Illustrations

Christian Teubner
Silvio Rizzi & Tan Lee Leng

whitecap

Contents

First published by Penguin Studio, an imprint of
Penguin Books USA Inc. in 1996.

Original edition published under title
"Das Grosse Buch der Teigwaren – Pasta, Knödel,
Gnocchi"
© 1994 Teubner Edition, Germany

English language text
© 1996 Transedition Ltd., England
All rights reserved

ISBN 1-55285-433-7

Printed & Bound in Dubai
by Emirates Printing Press.

All recipes serve 4 unless stated otherwise.

A tale of pasta

Is the history of pasta at all important? After all, eating and drinking are part of life, and all that really matters after a meal is whether or not it was enjoyable and sustaining. Few classic dishes can be attributed to a creator who might be worthy of a monument; perhaps the only examples are mayonnaise and French *praline*, whose originators are named in the *Larousse Gastronomique*. Even in the case of more recent creations, *cordon bleu* for example, the trail ends somewhere in the grand European hotels of the turn of the century. And from old recipe collections it has been proved that it was not the Tatin sisters who "invented" the upside-down apple and caramel tart, in the sense that Edison invented the light bulb.

There has also been a great deal of bluster about the discovery of pasta, with national pride playing no small part, particularly among the Italians. If dough can be said to be amorphous or unshaped, then pasta becomes a synonym for shaping or designing. There is, in fact, etymological justification for this. The word "dough" is related to the Sanskrit *dheigh*, which means to knead or to work. Thus the dough is an undefined mass waiting to be shaped into noodles and so on. And the word "noodle" itself goes back to the Latin *nodus* or *nodellus*, meaning "node" or "nodule." Remarkably, however, this

"Pasta needs careful preparation" has been the recommendation since time immemorial. *(From the 14th century Domestic manual of the Cerruti family, Austrian National Library, Vienna.)*

loan-word has survived only in English, French (*nouilles*), and German (*Nudeln*).

The German word for knot or node has the same root, and gave rise to the name for another kind of food made of dough, the *Knödel*, or dumplings, of southern Germany and Austria.

"Roll it out on a bench" used to be the instruction for rolling out pasta dough. In the course of time, the "bench" became the kitchen table or the sideboard and, today, a pastry board.

In front of a pasta shop in Apulia, Italy, 1909. As the region developed economically, the spaghetti-maker and -seller played an increasingly important role in the community.

Apicius was one of the first to describe pasta as dough cut into flat strips.

The dim and distant past

The story of the Venetian Marco Polo, who is said to have seen noodles being made in China, and then to have brought some of this new food home with him, is probably just an entertaining anecdote: his account of his journey, dictated in prison in Genoa in 1298, did not become widely available until the invention of printing toward the end of the 15th century. By this time people in southern Italy had long been devouring "*maccheroni*," which is what all pasta, of whatever shape, were called in Naples and Sicily. It seems reasonable to suppose that the idea of making something as simple as pasta dough would occur to all people able to grind wheat sufficiently finely. Making bread by adding yeast seems a positive stroke of genius in comparison.

Something approximating pasta is said to have been identified on Etruscan funerary plaques. And it is now accepted that the Arabs, who knew about durum wheat before the Italians, used to cook thinly rolled sheets of dough. The technique of rolling wheat paste into thin sticks in order to dry it in the sun and thus preserve it has also been attributed to the Arabs. Is that how the hole got into macaroni? The origin of documents in the Museum of Pasta – once located in Pontedassio, a town on the Ligurian Riviera, and now in Rome – is still uncertain. What is curious, however, is that the ancient Romans, on the evidence of recipe collections that have come down to us, do not seem to have prepared any pasta dishes. Perhaps they were simply unsuited to the cuisine of the polite society of that time, whose eating habits were detailed in the writings of both Petronius and Apicius.

Spaghetti eating as a spectator sport

In fact, pasta has never been polite or refined. The *lazzaroni* of Naples, a horde of good-for-nothings and idlers, are said to have subsisted largely on pasta. The scope this offered for showing off can well be imagined: until the 16th century few people used table cutlery, least of all forks, so diners would take long strips of pasta in their hands, tilt their heads backward, and let the pasta slide into their mouths; often they did not even chew it, but simply swallowed it whole. Such artistry was undoubtedly congenial to those of an exhibitionist temperament.

For rich and poor

So we are in Italy. Where else? It was only in that country, not in China or Japan, that pasta became a cult object, the focus of culinary attention, comparable in status with rice in the Far East. The dumplings of Germany can lay no claim to such a success story, and in France there has never been a food of such fundamental, to a certain extent "national," importance. Pasta dishes even reflected the social order in Italy: egg noodles, and meat encased in sheets of pasta, were available for the rich, while the poor had to make do with pasta made from just flour and water, the so-called *pasta asciutta*.

Cutters for making a wide range of stuffed pastas were developed by manufacturers, providing cooks with tools that made it simpler to produce a variety of shapes.

Interior view of a pasta plant around the turn of the century. In this machine room, the dough ingredients were first combined in a mixing machine and then kneaded in a sort of press into a smooth dough before further processing.

Pasta wheels reflect the Italian love of detail. Made of wood, iron, and brass, they cut decorative edges on pasta strips and shapes.

What about the tomatoes?

Nowadays we think of the marriage of pasta and tomatoes as authentically Italian. Of course, the combination cannot be very deeply rooted in the past, since tomatoes were not cultivated in Italy until the 19th century. The abundance and powerful flavor of this solanaceous plant, which includes the deadly nightshade among its relatives, have made it both cheap and popular. However, the tomato was not available all year round until it became an industrial product, first as a concentrated paste in cans or tubes and then peeled, chopped or whole, in cans. Prior to this, the only way of preserving tomatoes was to dry them and keep them in oil, or to seal a ready-made sauce in glass jars especially made for the purpose.

But the producers have not been idle. *Pomodori* – literally, golden apples – now ripen all year round; however, their flavor and texture often leave something to be desired, even in Italy.

The industrial age

The wide range of pasta shapes familiar to us today became possible only through industrial production, which is a relatively recent phenomenon. It is true that, at an early stage, the pasta-obsessed people of

Naples developed various means of hastening the production process, but it wasn't until the early years of the 20th century that the attractively grooved or curved pasta shapes, with their highly imaginative names, were first produced. Large, high-speed presses, designed by inspired engineers in France, Switzerland, and Italy, made this possible.

The French have a saying: there is no cooking without cooks, meaning that culinary discoveries are always made in the kitchen. But this is not the case with dried pasta: certainly as far as shape is concerned, it is a purely industrial product. The Italians do not consider this to be a flaw in any way. Even while fresh pasta continued to be made in many households, factory-made spaghetti, at least, absolutely straight and incredibly long, soon replaced the homemade variety. Older people will remember

that the commercial spaghetti of their youth was bent at one end, as if it had been dried on a rail – a notion that still made sense during the transition from manual to machine production. (You still see some of this spaghetti today.) Italians are not at all suspicious of machines. Indeed, the pride and joy of many Italian restaurateurs is still a device that produces noodles or presses and shapes ravioli. Of course, there are many connoisseurs who are persuaded of the quality of handmade pasta. They avoid machines and willingly accept that making pasta by hand requires extra time and effort.

Pasta spreads throughout the world

The spread of pasta beyond Italy is also part of its history. It is very difficult to explain why the French have never really taken to pasta, even though French cuisine is said to have its roots in the Italy of Catherine De' Medici. She introduced the cooking of her native country to the court of Henri II – and pasta was undoubtedly known in late Renaissance Italy. The reason why Catherine did not bring pasta with her can only be that it was a food for the poor and therefore not suitable for the court. Even Escoffier, who is said to have revitalized 20th-century cooking, includes no pasta dishes in his *Guide Culinaire*, apart from a few Italian-style

Spaghetti can be dried in the open air in Naples thanks to its mild climate; in the damper north of Italy, heated drying rooms are required.

Pasta shapes given their traditional local names. These pages are from catalogs dating from 1916.

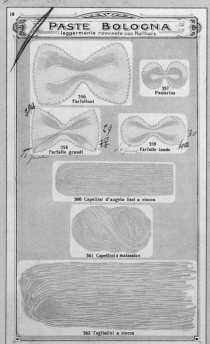

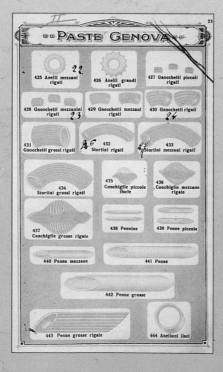

gnocchi and macaroni recipes. It is interesting to note, however, that it was in France that Thomas Jefferson first encountered pasta; he took some macaroni back to the United States in 1786.

All other countries north of the Alps proved to be more receptive, though mainly to industrial pasta, which was cheap and very popular with children. Only in southern Germany and in Alpine regions was there any resistance: the traditional types of German pasta, such as *Spätzle* and *Maultaschen*, a sort of large ravioli, were not completely ousted, not even by really good egg noodles, which are not dissimilar to *Spätzle* in flavor.

Apart from the Chinese, the Italians are the most successful exporters of their national cuisine. Everywhere they open a restaurant – and where are there no Italian restaurants? – they also spread their pasta culture, from North America to Australia, from northern Europe to South Africa. Their most popular export, pizza, is so far ahead in the race as to be unbeatable, but spaghetti is hot on its heels. Even the French are now beginning to learn how to wrap the long strands around their forks and raise them to their mouths. Asian noodles, like the colorless cellophane or bean thread noodles, for example, or soba buckwheat noodles, are gaining in popularity, but they are eaten most often in restaurants, where diners fish the slippery strands out of soups or, when they are served fried, enjoy their crunchiness.

Astonishingly, the development of stuffed pasta followed virtually the same path in Italy and in China. Chinese ravioli differ only slightly from the Italian version. Who learned what from whom remains unclear to this day. The only thing the Italians have never tried their hand at, despite their passion for things artistic, is the technique of repeatedly stretching a ball of dough until it forms thin noodles.

Pasta makes it to the top

The multicultural cuisine of our time has certainly muddled everything up. The Japanese now eat spaghetti, the Italians eat cellophane noodles, and the top cooks in all countries have discovered that pasta stuffed with various fillings is a great delicacy, regardless of whether it is called "*raviolis*," as in France, or wonton, or whether it is boiled, steamed, or fried. And a few paper-thin noodles – homemade of course – enliven the ambitious menus of leading chefs everywhere. Fresh pasta, whether commercially prepared or homemade, has even penetrated the domestic kitchen, with more and more cooks trying to emulate the Italian pasta specialists.

Pasta beyond Italy

Everyone is now aware that pasta is treated differently at mealtimes in Italy. The Italians have always considered pasta to be worthy of a course in its own right, the *primo*, which comes before the *secondo*, or entrée. The three-course meal, consisting of *antipasti* (hors d'oeuvres), *primo* (pasta or risotto), and *secondo* (meat or fish, possibly accompanied by vegetables), has remained more or less unchanged, even in the upper reaches of Italian gastronomy, while to the north of the Alps, and elsewhere in the world, different customs have emerged. There, pasta is either used as an accompaniment to meat and as a vehicle for sauces of all kinds, or forms the main course, whether as a dish of spaghetti or other pasta with various ingredients or as part of a dish baked in the oven.

There is not a great deal to be said about noodles as a side-dish, and every cook knows they are delicious simply dressed with a little melted butter or extra-virgin olive oil. Egg noodles are the favorite choice as a side-dish for roasts and their gravy. And for those seeking a little more variety in their side-dishes, the imaginatively shaped products of the pasta industry, such as bow ties (*farfalle*) or wagon wheels (*rotelle*), can be recommended, as can the combinations of yellow, red, green, and other colored pastas that are now available.

One-dish meals for hungry families include the familiar and well-loved macaroni and cheese, lasagne of all kinds, manicotti and cannelloni, spaghetti and meatballs, an endless variety of pasta casseroles, and traditional German types of pasta, such as *spätzle*, that are often served with browned onions and rich, melting cheese.

A page from an Art Nouveau calendar – an allegorical representation of Ceres, the Roman goddess of agriculture. She is fertilizing the Earth with a cascade of golden pasta.

North of the Alps noodles are often served separately, as a side-dish, for example as an accompaniment to meat stews. They are a delicious way of soaking up the gravy.

The grain

This is the basis of pasta; water is all that is necessary to make dough from flour

From a botanical point of view, the term "cereal" denotes cultivated or semi-cultivated plants that belong to the grass family (Gramineae, Poaceae). The fruits of these plants are called grains, and are an important foodstuff for both human beings and animals. Other plants with grain-like fruits, such as buckwheat, a member of the genus *Fagopyrun*, are usually defined as suborders of the cereals. Cereals are the most important agricultural crops in the world. In addition to their use in the production of bread, they are used all over the world to make pasta. Wheat and rice play a particularly important role in this respect.

A BOTANICAL STUDY

The grain of cereals is a monospermous, or one-seeded, fruit that belongs botanically to the group of indehiscent fruits, because on ripening it does not automatically split open in order to release the seed. Since the three layers of the pericarp (the epicarp, mesocarp, and endocarp) not only form a hard, woody husk but are also so tightly fused to the testa, or seed coat, that they cannot be separated, the fruit is a "caryopsis."

The grains of the various cereals are similar in appearance and structure. They consist of the outer covering or husk (the pericarp and seed coat), the endosperm, and the embyro or germ. The grains of barley, oats, rice, and millet have glumes with pointed, needle-shaped projections tightly fused to the pericarp, known as awns; these are not detached from the grain even during threshing. Wheat and rye, however, have no glumes. The diagram on page 13 uses the example of wheat to depict the structure of a cereal grain. Bran, which is rich in fiber or roughage, an aid to digestion and thus of great importance to the human diet, consists of the outer covering and the aleurone layer. The endosperm – to which the aleurone layer belongs in botanical terms – contains starch grains, which are enclosed in a thin layer of protein. The embryo or germ is the primary store of substances essential to a newly developing plant, and contains everything required for building new life. This unique combination of foods is also of value to human beings, since it provides everything needed for a nutritious diet. The high-quality store of nutrients can be made available for human use either by grinding (milling) the whole grain to make flour or by waiting for germination to start and then eating the grains and the shoots growing from them. Flour obtained solely from the endosperm is best suited to making dough and for baking, but it lacks the nutrients contained in the bran and germ.

Wheat (*Triticum*). Various forms of wheat have been the most important cereal in many parts of the world for thousands of years. It is native to Eurasia. Breeding and selection have led to the development of cultivated forms whose different qualities are used in a variety of ways in the kitchen. Commercial pasta is produced mainly from hard durum wheat (*Triticum durum*). As a summer wheat, it prefers warmth and can survive with little rain, conditions that prevail especially throughout the summer in the northern part of the United States and in Canada. The gluten-rich flour it provides produces a firm dough ideally suited to being kneaded or cut into shape. Mixed with starchy soft wheat (*Triticum aestivum*), it also fulfills all the demands made by baking. **Spelt** (*Triticum spelta*) is closely related to soft wheat. Unlike soft wheat, however, the grains of spelt are enclosed by glumes. Its gluten-rich flour was for a long time the basis for the flour-based desserts and baked goods of parts of Germany. **Unripe spelt grain**, called *grain de blé vert* in France, is spelt that has been harvested while it is still unripe and green. It is dried in kilns, which gives it a robust, full-bodied flavor. **Rice** (*Oryza sativa*) is the staple food of many parts of Asia. Rice grows in the humid tropics and subtropics. Because of its high rate

of transpiration it requires a plentiful supply of water. For this reason, it is grown mainly in paddy fields which are flooded for a large part of the growing period. There are many different species of rice, divided according to the shape and size of the grain into long-grain, medium-grain, and short or round-grain rice. **Buckwheat** (*Fagopyrum esculentum*). A close relative of sorrel and rhubarb, buckwheat produces reddish-brown, triangular seeds, $1/8$ to $1/4$ inch in length and similar in appearance to beechnuts. The flour obtained by grinding the seeds is used in breads and pancakes, including blini, and to make noodles. **Millet** (*Panicum miliaceum*). The term millet denotes a number of tropical and subtropical cereals that produce small seeds or grains on drooping, loosely branched flower clusters.

Millet flour lacks gluten, so is usually mixed with wheat flour for baking breads. **Barley** (*Hordeum vulgare*) is not of great importance in the production of pasta. In many countries, barley flour is used on its own, to make round, flat loaves, but it is usually mixed with durum wheat for noodles and similar products, since it contains no gluten. Malting barley is of great importance throughout the world as a basic ingredient for beer. **Oats** (*Avena sativa*) are also of little significance in the manufacture of pasta. However, wholegrain products made from oat bran and durum wheat are available commercially. **Corn** (*Zea mays*) is a basic foodstuff for millions of people, particularly in the Americas and parts of Italy. The different varieties of corn are classified according to the starch content of the grains. The various types

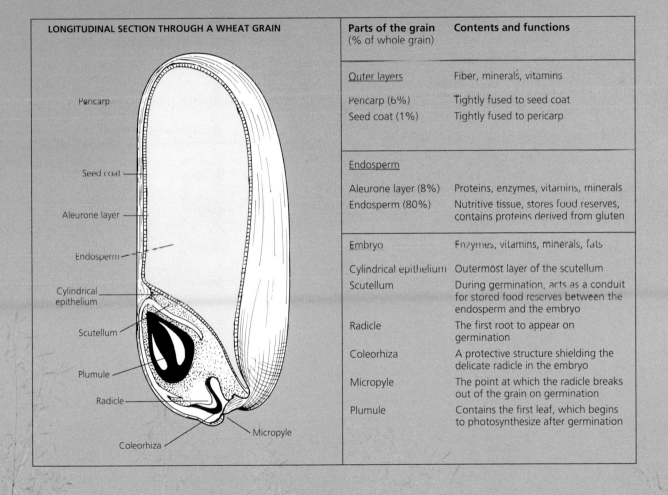

LONGITUDINAL SECTION THROUGH A WHEAT GRAIN	Parts of the grain (% of whole grain)	Contents and functions
Pericarp	Outer layers	Fiber, minerals, vitamins
	Pericarp (6%)	Tightly fused to seed coat
	Seed coat (1%)	Tightly fused to pericarp
Seed coat	Endosperm	
Aleurone layer	Aleurone layer (8%)	Proteins, enzymes, vitamins, minerals
	Endosperm (80%)	Nutritive tissue, stores food reserves, contains proteins derived from gluten
Endosperm	Embryo	Enzymes, vitamins, minerals, fats
Cylindrical epithelium	Cylindrical epithelium	Outermost layer of the scutellum
Scutellum	Scutellum	During germination, acts as a conduit for stored food reserves between the endosperm and the embryo
Plumule	Radicle	The first root to appear on germination
Radicle	Coleorhiza	A protective structure shielding the delicate radicle in the embryo
Micropyle	Micropyle	The point at which the radicle breaks out of the grain on germination
Coleorhiza	Plumule	Contains the first leaf, which begins to photosynthesize after germination

include dent corn, in which the inner part of the endosperm is soft; flint corn, which has a hard endosperm; sweet corn; and waxy corn. Corn is used in a great variety of ways in the kitchen, including as a vegetable, in breakfast cereals, as a coarse or fine meal used in breads and muffins and in polenta and grits, and as cornstarch, corn syrup, and corn oil. It is also widely used as an animal feed.

GLUTEN

The endosperm of a grain of wheat contains special proteins that make the wheat suitable for baking, even though they have no particular nutritive properties. Gluten, as these proteins are called, gives wheat flour the right "feel" and influences its baking performance; it also gives pasta, breads, and cakes the right texture because the proteins turn thready and sticky on contact with water. The most important of these proteins, in volume terms, are gliadin and glutelin. As soon as the flour comes into contact with water, the proteins swell. They bind the liquid in the dough and at the same time combine with the fats in the wheat itself. During the baking of bread, for example, the liquid bound by the gluten turns into steam. The air contained in the dough expands, thus producing an open, porous texture. At about 158°F, the gluten coagulates and combines with the starch in the flour to form the desired crumb texture.

Wheat contains a considerably higher proportion of gluten than rye or other cereals, which is why wheat has been known for hundreds of years as the best cereal for baking. Rye contains little gluten, thus rye flour needs to be supplemented with a leaven of fermented wheat dough in order to make a dough that is sufficiently elastic to be worked and remain in shape. Corn, rice, millet, and buckwheat contain no gluten and therefore cannot be used on their own to make flour for baking bread. Nevertheless, the starch they contain makes them suitable for gluten-free products, which are important in the diet of people who suffer from celiac disease, a disorder of the small intestine triggered by cereal protein.

Gluten content is of great importance in the manufacture of pasta. Durum wheat, being very high in gluten, makes the best pasta flour, which is why it is often added to other flours in order to improve their structure for pasta-making. Thus noodles made with soy or millet flour will contain a high proportion of semolina flour milled from the endosperm of hard durum wheat.

FROM GRAIN TO FLOUR

The various types of flour made from each cereal can be clearly distinguished from each other at a glance: light-colored flours are produced solely from the white endosperm, while darker flours also include the outer coverings of the grain (it is the bran that gives color). A dark flour is a "wholefood" product in the truest sense of the term, since it contains not only the starchy part of the grain but also the nutritionally important bran and germ, i.e. the aleurone layer, the pericarp and seed coat, and the highly nutritious embryo. However, since the fat in the embryo becomes rancid and bitter very soon after crushing, whole-wheat flour does not have a very long shelf life.

The process of milling flour begins by cracking the wheat kernels, and separating the bran and germ from the endosperm. For white flours, all of the bran and germ are sifted out, and the endosperm only is ground to the desired degree of fineness. As a result, white flour retains only about 25 percent of the original nutrients. U.S. law requires that any wheat flour not containing the germ must have certain nutrients added back (niacin, riboflavin, thiamin, and iron, as well as vitamins A and D in some cases); this flour is labeled "enriched." In whole-wheat flour, 100 percent of the husked kernel is retained – the bran, germ, and endosperm – by being recombined after grinding.

After milling, white wheat flour is light yellow in color. It will turn white naturally, through oxidation, in a month or two (such flours will be labeled "unbleached"), but to speed up the process, flour is often bleached with chlorine dioxide. While the color is purely an aesthetic consideration, the age of the flour is of importance, because maturation does improve the flour's baking qualities. Again, this natural process is normally hastened by means of chemicals.

White wheat flour type 00 *The type of flour most commonly used for making pasta in Italy.*

All-purpose flour *Fine-textured blend of hard and soft wheats; suitable for all cooking and for making pasta.*

Cake or pastry flour *Soft-wheat, low-gluten flour; makes tender cakes and pastries, but is not suitable for pasta.*

Semolina flour for pasta *Durum wheat flour, more coarsely ground than normal wheat flours.*

Whole-wheat flour *Contains the wheat germ. It makes pasta with a nutty flavor, and firm texture.*

Wheat bran *Has the highest vitamin and mineral content. It is often added to breads and breakfast cereals.*

Rye flour *Contains less gluten than wheat flours. It produces pasta that retains a slight chewiness when cooked.*

Corn meal *When mixed with flour containing gluten, it is suitable for making pasta and noodles.*

Rice flour *An important starch in Asian countries, where it is the basis for noodles and rice-paper wrappers.*

Oat flour *When used in baked goods, it must be combined with a flour that contains gluten.*

Spelt flour. *A protein-rich flour. Pasta dough produced from it has a pleasant smell and a mellow, nutty flavor.*

Unripe spelt flour. *Produced from spelt grain harvested when still unripe. It has a more robust flavor.*

Dried pasta

Bakers tend to be somewhat envious of pasta-makers. Bread does not taste at its best unless it is freshly baked every morning. Pasta, on the other hand, can be dried and stored for a long time – but not for years and years, as the "use-before" dates on the packages would have us believe. Dried egg noodles in particular quickly lose their flavor and should be consumed within six months.

Dried pasta is not only a popular product but is also very simple, consisting only of durum wheat flour and water, or of durum wheat flour, water, and eggs (pasteurized or dried). In recent years, the familiar pale yellow color has been supplemented by green, red, and even chocolate-brown pastas and by the dark gray of whole-wheat and other wholegrain pastas. The latter are made of coarsely ground flour, from the entire kernel of wheat or other cereals, whose vitamin and fiber content make it more nutritious than pastas made from white flour.

Although fresh pasta is becoming increasingly popular, particularly in restaurants, commercial dried pasta is still the ultimate convenience food. It is cheap, it can be prepared without any great culinary skill, and it is popular with children and adults alike. Italian restaurants are now found almost everywhere, and as a result spaghetti has conquered the world. It is even making inroads in France, a country hitherto unreceptive to pasta. The boom in fresh pasta has done nothing to reduce its popularity. Anyone who has ever been to Tuscany, and seen how *pinci* are laboriously rolled and thrown over the shoulder, will breathe a sigh of relief the next time they shake the brittle sticks of pasta from their bag or box into boiling water.

Dried noodles are also a familiar sight in Asia, particularly in China and Japan. Some are made from wheat flour and eggs, as in Europe, while others, like the remarkable cellophane noodles, are fashioned from mung beans. From Japan come milky-white rice noodles and somen noodles, which look as though they have been varnished but lose their sheen when cooked. In Asia, it is said that long noodles, whether flat or rounded, promise long life. And who would want to shorten it by eating pasta in the shape of little crescents or ears? However, the real reason for their popularity is probably that long noodles are easier to eat with chopsticks than small, slippery shapes.

The stream in Fara San Martino *is a picturesque sight. Its water is used in the production of dried pasta.*

Absolutely natural

And yet a wholly industrial product

This seems at first sight to be a contradictory assertion. However, it is accurate to the extent that the ingredients of pasta, namely flour, water, and, in some cases, eggs, are natural products that are simply combined with each other and processed into pasta. In this sense, industrial technology is merely an aid to the production of large quantities of this simple yet immensely versatile food. In Italy, the pasta industry became established in those areas where the best conditions for pasta-making existed, and particularly in regions where climatic conditions meant that pasta could be dried outdoors. Such conditions exist in the Parma area, in Naples, and in Abruzzi. Among the rocky slopes of Abruzzi, there is a small town where nature is still largely undisturbed. The River Verde has its source here, and its fresh, perpetually cool, crystal-clear spring water flows directly into the factories where much of Italy's pasta is made. For decades, amid the magnificent scenery of a national park, a food has been manufactured that is as simple and natural as it is possible to be, although in fact it is a wholly industrial product.

The durum wheat used to make pasta comes from Italy, as well as from North America and from Britain – wherever conditions guarantee a high-quality crop.

While the ingredients of pasta are highly standardized, the shapes and names of pasta products are extremely varied. In Italy, the term *"pasta secca"* includes all dried pasta, both *"pasta lunga,"* or long pasta, and *"pasta corta,"* short pasta. Some names,

Durum wheat and eggs, *plus water, are the ingredients of most pasta doughs in Europe and North America.*

each grade having its own number. As already noted, however, the same numbers are not used by all manufacturers. It is also possible to exploit the elasticity of the Italian language to good effect: thus, among the ribbon noodles, *tagliolini* are narrower than *taglierini,* which in turn are narrower than tagliatelle. The confusion is complete when narrow ribbon noodles are also sold as lasagne. As with the numbers, the names for ribbon noodles of varying widths are far from standardized.

Consumers should therefore seek reassurance in the following motto: if it tastes good, it is good, irrespective of what it's called. And yet the shape of pasta is more important than is often thought. Simply achieving a balanced combination of texture, taste, and sauce turns a pasta meal into an exquisite culinary experience.

Eggs are an important ingredient in certain types of pasta. They make them light and pliable, give them a warm yellow color, increase their nutritional value, and impart a full-bodied taste. Hens' eggs are undoubtedly an important source of food for human beings, but those who would make fresh egg pasta need to take account of the fact that fresh eggs and food made from them have a limited shelf life. When purchasing eggs, it is necessary to ensure that the shells are clean and undamaged: bacteria and other disease-causing agents contained in dirt, particularly salmonella, can penetrate the porous shell and make the eggs unfit for consumption. The longer eggs are stored, the greater the risk of contamination. Regulations ensure that eggs sold

Fresh mountain air for drying pasta is a relic of the past. Fully automated climatic chambers now provide constantly monitored, standardized conditions for the drying of pasta. Machines are also used to cut the dough into shape. Nothing is left to chance.

such as spaghetti, macaroni, tagliatelle or fettuccine, and pappardelle, are known everywhere, while others are much less familiar.

In order to distinguish their products from those of their competitors, individual pasta manufacturers also give their varieties numbers. Thus, various grades of spaghetti are available, ranging from the very fine *capellini* through *spaghettini, spaghetti,* and *spaghettoni* to the flatter *linguine* and *fettucelle,* with

commercially be marked with either the date on which they were laid or the date by which they should be consumed. The same regulations decree that all eggs should be kept under refrigeration. Nevertheless, it is strongly recommended that all homemade pasta containing fresh eggs be consumed immediately and not dried for future use. The pasta industry offers a wide range of perfectly safe products for the pantry.

• Spaghetti

• Vermicelli

• Whole–wheat spaghetti

• Spaghetti

• Spaghetti

Spaghetti and macaroni

Shapes synonymous with pasta

Spaghetti is long, usually round, and of variable thickness. Thicker types, with a hole running through them, turning them, so to speak, into tubes, are called macaroni. Pasta shapes made from the same kind of dough taste exactly the same, however they look. Thus it is the shapes – basically the diameter in the case of long noodles – and hence the names that bring variety to the range of pastas. Diversity is also achieved through different types of dough, some made from wholegrain flours.

• Capellini

• Capellini

• Fedelini

• Spaghettini

• Spaghettini

• Spaghettini, vermicelli

• Spaghetti verdi – with spinach

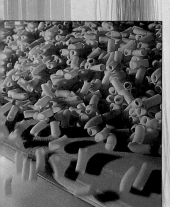

High-quality pasta demands optimal drying conditions: low temperatures from 140° to 160°F and up to 15 hours' drying time. Spaghetti hangs like a curtain on long iron bars. Tagliatelle and fettuccine are placed in pipes through which currents of air rise, first shaping the pasta into nests and then drying it.

• Spaghettoni

■ Spaghetti alla chitarra

○ Perciatellini

○ Bucatini, perciatelli

○ Perciatelloni

○ Fusilli lunghi

○ Mezze zite

○ Macaroni (Germany)

○ Zite, mezzanelli

○ Zite

Infinite care and great attention to detail are essential parts of the production process. In the picture above, dried lumaconi rigati are passing over a belt that shakes and separates them before they are finally weighed and packed.

Zite, ziti

○ Zitoni

Maccheroni alla genovese

Linguine, bavette

Linguine

Linguine integrali – whole-wheat

Linguine

Trenette

Fettucelle ovale

Fettucelle integrali – whole-wheat

Taglioni fini

Taglieri

Tagliatelle

Tagliatelline

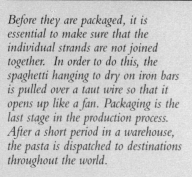

Before they are packaged, it is essential to make sure that the individual strands are not joined together. In order to do this, the spaghetti hanging to dry on iron bars is pulled over a taut wire so that it opens up like a fan. Packaging is the last stage in the production process. After a short period in a warehouse, the pasta is dispatched to destinations throughout the world.

— Fettucelle

— Tagliatelle
— Tagliatelle integrali – whole-wheat

— Capelli d'angelo

— Fettuccine

— Fettuccine verdi – with spinach

— Lasagnette

— Lasagne

Riccitelle, tripolini

— Pappardelle

— Pappardelle festonate

— Pappardelle

— Pappardelle

Lasagne integrali – whole-wheat

Trinette, mafalda

Reginette

Lasagne festonate lunghe

Lasagne ondine

Lasagne

Tagliardi, green

Tagliardi, white

Sagnarelli

Farfalline
(small bow ties

Tacconelli

Maltagliati, large

Farfalloni

Nastrini,
farfalline

Tortelli

Maltagliati, small

Farfalle
(bow ties)

Galle rotonde

Cannelloni integrali – whole-wheat

Pasta squares
(Israel)

Farfalle
(bow ties)

Canestrini

Cannelloni

Quadrucci

Cravattine

Galle quadre

Riccioli

Casereccie, gemelli

Cappelletti

Banane

Casereccie

Sorprese

Conchiglie (jumbo shells)

Strozzapreti

Conchiglie (small shells)

Conchiglioni da ripieno

Fileia del Calabrese

anierine

Conchiglie (medium shells)

Conchiglioni

Radiatori

Lumaconi
rigati grandi

Hörnchen – whole-wheat
(Germany)

Hütli, trulli (Switzerland)

Gramigna

Tortiglioni, elicoidali

Lumaconi rigati medie

Hörnchen (Germany)

Dischi volanti

Spaccatelle

Rigatini

Pipette, fischiotti,
chiocciole

Creste di gallo

Spiralen (Germany)

Spaccatelle integrali –
whole-wheat

Pipette integrali –
whole-wheat

Chifferi rigati

Fusilli rigati, cellentani

Fusilli col buco,
fusilli corti

Eliche, thick

Lumacine

Chifferotti rigati

Sigarette mezzini

Eliche, thin

Eliche integrali
– whole-wheat

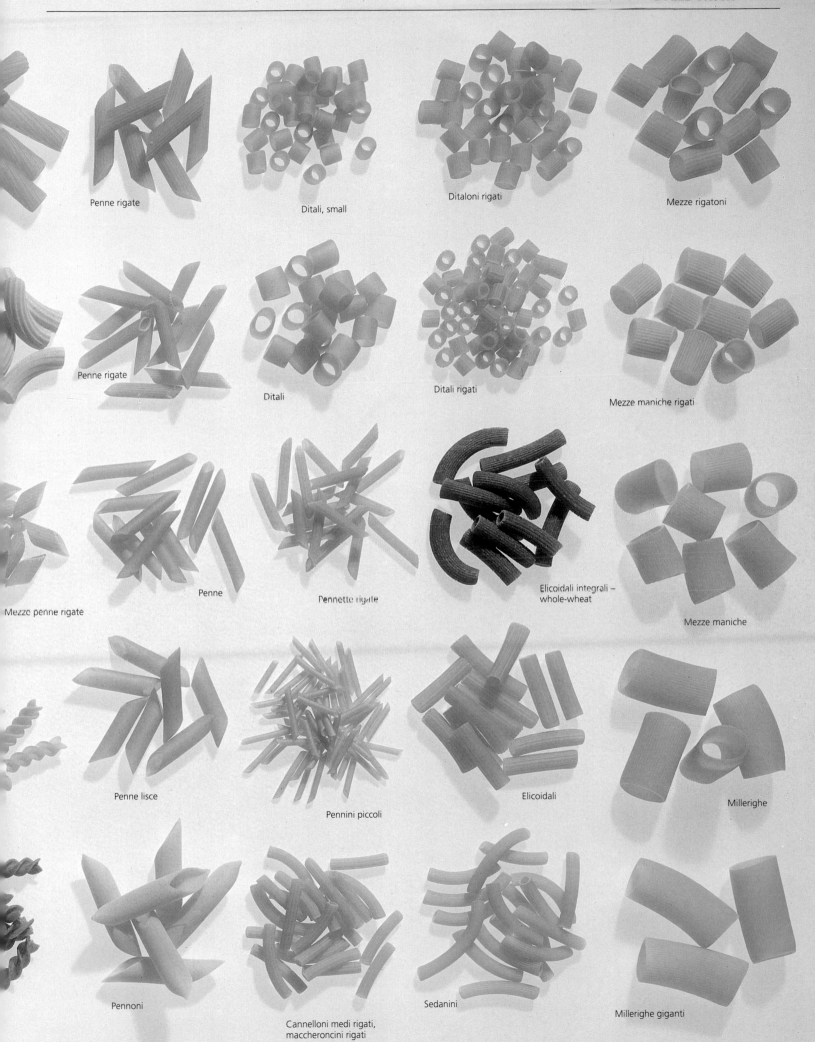

Penne rigate

Ditali, small

Ditaloni rigati

Mezze rigatoni

Penne rigate

Ditali

Ditali rigati

Mezze maniche rigati

Mezze penne rigate

Penne

Pennette rigate

Elicoidali integrali –
whole-wheat

Mezze maniche

Penne lisce

Pennini piccoli

Elicoidali

Millerighe

Pennoni

Cannelloni medi rigati,
maccheroncini rigati

Sedanini

Millerighe giganti

Gnocchi

Gnocchetti sardi

Essentially a substitute

Pasta for cooks in a hurry

Commercially made dried pasta is a boon for all cooks who are short of time, but it must be said that many dried pastas cannot compare with fresh in terms of taste. Dried Sardinian *gnocchi* and dried *orecchiette*, for example, never taste as good as their fresh counterparts: they are, and always will be, a substitute. In the case of dried *spätzle*, even this does not apply, since they have nothing at all in common with the fresh product and have to be regarded as a new and different form of pasta altogether.

Gnocchi rigati

Malloreddus, fini

Gnocchi integrali
– whole-wheat

Garganelli

Orecchiette

Gnobetti

Rotelle rigate
(wagon wheels)

Spätzle

Orecchiette
(little ears)

Gnobette d'Abruzzo

Rotelle, ruote
(wagon wheels)

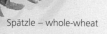

Spätzle – whole-wheat

Cavatielli

Gnobetti, larg
(Sardinia)

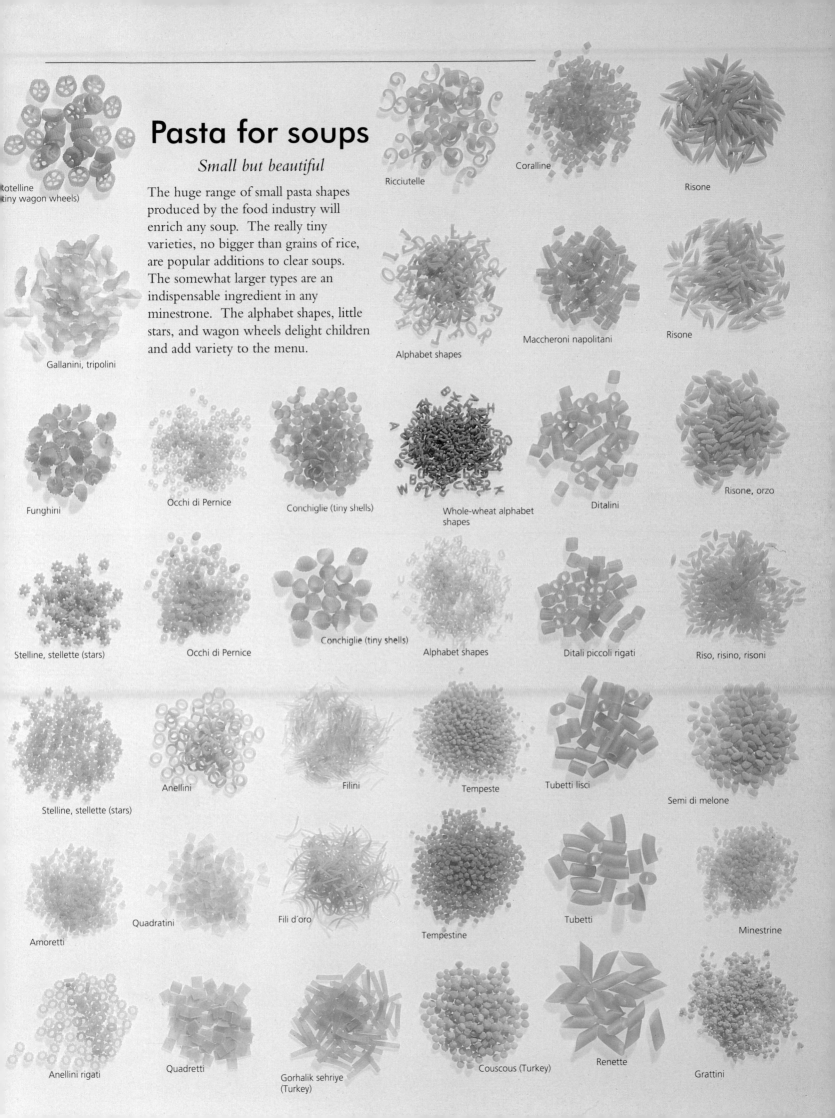

Pasta for soups

Small but beautiful

The huge range of small pasta shapes produced by the food industry will enrich any soup. The really tiny varieties, no bigger than grains of rice, are popular additions to clear soups. The somewhat larger types are an indispensable ingredient in any minestrone. The alphabet shapes, little stars, and wagon wheels delight children and add variety to the menu.

Rotelline
(tiny wagon wheels)

Gallanini, tripolini

Funghini

Occhi di Pernice

Conchiglie (tiny shells)

Whole-wheat alphabet
shapes

Ditalini

Risone, orzo

Stelline, stellette (stars)

Occhi di Pernice

Conchiglie (tiny shells)

Alphabet shapes

Ditali piccoli rigati

Riso, risino, risoni

Stelline, stellette (stars)

Anellini

Filini

Tempeste

Tubetti lisci

Semi di melone

Amoretti

Quadratini

Fili d'oro

Tempestine

Tubetti

Minestrine

Anellini rigati

Quadretti

Gorhalik sehriye
(Turkey)

Couscous (Turkey)

Renette

Grattini

Ricciutelle

Coralline

Risone

Alphabet shapes

Maccheroni napolitani

Risone

Penne rigate

Eliche – with oat bran

Twisted ribbon noodles

Taglierini – with millet

Casarecce, strozzapreti, gemelli

Eliche – with coarsely ground rye

Whole-wheat noodles – with soy

Taglierini – with spelt

• Spaghetti – with cornmeal

Mezze penne rigate – with buckwheat

Eliche – with spinach

Curly noodles

Tagliolini

Tagliatelline – with dried cèpe

Pasta curls

Eliche – with unripe spelt

Farfalle

Whole-wheat noodles – with spinach

Tagliatelline – with spelt and unripe spelt

Sigarette

Fusilli – with cornmeal

Radiatore – with onion

Tagliolini – with soy

Fettuccine – with soy

Gramignina – with soy

Fusilli – with cornmeal and spelt

Radiatore – with nettle and carrot

Fettuccine – with soy

Whole-wheat noodles – with spelt

Whole-wheat pasta

A wide range of shapes to choose from

These are mainly made from durum wheat flour and/or durum wheat semolina. There are also whole-wheat pastas made from other kinds of flours, but, since wheat flour is the only one that contains the gluten that gives the dough the required texture, it will be included to some degree. Whole-wheat pasta is becoming increasingly available, in wholefood markets, health-food stores, and supermarkets.

- Spaghetti – with rye

Linguine

- Spaghetti – with soy

- Spaghetti – with cornmeal

- Spaghetti – with wheatgerm

- Spaghetti – with seaweed

○ Spaghetti – with soy

- Spaghetti

○ Macccheroni – with wheatgerm

Lasagne

Tagliatelle – with squid ink

Tagliolini al peperoncino –
with hot chili

Fettuccine con spinaci –
with spinach

Tagliatelle with hot chili

Nidi di taglioni
– with squid ink

Tagliatelle – with tomato

Spaghetti al
peperoncino rosso
– with red pepper

Tagliatelle con orticia –
with nettle

Lasagne verdi – with
spinach

Nidi di taglioni – with
salmon

Tagliatelle
– with spinach

Penne rigate con spinaci –
with spinach

Fettuccine – with beet

Tagliolino, taglierini – with
spinach

Penne al
peperoncino
– with hot ch

Matasse – with spinach

Matassine
– with spinach

Cannelloni verdi – with
spinach

Orecchiette – with spinach

Colored pasta

A feast for the eyes

The pasta industry has not only produced a wide range of shapes but also introduced even greater diversity by adding a variety of colors. The main purpose here is to delight the eye. The addition of spinach, tomato, beet, squid ink, or saffron gives the most familiar pasta shapes an attractive color; true, it loses intensity during cooking, but it still offers innovative cooks a chance to create pleasing designs on the plate. The taste of these colorings in the finished dish is not generally very noticeable, unless the coloring agent is also added to the water used to boil the pasta or the pasta is cooked in an appropriately flavored stock.

Cappelletti – plain, with tomato, with spinach

Farfalline – plain, with tomato, with spinach

Gnocchetti sardi – plain, with tomato, with spinach, with saffron

Conchigliette – plain, with tomato, with spinach

Rotelline – plain, with tomato, with spinach

Hearts – plain, with tomato, with spinach

Farfalle – plain, with tomato, with spinach

Malloreddus sardi – plain, with tomato, with spinach

Radiatori – plain, with beet, with spinach

Conchiglie – with tomato, with spinach

Eliche – plain, with tomato, with spinach

Creste di gallo – plain, with tomato, with spinach

Hörnchen – plain, with beet, with spinach

Sedanini – plain, with tomato, with spinach

Fusilli – with pumpkin, with cornmeal, with tomato

• Spaghetti – with tomato

• Spaghetti – with spinach

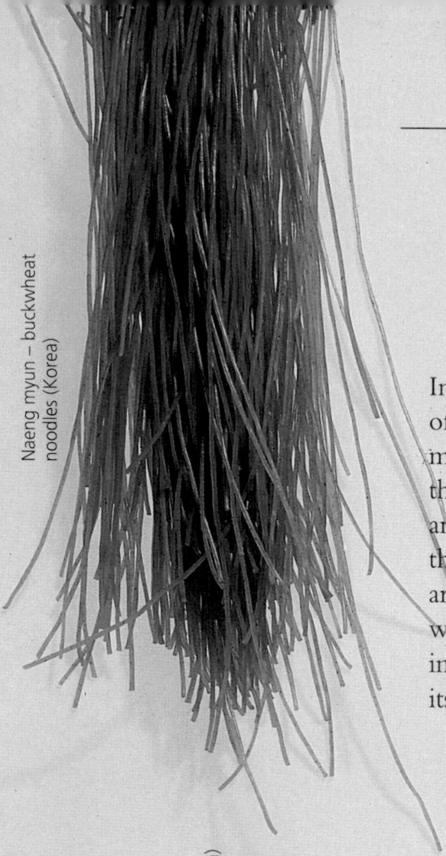

Naeng myun – buckwheat noodles (Korea)

Noodles from Asia

A staple foodstuff in Asia

In the cuisines of Asia, there is a multitude of noodles. Unlike pasta in the West, many of these are made from cereals other than wheat; flavorings include green tea and spinach, as well as red shiso, a plant that is also often pickled. Soba noodles are made mainly from buckwheat flour, with wheat flour being added simply to improve their cooking performance with its gluten. These noodles look like light-gray spaghetti, and they have a very distinctive taste. Japanese somen noodles, made from durum wheat, are produced by pulling long threads only 1 millimeter thick from the dough. After drying, they are cut into pieces. Raw somen noodles have a beautiful sheen that is unfortunately lost when they are cooked. Udon noodles, also from Japan, are less than 1/5 inch in diameter, round, squared, or flat, and often very long. They are available either fresh or partially or fully dried.

Very thin wheat noodles (Japan)

Somen – wheat noodles (Japan)

Thin wheat noodles (Japan)

Chasoba – buckwheat and green tea noodles (Japan)

Buckwheat and wheat noodles (Japan)

Ikeshima shiso somen – wheat noodles with red shiso (Japan)

Ikeshima cha somen – wheat noodles with green tea (Japan)

Zaru soba – buckwheat noodles with yam (Japan)

Aji no udon – wheat noodles (Japan)

Flat wheat noodles (Japan)

Kishimen, sanuki udon – wheat noodles (Japan)

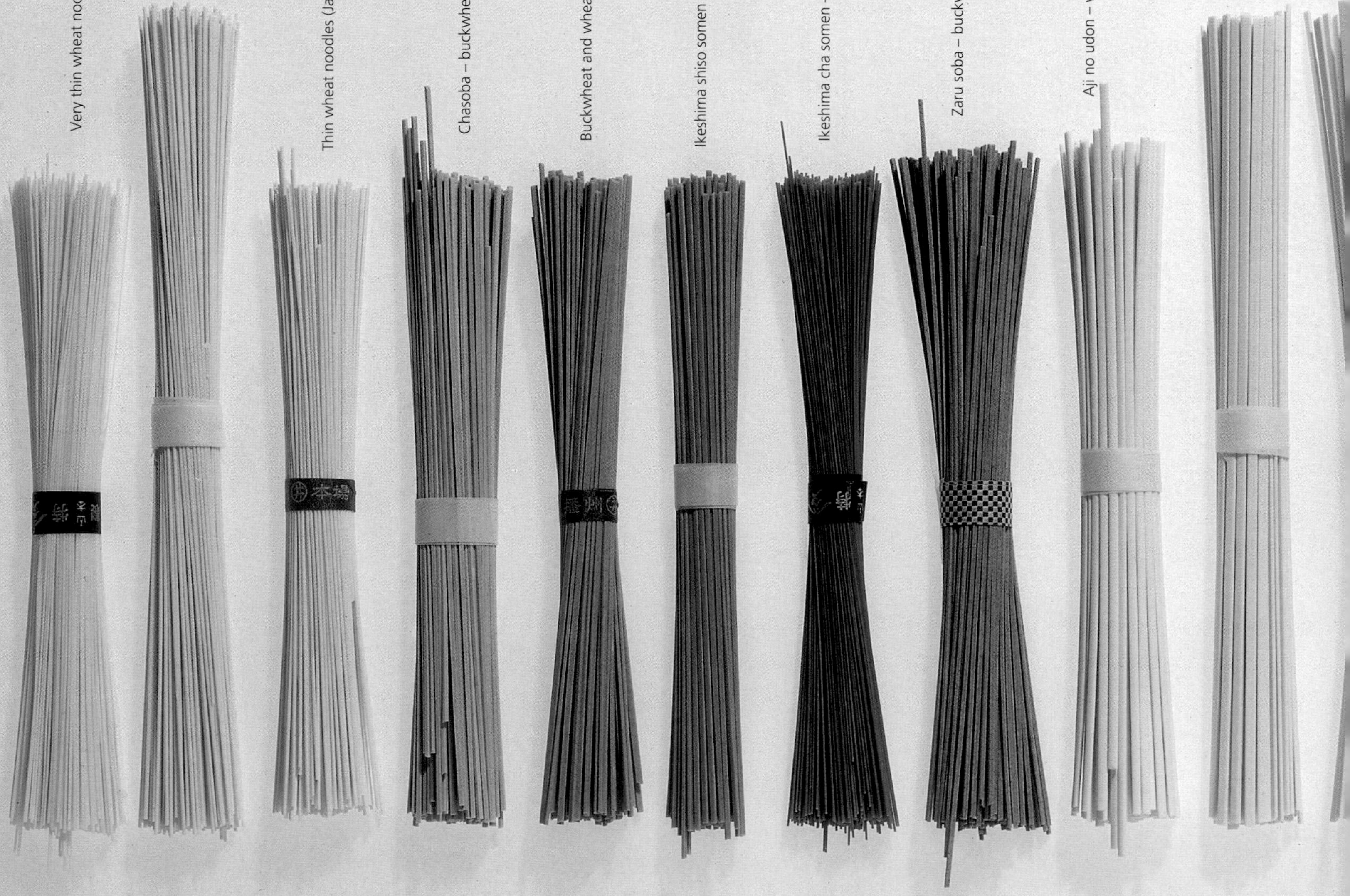

Hime chuka soba – Chinese-style
noodles (Japan)

Woh hup longevity noodles
(Malaysia)

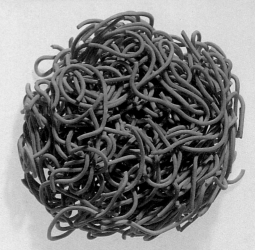

Poh chai mee (Hong Kong)

Longevity noodles, egg noodles (China)

Noodles with spinach (China)

Partially dried noodles (Malaysia)

Mee – whole-wheat noodles (China)

Mee (China)

Cantonese noodles
(China)

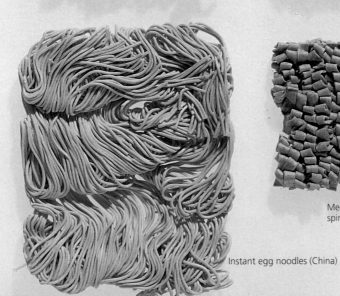

Instant egg noodles (China)

Mee – noodles with
spinach (China)

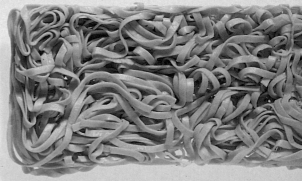

Mee – noodles without egg
(China)

Two sizes of rice-paper wrappers

Rice noodles, mung bean noodles

Semi-industrial noodle production in Asia

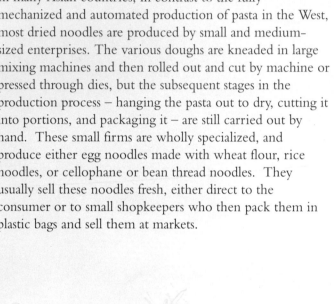

In many Asian countries, in contrast to the fully mechanized and automated production of pasta in the West, most dried noodles are produced by small and medium-sized enterprises. The various doughs are kneaded in large mixing machines and then rolled out and cut by machine or pressed through dies, but the subsequent stages in the production process – hanging the pasta out to dry, cutting it into portions, and packaging it – are still carried out by hand. These small firms are wholly specialized, and produce either egg noodles made with wheat flour, rice noodles, or cellophane or bean thread noodles. They usually sell these noodles fresh, either direct to the consumer or to small shopkeepers who then pack them in plastic bags and sell them at markets.

Flat rice noodles, chantaboon rice sticks (Thai: bánh pho'thu'o'ng hang)

Medium rice noodles, rice sticks (Thai: bánh phó)

Narrow rice noodles, chantaboon rice sticks (Thai: Bánh pho'thu'o'ng hang)

Fine rice noodles, rice vermicelli (Thai: wa wai brand)

Mitsukan saifun –
cellophane noodles
with sweet potato
and potato starch
(Japan)

Mitsukan kuzukiri –
cellophane noodles
with arrowroot and
potato starch (Japan)

Cellophane noodles –
with potato and mung
bean starch (Taiwan)

***Rice noodles being prepared for
drying.*** *In a small Chinese factory in
Singapore, this is all still done by hand.
With great skill, the slippery fresh noodles
are hung on rails before being dried in
large ovens.*

Choung soo dang
myun – cellophane
noodles (Korea)

Fresh pasta

"The taste of fresh pasta, made from a pliable dough and cooked for a short time in boiling water, is unsurpassed and cannot be compared with dried pasta." The enthusings of gourmets are justified, of course, but it is worth remembering that a lot of hard work has been done beforehand, and that the cook's hands and arms will be aching from all the kneading and rolling. There are machines that spare the cook all this effort, but they never produce pasta as good as handmade, at least not in the domestic kitchen. In particular, the machines that claim to both knead the dough and extrude it through nozzles, like the machines in pasta factories, never produce satisfactory results.

Whether the dough should be made from hard or soft wheat flour or semolina, or from a mixture of both, whether whole eggs should be used, or more yolk than white or just yolk, whether water should be the only liquid added or whether a spoonful of olive oil is also needed, or even whether it is worthwhile experimenting with whole-wheat or highly refined flours – these are all matters of endless dispute. The only thing not at issue is that the ball of dough should, as one chef puts it, be "kneaded to death," in other words worked for as long as is required for it to feel like silk to the touch. Nor is there any doubt that the dough should be wrapped in plastic wrap and left to rest in a cool place before any further handling – though not for days, of course, since fresh eggs cannot be kept indefinitely.

It is difficult to understand why, despite centuries of experience, there are still

problems to be solved in the cooking of pasta. They concern those kinds of pastas to which flavoring and colorings have been added. Most commonly these are spinach, tomato paste, or squid ink, although unsweetened cocoa powder or dried mushrooms, usually ground to a floury consistency, are also used. The boiling water mercilessly extracts the flavor of these additives from the green, red, or black pasta or noodles, leaving only the color. The only way of preserving the taste is to cook the pasta in flavored water – by blanching spinach in boiling water before cooking spinach pasta, or by using dried *cèpes* or *porcini* to prepare a stock in which to cook pasta containing wild mushrooms. This technique has by no means been fully exploited yet.

Fresh pasta comes in a rather more restricted range of shapes than the commercial dried product. And any cook who is not content with pasta shapes of differing width and thickness, or who would like to offer guests fresh *penne* or *orecchiette*, or stuffed pasta of any kind, will have to be prepared to spend half a day in the kitchen.

Asked how the quality of freshly made pasta could be identified, one Italian chef replied, "If it is so slippery that it seems to slide more easily out of the mouth and back onto the plate than down the throat, then it's perfect."

Homemade pasta is made fresh every day for their own restaurants by pastaie, Italian pasta cooks. This pasta fresca is made solely by women and is also sold for consumption off the premises.

such as marble or plastic, simply because wood stores heat well. In a well-heated kitchen, however, this is not of any great importance.

The flour is crucial to the success of good pasta. Fortunately, the quality of a given brand of flour will not vary much. The Italian flours used for pasta are known as "*farina bianca 00*" or "*Tipo 00*" (type 00) and "*farina di semola fine.*" The American counterpart to the latter is often labeled "semolina flour for pasta" (which should not be confused with semolina meal). Good results can be obtained with unbleached all-purpose flour. It is worth experimenting until you find the brand best suited to your purposes.

HOMEMADE PASTA DOUGHS

This usually means using eggs

Pasta dough consisting only of flour and water is made much better in factories than it can ever be at home. This is due to the selection and mixture of the right kinds of wheat in the commercial product. However, the home cook still has to choose among the various kinds of dough made with eggs, since different sorts of pasta require doughs made from specific ingredients. These are determined both by the kind of flour used and the ratio of egg white to yolk or of egg to water.

Adding salt to pasta dough is eschewed by some pasta experts, since it can make white spots in the dough. This can be avoided by using very fine-grained salt.

All the ingredients for pasta dough should be brought to room temperature before mixing, since only then can flour, eggs, and other liquids be quickly and easily combined to form a smooth dough. So do not use eggs straight from the refrigerator.

A solid wooden board is preferred by Italian pasta experts to a work surface made of any other material,

PASTA DOUGH NO. 1

This is a standard dough for most kinds of pasta. It can be used for cut pasta and stuffed pasta shapes.

2$^{1}/_{3}$ cups all-purpose flour
3 eggs
1 tablespoon olive oil
$^{1}/_{2}$ teaspoon salt
1 tablespoon water if required

PASTA DOUGH NO. 2

A dough for "country-style" pasta that remains firm when cooked. It owes its characteristic consistency to the addition of durum wheat semolina.

1 cup finely ground semolina flour for pasta
1 cup all-purpose flour
2 eggs, 1 egg yolk
$^{1}/_{2}$ teaspoon salt

PASTA DOUGH NO. 3

For stuffed pastas, such as ravioli, *agnolotti*, *tortellini*, *pansoti*, and many others.

2$^{1}/_{3}$ cups all-purpose flour
2 eggs, 4 egg yolks
$^{1}/_{2}$ teaspoon salt

PASTA DOUGH NO. 4

A rich dough with a distinctive taste of its own, which swells up on cooking. Ideal for tagliatelle, fettuccine, and other ribbon noodles.

2$^{1}/_{3}$ cups all-purpose flour
1 egg
7 egg yolks
1 tablespoon olive oil
$^{1}/_{2}$ teaspoon salt

1 Sift the flour onto the work surface in a mound and make a hollow in the middle. Break the eggs into the hollow. Add the olive oil and salt to the eggs. With a fork, first mix the ingredients in the hollow together and then start to mix in the flour from the edge.

2 Gradually incorporate more of the flour until a viscous paste begins to form. Put the fork to one side and, using both hands, heap the remaining flour from the outside over the paste in the middle. Work the flour into the paste. If the paste does not absorb all the flour, and if the ingredients cannot be easily worked, add a little water.

3 Work in the water with both thumbs, then press the dough into a ball and work in the rest of the flour. Now the actual kneading begins. Push out the dough with the heels of the hands, then form it into a ball again. Repeat this kneading action until the dough has a firm but slightly elastic consistency and no longer changes shape when you remove your hands. Cover with plastic wrap and let rest about 1 hour.

Whole-wheat, cornmeal, and chestnut flour

Pasta doughs that offer the cook greater variety – some with a very distinctive flavor of their own

Corn or maize (Zea mays) *is a tropical and subtropical cereal belonging to the grass family. Whether in the form of whole ears or individual kernels, it has many uses in the kitchen, particularly as a vegetable. Cornmeal is used to make pasta and polenta.*

WHOLE-WHEAT PASTA DOUGH

Whole-wheat flour is made from the entire wheat kernel (berry), particularly the highly nutritious embryo (germ) and the husk (bran), which is a good source of fiber. The flour develops its full flavor if used immediately after grinding. All whole-wheat flours require the addition of refined white flour to make a dough that is easy to work.

2 cups whole-wheat flour
2 cups all-purpose flour
$^1/_2$ teaspoon salt, 2 eggs, 1 tablespoon olive oil
about $^7/_8$ cup lukewarm water

Preparing whole-wheat pasta dough:

Mix the two types of flour with the salt on a work surface, shape into a mound, and make a hollow in the middle. Break the eggs into it.

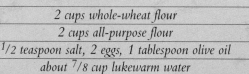

Measure the tablespoon of olive oil and add it to the eggs in the hollow.

Mix the ingredients in the hollow together, then begin to stir in the flour from the edge.

As soon as a viscous paste begins to form in the hollow, use both hands to heap the remaining flour over the paste.

Mix the flour into the paste, using both thumbs to work in enough water to bind together into a dough. Shape the dough into a ball.

Push out the dough with the heel of the hands and form it into a ball again. Repeat this kneading action until the dough retains its shape.

Roll the dough into a ball, cover with plastic wrap, and let rest at least 1 hour.

Whole-wheat pasta dough

CORNMEAL PASTA DOUGH

The addition of cornmeal produces a pasta dough with quite astonishing qualities. First, it is more robust, with a pleasantly firm texture; second, it is easy to mold or cut because it retains its shape and does not stick.

1 cup + 3 tablespoons cornmeal
1 cup + 3 tablespoons all-purpose flour
3 eggs, 3 egg yolks
1 tablespoon olive oil, $^1/_2$ teaspoon salt
freshly grated nutmeg

Preparing cornmeal pasta dough:

Sift the two flours onto the work surface, shape into a mound, and form a hollow in the middle. Add the remaining ingredients to the hollow.

Mix the ingredients in the hollow with a fork and then begin to stir in the flour from the edge.

Using both hands, work in the remaining flour. Knead the mixture with the heels of the hands into a smooth dough.

CHESTNUT-FLOUR PASTA DOUGH

Chestnut flour is milled from dried chestnuts, *Castanea sativa*. Its distinctive taste is brought out to best advantage if the pasta made from it is served with browned butter and a mild cheese. Chestnut flour can be found in health-food stores and Italian grocers.

$1^2/_3$ cups chestnut flour
3 cups + 3 tablespoons all-purpose flour
4 eggs
5 egg yolks
$^1/_2$ teaspoon salt

Preparing chestnut pasta dough:

Sift the two flours onto a work surface, shape into a mound, and form a hollow in the middle. Add the eggs, egg yolks, and salt to the hollow.

Mix the ingredients in the hollow with a fork and then begin to stir in the flour from the edge.

Using both hands, work in the remaining flour, then knead the mixture with the heels of the hands into a smooth dough.

Cornmeal pasta dough

Chestnut-flour pasta dough

Fields of buckwheat are no longer a rarity in Europe: in the trend toward healthy eating, this plant is making a comeback. It is an undemanding crop that thrives even in poor soil.

Buckwheat noodles

Flour made from buckwheat (*Fagopyrum esculentum*), which incidentally is not a cereal, is used to make breads, pancakes, Russian blini, and crêpes in Brittany. In the Balkans and in some parts of Italy, it is also used to make noodles, at least at home.

The situation in Asia is completely different, particularly in Korea and Japan. In these two countries, the making of soba – buckwheat noodles – is a tradition going back more than 400 years. The word *soba* in Japanese denotes both the buckwheat plant and its seeds and the thin, brownish noodles made from them. The continued popularity of these noodles is due to their undisputed nutritional value, as well as to their pleasant, sweetish flavor.

Buckwheat is normally ground quite coarsely when used in Europe and North America. In Japan, on the other hand, there are five or six different grades of buckwheat flour, ranging from coarse,

wholegrain flour to the finest flour, which is ideal for making the most delicate, pale noodles. Soba noodles are as popular in hearty dishes during the cold periods of the year as during the heat of summer, when they are served cold with salads or with nothing more than wasabi or a dipping sauce. They can also be served as a dessert, either with fruit or with ice cream. In Tokyo alone, there are 7,000 shops selling soba noodles, and many of them still offer genuine handmade noodles. There, customers can watch the somewhat complicated process by which soba noodles are made.

There are various means by which one can obtain a smooth dough from buckwheat flour, which, after all, has none of the gluten that is so important for producing a malleable dough. Those wishing to make soba noodles at home are advised to use a mixture containing three or four parts buckwheat flour to one of wheat flour. However, it is possible to increase the proportion of buckwheat flour without the dough becoming impossibly crumbly. In Japan, this is done by using boiling water, which partially compensates for the lack of gluten in buckwheat flour by penetrating the starch in the flour more quickly and thus binding the dough ("*kiko-uchi*," which translates roughly as "pure buckwheat noodles", is a stamp of quality in Japan). An alternative, very simple method of achieving the same effect is to use an egg. First, whisk it with cold water and then mix it into the dough. This does not alter the taste significantly, but it does make the dough smooth and pliable. The particular flavor of the noodles that can be made with the buckwheat flour available in North America and Europe is full-bodied and earthy, best suited to combinations with vegetables, particularly cabbage, as well as bacon and strong cheeses.

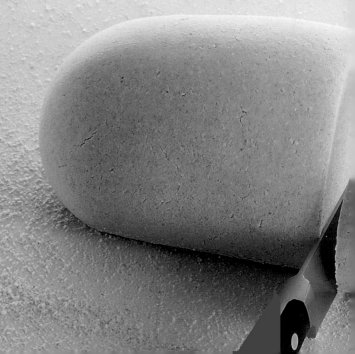

BUCKWHEAT PASTA DOUGH

This dough is always made from a mixture of buckwheat and wheat flours, sifted together into the mixing bowl. By sifting, the two kinds of flour are mixed evenly and are aerated. This is important, since it means that the water can be worked into the flour quickly, thus avoiding the formation of any hard lumps.

3 cups buckwheat flour
1 cup + 3 tablespoons all-purpose flour
¹/2 teaspoon salt, 1¹/4 cups water

Preparing buckwheat pasta dough:

Sift the two kinds of flour and the salt together into a bowl. Stir in the water with a fork.

As soon as the water is absorbed, place the resulting paste on a floured wooden board and knead it into a smooth dough, as described on page 41.

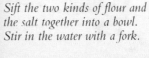
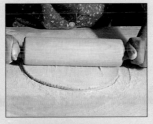

Divide the dough into four equal pieces. Roll out each piece into a disk ¹/8 inch thick, sprinkling it frequently with flour while rolling.

Dust the disks with buckwheat flour and let them dry out a little. To make noodles, cut the first disk into strips 2 inches wide.

Stack the cut strips on top of each other, so that the edges are flush. Then cut the strips across into short noodles about ¹/4 inch wide.

Place the cut noodles on a clean dish towel. Cut the remaining disks into noodles in the same way.

This is the critical phase in the making of buckwheat dough. *After the water has been added to the flour, it must be mixed in quickly in order to avoid hard lumps forming. One tried and tested way of preventing this, used in Europe and in Asia, is to add an egg whisked with water.*

Pasta with color and flavor

Color is not all that is required

In the view of many pasta lovers, pasta should taste of pasta. They prefer to use the sauce to add the flavor of tomatoes or mushrooms or whatever, rather than add it to the pasta itself, and they reject colored pasta on the same grounds. In fact, however, colored pasta offers the creative cook many new opportunities for variations on a theme.

GREEN PASTA DOUGH

Green is the most frequently used coloring for pasta. This may be due to the fact that green is the color that best sets off a tomato or white sauce. The production process is far from simple, since the color has first to be taken from the spinach that is the principal coloring agent. This is done by making spinach pulp, which involves extracting chlorophyll from spinach. Chlorophyll has virtually no taste and is therefore well suited for use in sauces, stuffings, and even sweet dishes. Green pasta should not be confused with spinach pasta, also green, which is made with finely puréed spinach and has its own distinctive flavor.

For the spinach pulp:
¹/2 pound spinach, 2 to 3 tablespoons water
For the pasta dough:
1¹/4 cups all-purpose flour
5 to 6 egg yolks
1 tablespoon olive oil, ¹/2 teaspoon salt
3 tablespoons butter
freshly grated nutmeg, salt

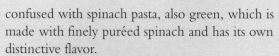

Making spinach pulp: *Place a few of the spinach leaves in the blender, add the water, and blend to a smooth purée. Gradually add the rest of the spinach leaves, blending until smooth. Place the purée in a piece of cheesecloth. Squeeze the juice out into a saucepan.*

Heat the spinach juice to about 150°F, but do not let it boil. Skim off the pulp with a small strainer as it rises to the surface.

Preparing the dough:

Pour the flour onto a work surface, shape into a mound, and make a hollow in the middle. Add the egg yolks and the spinach pulp, pressing it through the strainer.

Using first a fork and then your hands, mix all the ingredients into a smooth dough, as described on page 41.

Roll the dough into a ball, cover with plastic wrap, and let rest 1 hour.

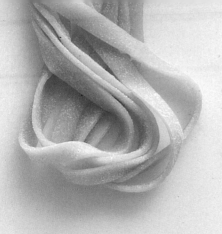

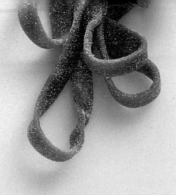

SAFFRON PASTA DOUGH

This is a perfect combination of color and taste.

1/4 teaspoon saffron threads
2 cups all-purpose flour
2 eggs, 1 egg yolk
2 tablespoons olive oil
1/2 teaspoon salt

Mix the saffron with 2 tablespoons water. Prepare the dough as described on page 41, adding the saffron liquid to the hollow with the other ingredients.

BEET PASTA DOUGH

Very beautiful pasta, almost purple in color, but virtually without beet taste.

2 cups all-purpose flour
2 eggs, 1 egg yolk
2 tablespoons olive oil
1/2 teaspoon salt
1/3 cup beet juice

Prepare the dough as described on page 41. Using a vegetable juicer, extract 1/3 cup juice from fresh beets, and boil down to 2 tablespoons. Work the concentrated beet juice into the dough.

MUSHROOM PASTA DOUGH

The uniquely intense flavor of this pasta makes it a culinary treat.

1/3 ounce dried porcini or cèpes
2 cups all-purpose flour
2 eggs, 1 egg yolk
2 tablespoons olive oil, 1/2 teaspoon salt
1 tablespoon minced fresh parsley
water as required

Mince the porcini finely with a knife or grind them coarsely. Prepare the dough as described on page 41, adding the porcini and minced parsley to the ingredients in the hollow.

HOT-PEPPER PASTA DOUGH

This pasta has a hot, spicy flavor.

6 small dried hot red chili peppers
2 cups all-purpose flour
2 eggs, 1 egg yolk
2 tablespoons olive oil
$^1/2$ teaspoon salt, water as required

Slit open the chilies, remove the seeds, and mince the pods or grind them in a mortar and pestle. Prepare the dough as described on page 41, adding the chilies to the hollow in the flour.

SHRIMP PASTA DOUGH

Aromatic pasta, with a delicate, unmistakable flavor. The recipe uses dried shrimp, which should not be confused with the dried shrimp used as a seasoning in Asian cooking.

1 ounce dried shrimp
2 cups all-purpose flour
2 eggs, 1 egg yolk
2 tablespoons olive oil
$^1/2$ teaspoon salt
water as required

Mince the shrimp. Prepare the dough as described on page 41, adding the shrimp to the ingredients in the hollow.

BLACK PASTA DOUGH

The color is the focus of attention here, and can inspire cooks to create dishes full of visual contrast. None of the rich color is lost during cooking: the water remains completely clear. Squid ink, which has virtually no taste, can be bought in gourmet shops, or extracted from the ink sacs of fresh squid.

$2^1/3$ cups all-purpose flour
2 eggs
2 teaspoons olive oil
$^1/2$ teaspoon salt
$^3/4$ ounce squid ink

Prepare the dough as described on page 41, adding the squid ink with the eggs.

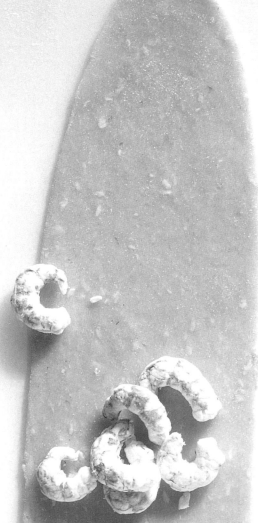

HERB PASTA DOUGH

This pasta has an intense herby flavor. A single herb, such as basil, can be used instead of a mixture.

1/2 cup mixed fresh herbs: sage, thyme, parsley, chives
2 cups all-purpose flour
2 eggs, 1 egg yolk
2 tablespoons olive oil
1/2 teaspoon salt
water as required

Mince the herbs. Prepare the dough as described on page 41, adding the herbs to the ingredients in the hollow.

GARLIC PASTA DOUGH

Garlic makes the most strongly flavored pasta of all.

3 garlic cloves
1/2 teaspoon salt
2 tablespoons olive oil
2 cups all-purpose flour
2 eggs, 1 egg yolk
2 tablespoons olive oil
water as required

Crush the garlic with the salt and oil in a mortar and pestle. Prepare the dough as described on page 41, adding the garlic paste to the ingredients in the hollow.

TOMATO PASTA DOUGH

Pasta with a fresh aroma and striking color.

2 cups all-purpose flour
3 to 4 egg yolks, 3 tablespoons clarified butter
1/2 teaspoon salt
2 to 2 1/2 tablespoons tomato paste
about 3 tablespoons water

Prepare the dough as described on page 41, with the butter replacing the oil and the tomato paste added with the yolks.

Pasta fresca all'uovo

In Bologna, the pasta center of Emilia-Romagna, fresh egg pasta is prized above all else

Handmade pasta is, of course, to be cherished, but there are certain shapes that absolutely have to be made by machine, because they would otherwise not be made at all, or only with great difficulty. These include the various sizes of spaghetti and macaroni and many others. So lovers of fresh egg pasta have no alternative but to resort to a machine if they wish to produce these shapes. Hand-operated machines are available, similar in shape to a meat grinder. The pasta is propelled along a shaft to a suitably perforated disk and extruded through it. Such simple devices exist for making *bigoli*, for example, a Venetian whole-wheat pasta. There are also electric pasta machines with a very wide range of perforations that can produce all the usual long noodles without any difficulty at all. These machines are as suitable for use in domestic kitchens as in restaurants.

With pasta, "homemade" is still synonymous with "good quality." Homemade pasta is good pasta. This applies not only to the making of the dough but also to the subsequent stages of the process – the rolling out and cutting, the stuffing and shaping. And yet in Italy, particularly in Emilia-Romagna, fresh pasta does not necessarily mean homemade pasta. There are still

Rolling out the dough into a sfoglia – *a thin sheet of even thickness – is exhausting work, and requires years of experience.*

To make tagliatelle, the sfoglia *is left to dry slightly and then folded over and cut to size. At Gigina's in Bologna, Italy, the whole process is performed with machine-like accuracy.*

Loosely curled bundles of tagliatelle are placed in a small bowl and then turned out carefully onto a board. The pasta "nests" are then left to dry.

The choice in Italian pasta shops is not very wide, but everything is guaranteed fresh, from the ribbon noodles of varying widths to the house specialties. The picture shows, from left to right, passatelli, gramigna, and strozzapreti.

specialists there, the so-called "*pastaie*," who produce fresh pasta day in, day out, whether for their own restaurants or for consumption off the premises. It is advisable to order in advance if you want to be certain of having your fresh tortellini or tagliatelle the next day, since nobody in the pasta region around Bologna will voluntarily forego their *pasta fresca*. And it can be expected that in every good restaurant the pasta "*fatta in casa*" is indeed homemade.

The interesting thing is that the vast majority of *pastaie* are women. Pasta-making is not something to be entrusted to men or to machines; it is the province of the female pasta cook, who kneads the dough and, with incredible speed and skill, rolls it out into *sfoglie*. These thin sheets are then hung on rails and dried for a precisely defined time, since the dough should be neither too soft nor too dry when it is folded over for cutting. With machine-like precision, it is cut into the desired width for tagliatelle and taglierini or into broad strips for pappardelle. Loosely curled into nests, the pasta is then ready for the cooking pot.

Fresh pasta should always be cooked on the same day it is made, since it is then dry enough to retain its shape while it cooks but also soft enough to need only a short cooking time. This is just as important for the various forms of cut pasta as it is for the stuffed varieties, which are in any case highly perishable if they have a meat filling.

"Alla chitarra" *is the term used to describe noodles cut with the device shown above, the chitarra or "guitar." These noodles, known as "pasta alla chitarra," "spaghetti alla chitarra," or "spaghetti quadrati," ("square spaghetti") come from the Abruzzi region of Italy and are still produced there today. The chitarra consists of a wooden frame with thin wires stretched across the top. A sheet of pasta dough, rolled out to a thickness approximately equal to the distance between the wires, is laid over the top of the chitarra and a rolling pin is used to press the dough down through the wires. The strips of cut pasta, which now have a square cross section, drop through the wires onto the board that forms the bottom of the frame.*

With knife or machine

Method makes no difference to taste, but it is important for consistent results

With a knife:

Dust the work surface evenly with flour and roll out the dough into a sheet, rolling from the center alternately in both directions.

For ribbon noodles, fold the sheet of dough over several times. Dust it with flour first, so that the layers do not stick together.

Pappardelle, lasagnette *are cut in broad strips 5/8 to 3/4 inch across. Unfold immediately so they do not stick together.*

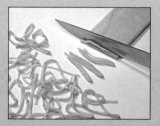

Tagliatelle *are cut in strips about 1/4 inch across. Fettuccine are a little wider: 3/8 inch across.*

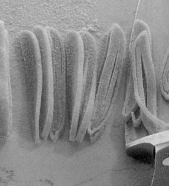

Tagliolini or taglierini *are narrow ribbon noodles less than 1/8 inch in width. In Piedmont they are sold under the name "tajarin."*

Fresh pasta can be cut by hand or by machine. By hand means the pasta is cut with a knife. However, this should be done only if you can achieve results similar to those produced by machine. Thus the pasta has to be rolled out evenly and cut into strips of approximately the same width. Strips of differing widths and thicknesses would cook unevenly, which would spoil the taste and texture of the pasta.

Proper tools are essential for both methods. For the first one, this is a knife of appropriate length and

sharpness with a blade that is not too thick. The ideal material for the work surface is wood, although plastic boards are now very popular. They are easier to keep clean and are also less damaging to a knife than marble or other surfaces.

Anyone whose skill and artistry with a knife do not match those of the professional pasta cook should consider purchasing a pasta machine. They are generally easy to use, and they produce perfect pasta in a huge variety of shapes and sizes. As shown in

By machine:

Put the strip of dough through the machine's smooth rollers several times, narrowing the setting each time, until the desired thickness is achieved.

Pappardelle, lasagnette are made using a cutting roller to produce $^5/8$- to $^3/4$-inch strips. Toss with flour and shape into loose nests.

Tagliatelle and fettuccine are cut $^1/4$ inch and $^3/8$ inch wide respectively. If they are not to be cooked immediately, curl them into loose nests and store.

Tagliolini or taglierini, narrow ribbon noodles, are made using a cutting roller with a width just under $^1/8$ inch.

Drying noodles. A rack like this can be improvised with wooden spoons, and the pasta hung over their handles to dry.

the picture sequence above, the dough has first to be rolled out; then, when it has reached the desired thickness, it can be cut into sheets of lasagne or used to make stuffed pasta. Or it can be fed through one of the interchangeable sets of cutting rollers. Most machine manufacturers supply rollers to make all the common pasta shapes. There are also very sophisticated machines designed to produce filled and shaped ravioli.

Pasta-makers were very quick to appropriate technology for their own purposes, as the photograph above shows. In one process, this machine can roll out the dough to the required thickness and then feed it straight to the cutting roller.

Pasta shapes

Cutting fresh dough into shape: pasta doesn't get any more individual

Using a pastry wheel and a ruler, cut strips 3/4 inch wide. Moisten the edges of the strips.

Lay the natural and green strips side by side alternately, slightly overlapping, and roll to the desired thickness.

Sheets of two-tone dough look particularly attractive, but require a lot of effort to make. A machine makes the rolling easier. Roll out the two batches of dough a little thicker than ultimately required.

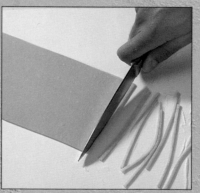

Fusilli are available commercially made in many different forms. Cut strips about 1/16 inch wide and 3 inches long.

Wind the strips around a floured wooden stick, then carefully slide the stick out. Let dry before cooking.

Quadrucci. Dust thin rounds with flour and let dry slightly, then stack and cut into 4 inch wide strips.

Cut these long strips across into equal strips of the desired width, then cut them into squares of the desired size.

Squares of any size can be cut. The most popular sizes have sides 3/8, 1/2, and 3/4 inch long.

Maltagliati is the name of these noodles and means "badly cut," so you do not have to be too careful cutting them.

Sprinkle the dough liberally with flour and fold it over. First cut off the corners and then cut across.

You will end up with shapes that taper off at each end. Unfold and let dry on a lightly floured surface.

Orecchiette are normally made from a flour and water dough. Roll into tubes about 3/8 inch thick.

Cut in even pieces about 3/8 inch across, so that all the orecchiette end up the same shape.

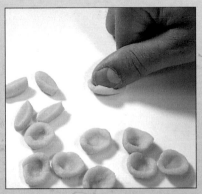

Sprinkle the work surface with flour, then press out each "ear" shape with your thumb. Let dry before cooking.

Garganelli are pasta tubes. Roll 2 1/2-inch squares of dough around a 1/4 inch diameter wooden stick.

Roll the tube of dough over a grooved board, like that used to shape pats of butter, pressing down firmly.

Carefully slide out the wooden stick without squeezing the tube of pasta. Let dry before cooking.

Farfalle or pasta bows, are made from rectangles, varying from 3/4 x 1 1/4 inches to 1 1/4 x 2 1/2 inches.

Cut long strips with a straight or fluted pastry wheel and then cut these across in rectangles of the desired size.

Pinch each rectangle of dough together in the middle. Let dry on a work surface sprinkled lightly with flour.

Cantonese noodles

Dexterity and a feel for the quality of the dough are required in order to make noodles as slender as threads of silk

So thin *it can pass through the eye of a needle! Here, Sang Koon Sung, a native of Canton and the noodle specialist at the Pine Court Restaurant in Singapore's Mandarin Hotel, proudly displays one of the products of his craft. Even the thinnest* capelli d'angelo *made in Italy cannot compete.*

The dough for these noodles consists solely of water and wheat flour. In order to make it, cooks shake flour onto a work surface, add salt, and gradually pour on cold water. The dough has the same consistency as normal flour and water dough, but is left to settle only a short time before the next stage of the noodle-making process begins, initially on an unfloured work surface. The dough is stretched into a skein, folded together, stretched out again, folded together again, and so on, over and over again. At the same time, it is tossed in the air and rotated. As the whole process proceeds, the individual strands begin to emerge, but at this stage they remain stuck together. When they are about 1/4 inch wide, they are sprinkled liberally with flour. The dough is then repeatedly stretched, folded together, and twisted into a spiral; from time to time it is rolled in flour, so that the noodles get gradually thinner and thinner and remain separate from each other. The process continues until the noodles are of the desired thickness. Finally, the thick ends of the skein of dough, which can make up about half its total weight, are cut off with a knife. The noodles are hung to dry over a rail, while the whole process is repeated with the second half of the dough. The surprising thing about these very fine noodles is that, provided they are not cooked too long, they retain a certain degree of firmness to the bite.

Like an evenly draped curtain *is how Cantonese noodles look when a hand is passed through them. It is a real pleasure to watch a Chinese cook making these unbelievably thin noodles, without any tools and almost as quickly as a machine. Having seen the process it is almost impossible to imagine that anyone other than the Chinese could have discovered pasta.*

How to cook pasta

It is certainly going too far to suggest that cooking pasta represents a serious challenge for the cook; however, cooking it properly is not such a simple matter

Great attention has to be paid to a few important points. This is why, for pasta experts, cooking pasta is as serious a matter as making the dough. Nothing can be left to chance.

The right pot The ideal pasta pot should be of good quality, taller than it is wide and big enough to hold suffient water, and its base must sit flat on the burner. As a rule of thumb, 1 generous quart of water is required for every 4 ounces of pasta, whatever shape it may be. This is the minimum water required to cook pasta properly. If the volume of water is increased by 25% or more, this can only be of benefit, since pasta requires as constant a temperature as possible during its relatively short cooking time, and this is easier to maintain with a large volume of water. The pasta also cooks more evenly. A tightly fitting lid is necessary, in order to cover the pot as soon as the pasta has been added to the boiling salted water. In this way, it will return more quickly to a boil. The lid should then be pushed to one side so that it covers about two-thirds of the pan, thus allowing steam to escape. Alternatively, the lid can be removed completely, so

that the cooking process can be monitored more closely. The surface of the water should be at a rolling boil, but it should no longer be bubbling vigorously. In this way, the pasta will automatically swirl around in the large volume of water. Nevertheless, it is a good idea to stir the water occasionally with a long wooden spoon or fork in order to avoid clumps of pasta forming that will then cook unevenly.

Al dente – or the right degree of resistance. It is not at all simple to predict the exact cooking time for pasta, so frequent testing is required as the end of the assumed cooking time draws close. As it cooks, pasta absorbs water at a variable rate, becoming increasingly soft and swelling up. It is cooked when it feels soft to the touch but is very slightly resistant and firm in the center (not raw) when bitten into. This is what Italian pasta cooks describe as "*al dente*," or "to the tooth." Obviously, the length of time required to achieve this state of doneness varies, depending on the shape of the pasta and whether it is fresh or dried.

Drain quickly. Some cooking times, particularly

A lot of water is needed. *As a rule of thumb, use at least 1 quart of water for every 4 ounces of pasta.*

Salt the water. *Add 1 teaspoon of salt for each quart of water. This is important for all types of pasta.*

Oil *is only needed when cooking pasta that tends to stick together, such as large sheets of lasagne and very fresh pasta.*

Long pasta *should be pushed in gently, and pasta shapes added a few handfuls at a time. The water must be bubbling.*

Stir *with a wooden fork so that the strands or shapes are separated and do not stick together.*

Put the lid on, *leaving about a third of the pot uncovered. In this way, steam can escape and the pasta will cook evenly.*

The surface of the water *should be rolling gently, but not bubbling, maintaining a constant temperature.*

Testing the pasta *should be done frequently toward the end of the cooking time. It should be cooked "al dente."*

Drain *the pasta as soon as it is cooked. Pour it into a colander and shake gently to drain it thoroughly.*

Rinse with cold water *only if the pasta is to be used in a salad or served as a side-dish.*

Rinse with the hot cooking water *to keep the pasta warm for a short period. This will keep the pieces separate.*

for fresh pasta, are very short, so the pot has to be removed from the heat at exactly the right moment and its contents emptied immediately into a colander in order to bring the cooking process to a halt. If large quantities of pasta are being cooked, this can be a somewhat difficult process; the use of a special perforated insert in a pasta pot, as shown in the picture sequence below, makes the task considerably easier.

The cold rinse. The decision whether or not to stop the cooking process by rinsing the pasta in cold water depends on what is to be done with it subsequently. Rinsing in cold water removes the glutinous starchy layer from pasta, which is fine if it is to be served cold in a salad or used as a side-dish or browned lightly in butter. However, if it is to be mixed with a sauce and served hot, then the starch layer is necessary in order to prevent the other ingredients simply sliding off the pasta and thus failing to bind properly with it.

Some types of commercial pasta have fluted surfaces – described in Italian as "*rigati*" – to which sauces and cheese adhere particularly well. However, this only works properly if the pasta is really hot and is not sticking together. If it does begin to stick,

Cooking pasta in a perforated insert has a number of advantages: since the boiling water can circulate between the pot and the insert, the pasta remains in constant motion without sticking to the bottom of the pot. When the pasta is cooked, it can be easily removed from the pot and drained. Large pans and stockpots with perforated inserts are available in a range of sizes.

Cooking pasta in a perforated insert:

Drop the pasta into the boiling water. The ratio of water to pasta should be the same as usual: 1 quart of water for every 4 ounces of pasta.

Whether you are cooking long or short pasta, it must be stirred frequently to prevent it from sticking together.

When the pasta is cooked, lift the insert out of the boiling water and hold it over the pot to drain, shaking the insert gently.

Tip the drained pasta it into a pre-warmed bowl and mix immediately with butter, olive oil, or a sauce.

break it up by pouring the hot cooking water over it, shaking the colander vigorously as you do so. Pasta and sauce should always be mixed in a pre-warmed bowl immediately after draining.

How much per person? This is a question to which there is no precise answer, since the size of each portion depends on many factors. Unless otherwise indicated, the quantities given in the recipe section are sufficient for 4 servings as an entrée. The rule of thumb is to allow 4 ounces of pasta per portion. The reason why not all the recipes require 1 pound of pasta is that the quantities of other ingredients required vary widely and sometimes even exceed the pasta in weight. Since pasta dishes are not only main dishes, but are also frequently served as first courses, calculating the quantity of pasta depends in part on how many courses are to be served.

COOKING TIMES

How to decide when pasta is properly cooked is described on page 58. The length of time it must cook before reaching that state cannot be indicated very precisely, so cooking times should always be treated as mere guidelines requiring constant checking.

Fresh pasta is always a problem when it comes to calculating cooking times, since these depend on the extent to which the pasta has been dried. So it makes a big difference whether the pasta is cooked immediately after cutting or several hours afterward. And the thickness of the dough affects the cooking time as well. Fresh dough naturally has a particularly short cooking time which, depending on the thickness and width of the cut pasta, can barely be measured in minutes. This means that thin pasta, in particular, should be watched constantly as it cooks so that it can be drained as soon as it is ready, bringing the cooking process to an immediate halt. *Capelli d'angelo* (angel's hair), for example, may need just 30 seconds' cooking, *taglierini* about a minute, and stuffed pasta such as tortellini, 4 to 5 minutes.

Commercial dried pasta is less problematic, since cooking times are considerably longer. Thus it is easier to intervene if testing shows the pasta to be ready before the suggested cooking time is up. It is essential to take the time indicated on the package as a guide, since even with the same shape of pasta the time can vary from manufacturer to manufacturer. The following table is intended as an aid to finding the guideline figure for a given kind of pasta. If the type you are cooking is not listed here, turn to the section of the book on dried and fresh pasta, find a variety similar in shape and size, and then use the table to find the recommended cooking time.

Recommended cooking times for dried pasta	
Pasta shape	**Cooking time in minutes**
Alphabet shapes	5
Anellini	5
Banane	8–20
Bavette	4
Bucatini	7–8 (depending on thickness)
Buckwheat noodles (soba)	
• thin, ribbon	4–5
• flat	5
Capelli d'angelo	3–5
Capellini	1–3 (depending on thickness)
Cavatappi	10
Cellophane or beanthread noodles	3–4
Chinese wheat noodles	
• thin (with egg)	3–5
• thin (without egg)	4–5
Conchiglie, 1-1 1/4 inch	14
Conchiglioni (for stuffing)	8 + 30–40 for baking
Ditali	up to 6 (depending on size)
Farfalle	7–9 (depending on size)
Fedelini	3–5 (depending on size)
Fettuccine	6
Fusilli	11
Gnocchetti sardi	10
Gnocchi	9
Japanese wheat noodles	
• thin (somen)	1
• thick (udon)	10
Lasagne sheets	7–9
Linguine	6–8
• whole-wheat linguine	9
Lumaconi	8–9
Maccheroni	10–12
Malloreddus	10–12
Orecchiette	12–15
Pappardelle	4
Penne	11–12
Quadrucci, 3/8 inch	7–8
Rice noodles	
• long, thin (vermicelli)	3–4
• flat	8
Rigatoni	10
Risoni	5
Sedanini	8
Spaccatelle	9
Spaghetti alla chitarra	15
Spaghetti	12
• whole-wheat spaghetti	10–12
Spaghettini	8
Tagliatelle	6–8
Trenette	13–15
Trinette	8
Tubetti	6–7
Ziti	7
Zitoni	9

Spätzle and Knöpfle

Soft-dough pasta specialties from Alsace and the southern Tyrol

If a truly regional variety of pasta exists at all outside of Italy, then it must be spätzle. It has its origins in southwestern Germany, where it is still made "by hand" in the traditional way, with each individual spätzle being cut from a board straight into boiling water. Similar varieties go under the name of *Knöpfli* in northern Switzerland, *Spatzlen* in the Tyrol, and *Pizokel* in the Engadine. There is now a commercially produced spätzle, dried and packed in plastic bags like noodles, but in flavor and texture it has so little in common with the original that it cannot even be regarded as a substitute.

SPÄTZLE DOUGH

The same dough is used for all three methods of making spätzle: scraping, pressing, and slicing. However, whether four, five, or even six eggs should be used for each pound of flour is a question that still gives rise to serious discussion in Germany. In any event, using more water than eggs would be unworthy of even the thriftiest spätzle cook. The following recipe is certainly a good compromise, and the proper consistency of the dough is actually

determined by the little bit of water that is added, for which, even with the best will in the world, it is impossible to specify an exact amount. And spätzle should be cooked in as much water as possible, so that they can expand properly without sticking.

4 cups all-purpose flour
5 eggs
1 teaspoon salt
about 7 tablespoons water

Make the dough as shown in the picture sequence below, and use whichever of the three methods you prefer to transfer it to a large pot of boiling salted water. As soon as the spätzle rise to the surface, lift them out with a slotted spoon. If they are to be served as a side-dish, they can be rinsed in warm water or tossed quickly in fresh butter. If they are to be served with cheese, put the cheese and spätzle in alternate layers in a dish

Making spätzle dough:

Pour the flour into a bowl, make a hollow in the middle, and break the eggs into it. Add the salt.

Pour in half the water to start with, and mix all the ingredients to a smooth paste using a wooden spoon.

Beat the paste thoroughly until it takes on a smooth, elastic consistency and falls in thick blobs from the spoon. Add more water if necessary.

Cheese spätzle *are enjoyed all over the world. Gourmet tourists who visit southwestern Germany take a spätzle press home with them as a souvenir, in preference to a cow bell. What makes this simple dish so delicious is the combination of the delicate spätzle with the melting cheese — Gruyère or Emmental — which stretches into long strings when lifted out of the serving dish. A popular addition is onion rings fried in plenty of butter.*

Spätzle scraped off a board by hand *are the really authentic kind. This method requires a board with a tapering front edge. Immediately prior to use, it should be plunged briefly into water. A portion of the spätzle dough is placed on the dampened board and cut into small pieces with a knife or,*

preferably, a metal spatula, which must be repeatedly wetted during the process. These strips of pasta should be of approximately the same thickness so that they require the same cooking time. As they are cut, the strips of dough are "scraped" off the board into the boiling water.

Partly machine-made spätzle *might be an accurate description of the strands of dough squeezed into boiling water from the type of spätzle press that is similar to a potato ricer. The bottom of the press has holes, about 1/16 inch in diameter, through which the spätzle dough is squeezed. This process*

produces long threads, similar in appearance to spaghetti, which at first sight seem to have little in common with genuine, "hand-scraped" spätzle. However, their lack of resistance to the bite reveals that they are made not from a pasta dough but from the softer spätzle dough.

Swiss Knöpfli *differ from German spätzle in their characteristic teardrop shape. Originally, the dough was pressed through a circular sieve with holes about 1/4 inch in diameter. However, the press shown here, which is similar to a vegetable grater, has been in use for a long time. It consists of*

a long strip of perforated metal on top of which sits a rectangular container for the dough. The container slides to and fro like a sledge along the perforated metal strip. The dough is forced through the perforations and then sliced off immediately as the container is pushed along the metal strip.

Equipment for the pasta cook

1 Machine for rolling out and cutting pasta dough

2 Rollers for cutting ribbon noodles in widths of ¹/16 inch (*capelli d'angelo*), ¹/4 inch (*trenette*), and ³/8 inch (*lasagnette*) and for making spaghetti.

3 Wide wooden spoon

4 Vegetable-grater-type spätzle press

5 Spätzle board

6 Metal spatula

7 Knives of various sizes

8 Shovel-type spatula for serving lasagne

9 Pastry brush

10 Plastic and metal dough scrapers

11 Ruler

12 Pizza cutting wheel, very sharp

13 Fluted pastry wheel

14 Roller for cutting ¹/4-inch tagliatelle

15 Fluted roller for cutting 1¹/2-inch squares

16 Smooth roller for cutting 1¹/2-inch squares

17 Roller for cutting out disks 2 inches in diameter

18 Smooth-edged pastry cutters, 1¹/4 to 3 inches in diameter

19 Fluted pastry cutters, 1¹/4 to 3 inches in diameter

20 Pastry cutters, 1¹/4, 2, and 2³/8 inches in diameter

21 Potato-ricer-type spätzle press

22 Flour sifter

23 Potato ricer

24 Italian rolling pin for pasta

25 Rolling pin with handles

26 Truffle slicer

27 Set of mixing bowls

28 Molds for stuffed pasta

29 Mortar and pestle

30 Parmesan mill

31 Parmesan grater

1 Large pot for cooking long noodles (*pasta lunga*)

2 Large pot for cooking short pasta, (*pasta corta*), stuffed pasta, gnocchi, etc.

3 Collapsible steamer insert

4 Colander and strainer

5 Measuring cups

6 Ladle

7–9 Slotted or skimming spoons of various lengths and diameters

10 Wire straining spoon

11 Wide wooden spoon

12 Wooden fork for lifting out pasta for testing

13 Spaghetti server

14 Aluminum foil

15 Ceramic baking dishes for lasagne and other baked pasta dishes

16 Stainless steel baking dish for lasagne

17 Perforated square spatula for lifting large sheets of pasta from boiling water

18 Cotton dish towel for draining cooked sheets of pasta

19 Chopsticks for Asian cooking

20 Wire strainer for Asian cooking, particularly suitable for removing food from a wok

21 Wok with spatula and cleaning brush

22, 23 Bamboo steamers for Chinese dishes

Pasta sauces

Most Italian cooks have little interest in creating scintillating new sauces for pasta; instead, they are very skilled at adding individual touches to the classics like tomato or bolognese sauce or pesto. Every Italian maintains he can recognize his mother's sauces immediately, and that they are the best he's ever eaten. And they probably are, because they are made at home, from scratch, using the best ingredients available.

For the basic pasta sauces, as for all other dishes, the ingredients are all-important. It is not only foodies who complain that tomatoes in supermarkets nowadays look appetizing but usually taste of nothing. What a joy it is, then, to discover a farmers' market or specialty produce market selling vine-ripened tomatoes that combine the familiar sweetness of tomatoes with a robust acidity. These tomatoes make the most delicious, full-flavored sauce. When it comes to making a bolognese sauce, the quality of

the meat used is paramount. And it must be freshly ground. Meat of an inferior quality will not give the requisite robustness to this sauce that simmers for hours.

Of course the food industry, with all its energy and competitive zeal, has thrown itself into the sauce business. Until a few years ago, canned tomato purée and paste were all the industry had to offer, apart from canned peeled tomatoes, the so-called "*pomodori pelati*," which often have more taste than fresh tomatoes. Today there are sauces of all kinds, both fresh and in cans or packages. Some are good, but many are not.

In contrast to the basic sauces of classic French cuisine, which can be difficult to produce in the domestic kitchen, Italian sauces are ideally suited to being made at home (some of the basic sauces, like béchamel, are dead easy). Anyone who owns a heavy cooking pot and shops carefully for the right ingredients can make a pasta sauce as successfully as any professional cook. Because the sauces usually simmer for a long time, there is always an opportunity to correct mistakes — unless, of course, you've been overenthusiastic with the salt. Sauce-making offers plenty of scope for anyone keen to experiment: countless amateur cooks have perfected pasta sauces of their own, of which they are justifiably proud. And don't forget that the delicious aromas permeating the house will whet your family's appetite.

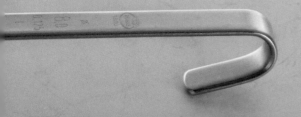

Good, ripe tomatoes

The number-one ingredient in Italian pasta sauces

With tomatoes, freshness is not always the most important criterion. If the choice is between freshly picked but green tomatoes from the greenhouse and those picked fully ripe and then canned or dried under the Mediterranean sun, then there's simply no contest.

Fresh tomatoes

The sauce is as simple as the pasta with which it is eaten, and this explains why the quality of the tomatoes is so important. The simplest tomato sauce consists of little more than ripe tomatoes, a little oil, and salt. The tomatoes must be really ripe and sweet, brought to maturity on the vine – in the sun, not in a greenhouse. Even in countries with the right climate, such perfection is available only for a limited period. In Italy, the tomato season lasts roughly from August to the end of October. The problem of obtaining good ripe tomatoes is a familiar one for Italian cooks, which is why they put by sufficient stocks of the best, ripest, and sweetest tomatoes during the late summer and early fall in the form of *conserva di pomodoro*, in order to have a constant supply of this fresh tomato purée.

Making fresh tomato purée

All you need is tomatoes – no seasonings or preservatives. First, plunge the tomatoes into boiling water for a brief blanch and then peel them. Next, press them through a large-meshed strainer or food mill, or purée in a blender or food processor (you can then strain out the seeds, if desired). Pack the resulting pulp into sterilized canning jars or bottles with wide necks and screw down the lids. Set the bottles in a large, deep pan, add enough water to come level with the purée in the jars, and simmer gently for about 50 minutes. Remove the pan from the heat and let the jars cool in the water.

Choosing the right tomatoes

Not all varieties of tomato can be used to make a good sauce, and Italian pasta experts are very choosy. In Italy, the very best tomatoes for sauce-making come from Campania, and it is said that those grown on volcanic soil around Vesuvius are the finest of all. The egg-shaped plum or roma tomatoes are particularly suitable for sauces. These are the Neapolitan or Roman varieties, very meaty and with few seeds. If they are picked when deep red and really ripe, they have a particularly intense flavor. When buying tomatoes, choose those with a rich color and noticeable fragrance. Don't worry if they are not perfectly shaped – this has no effect on their flavor.

Canned tomatoes

You can buy fresh tomatoes year round in supermarkets, but they are unlikely to have much flavor if they're not locally grown and in season. If tomatoes have been shipped any distance, they will generally have been harvested when still green in order to stop them spoiling during transport. It is true that they eventually turn a lovely red color (due to ripening in a warm room or with ethylene gas), but the flavor does not develop to the same extent as when they are left to ripen on the vine. So it is sensible to keep a stock of canned tomatoes in the pantry. Imported Italian brands, from the tomato-growing areas around Naples and Parma, often have better flavor than American brands because Italian packers tend to pick riper tomatoes. You can buy canned peeled whole tomatoes, peeled and crushed tomatoes, and tomatoes flavored with herbs such as basil and oregano, as well as canned tomato purée and the Italian tomato purée called *passata di pomodoro* or *polpa di pomodoro*. Passata is an ideal base for quick pasta sauces.

Sun-dried tomatoes, tomato paste

Sun-dried tomatoes, sold packed in oil or dry-packed, loose or in cellophane, have a particularly rich, highly concentrated flavor. They are well suited to those *sughi* (sauces) that require little liquid but need a concentrated tomato flavor. Tomato paste, available in cans and tubes, consists of tomatoes cooked down to a concentrate. The best is made from sun-dried tomatoes, which is still sold from earthenware pots in some parts of Italy.

FRESH TOMATO SAUCE

Of the many *sugo* recipes, the simplest are the best, as is so often the case. The following sauce is one of these, and it must be made only from the ripest fresh tomatoes. These need not be plum tomatoes – the round varieties are perfectly suitable, as long as they have been ripened in the sun. Their taste comes through pure and unadulterated, because the recipe includes neither onions nor garlic, nor any other dominant flavoring – just basil, which perfectly complements the fresh acidity of the tomatoes.

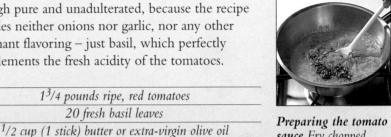

1³/4 pounds ripe, red tomatoes
20 fresh basil leaves
¹/2 cup (1 stick) butter or extra-virgin olive oil
1 teaspoon salt
freshly ground black pepper

Preparing the tomato sauce Fry chopped tomatoes in butter. Add fresh basil after simmering.

Blanch the tomatoes briefly, then peel them; remove the seeds and dice the tomatoes. Coarsely shred the basil leaves. Add the diced tomatoes to the hot butter or oil and simmer until thick. (How long will depend on their moisture content.) Season, stir in the basil, and serve.

Tomato sauces

From very simple and basic to piquant or luxuriously creamy, tomato sauces are an indispensable element in pasta cooking

BASIC TOMATO SAUCE

Its Italian name is "*La pommarola.*" A basic smooth sauce of this kind can be used for many *sughi*, instead of a ready-made sauce from a jar or can. This basic sauce can be seasoned to suit individual tastes, with fresh or dried herbs, or as much garlic as you like, and you can replace the olive oil with butter.

1 small carrot, 1 yellow onion
2 celery stalks, 1³/4 pounds ripe plum tomatoes
1 teaspoon salt, freshly ground black pepper
¹/4 cup olive oil
1 tablespoon chopped fresh basil

Peel the carrot and cut it first lengthwise into strips and then into small cubes. Peel and mince the onion. Trim and dice the celery. Prepare the sauce as shown in the picture sequence.

Preparing the tomato sauce:

Wash the tomatoes and trim out the cores. Using a sharp knife, cut the tomatoes in half, then in quarters, and, finally, in dice.

Put the tomatoes and diced carrot into a saucepan. It is important that the tomatoes be on the bottom of the pan, since they will exude liquid.

Add the minced onion and diced celery. Cover the pan and cook on a low heat until all the ingredients are soft, about 40 minutes.

Put the vegetable mixture into a large-mesh strainer set over a bowl and press through with a spoon. (Or you can use a food mill.) The sauce will be quite thin.

Scrape all pulp from the base of the strainer or food mill and add it to the sauce.

Pour the sauce into a pan and heat. Season to taste with salt and pepper. Add the oil to the sauce and stir in.

Add the chopped fresh basil to the sauce. Check the seasoning, adding more salt and pepper if required.

PIQUANT TOMATO SAUCE

A beautifully thick, rich *sugo*, best suited to tube-like pasta such as macaroni, penne, or ziti. If you prefer a thinner sauce, add a little extra meat stock.

1 pound ripe, juicy tomatoes, 1 small yellow onion
1 garlic clove, 1 small hot red chili pepper
5 tablespoons olive oil, 2 tablespoons chopped fresh parsley
1 tablespoon chopped fresh herbs: oregano, sage, rosemary
3 tablespoons meat stock
2 tablespoons ricotta salata (salted ricotta cheese), salt

Blanch the tomatoes, then peel. Cut in half, remove the seeds and core, and dice. Peel and chop the onion. Peel and thinly slice the garlic. Cut the chili pepper in half lengthwise, remove the seeds, and mince. Heat the oil in a wide pan and sauté the onion and garlic until they become translucent. Add the herbs, chili pepper, and diced tomatoes.

Pour in the stock and simmer over low heat about 20 minutes. Press the ricotta through a strainer into the pan and stir in. Taste the sauce and season with salt if necessary.

CREAMY TOMATO SAUCE

This is a perfect sauce for spaghetti. Serve with freshly grated cheese – Parmesan or pecorino romano.

1 3/4 pounds ripe tomatoes
1 yellow onion
2 slices of bacon, thick-cut
1 tablespoon olive oil
1/4 cup cream
salt and freshly ground black pepper

Wash the tomatoes, cut in half, and remove the seeds and core. Cut first in quarters and then in small pieces. Peel and chop the onion. Cut the bacon in small pieces. Fry the bacon with the oil in a saucepan until it begins to brown slightly. Pour off excess fat, if desired, then add the chopped onion and sauté until translucent. Add the tomatoes, cover the pan, and simmer 20 minutes.

Purée in a blender or food processor and then press through a strainer. Add the cream and season to taste with salt and pepper.

Ragù alla bolognese

The best example of fine Italian pasta cooking

BOLOGNESE MEAT SAUCE

Italian cooking certainly enjoys an outstanding reputation, but the specialties of Bologna represent a further step up the ladder of culinary excellence. One of these is tagliatelle with meat sauce. This versatile pasta sauce, perhaps the most famous one of all, is very often served in Italy with homemade tagliatelle. Outside Italy, it is indissolubly associated with spaghetti. The sauce must be cooked for a long time – the longer the better – so that all the ingredients can combine to create the unique blend of flavors.

2 carrots, 1 yellow onion
2 garlic cloves, 3 celery stalks
1/2 pound prosciutto, 1 3/4 pounds fresh tomatoes
1 28-ounce can whole tomatoes
10 ounces beef round, 7 ounces boneless pork
1/4 cup olive oil, 1/4 cup chopped fresh parsley
6 tablespoons (3/4 stick) butter, 6 tablespoons tomato paste
1 cup meat stock
1 teaspoon salt, freshly ground black pepper
1/2 teaspoon sugar (optional)

Peel the carrots; cut lengthwise in strips and then in small dice. Peel and mince the onion and garlic. Finely dice the celery. Cut the prosciutto in small cubes. Blanch the fresh tomatoes, then peel; cut in half, remove the seeds, and dice finely. Drain the canned tomatoes and chop coarsely. Grind the meat coarsely. Heat the oil in a saucepan and fry the carrot. Continue as shown in the picture sequence. Then season the sauce with salt and pepper and simmer at least 1 hour, leaving the lid slightly ajar so that steam can escape. Add sugar, if desired, and simmer 30 minutes longer. Add the rest of the butter, and check the seasoning.

Add the ground meat and lightly brown it, stirring and breaking it up so it becomes crumbly.

Add the prosciutto to the meat and vegetable mixture and cook 5 minutes, stirring constantly.

Add half of the butter and then the diced fresh tomatoes.

Add the canned tomatoes and stir all the ingredients together thoroughly. Simmer briefly, uncovered.

Bolognese sauce *is still made every day in its city of origin, for example at Gigina's, 1 via Stendhal, Bologna, where the traditional recipe is followed scrupulously. The process begins with the selection of the meat; each piece is carefully inspected before purchasing in order to ensure quality, even though it is only going to be put through the meat grinder. Connoisseurs are agreed that only the best meat should be used, although there is some debate about the ratio of beef to pork, or whether lamb or even rabbit should also be added. Some ragù purists swear by a sauce made just with beef. And just how long it should simmer on the lowest possible heat is a secret that nobody is prepared to divulge.*

Making bolognese sauce:

Add the onion and garlic to the carrots and cook until golden brown, stirring constantly.

Stir in the tomato paste. Let the sauce simmer a little to evaporate excess liquid.

Stir in the chopped celery, then add the chopped parsley and cook until all the vegetables are soft.

Add the meat stock and mix all the ingredients together thoroughly.

The white sauces

Béchamel and velouté, both thickened with flour, are the basis for many pasta sauces

FRESH HERB SAUCE

A creamy sauce is the perfect base for aromatic fresh herbs. Delicious with pasta.

2 tablespoons butter
3 tablespoons flour
2 cups beef or chicken stock
1/2 teaspoon salt, freshly ground white pepper
a pinch of freshly grated nutmeg
1 egg yolk
1/2 cup cream
2 tablespoons chopped fresh herbs: chives, parsley, oregano, thyme, sage

Melt the butter in a saucepan over medium heat, sprinkle in the flour, and cook gently, stirring, 1 to 2 minutes; do not brown. Pour in the stock, whisking constantly. Season with salt, pepper, and nutmeg, and simmer 20 minutes, whisking occasionally.

Remove the pan from the heat. Mix together the egg yolk and cream. Add a little of the hot sauce to the egg yolk and cream mixture, then stir into the rest of the sauce. Strain the sauce. Reheat gently (do not boil or the sauce will curdle), then add the herbs and blend thoroughly.

GORGONZOLA SAUCE

The same base can be transformed very simply into a cheese sauce. Just replace the herbs with 3 ounces of gorgonzola or other creamy blue cheese, cut in small cubes, letting it melt into the sauce. Gorgonzola is a particularly good blue cheese to use because it melts very easily.

This classic Italian blue cheese is available in two strengths – the mild *gorgonzola dolce* "sweet gorgonzola" and the stronger *gorgonzola piccante* "sharp gorgonzola."

SAUCE MORNAY

Swiss Gruyère or Emmental can be used instead of Parmesan and fontina.

For the béchamel sauce:
2 tablespoons butter, 3 tablespoons flour, 2 cups milk
1/2 teaspoon salt, freshly ground pepper
a pinch of freshly grated nutmeg
1 egg yolk, 1/2 cup cream
In addition:
1/4 cup each freshly grated Parmesan and fontina cheeses
1 to 2 heaping tablespoons whipped cream

Make the sauce Mornay as shown in the picture sequence below.

Making sauce Mornay:

Melt the butter in a saucepan, add the flour, and cook gently 1 to 2 minutes, stirring. Do not brown.

Add the milk and whisk to a smooth consistency. Add the salt, pepper, and nutmeg. Simmer 20 minutes, whisking occasionally.

Remove the pan from the heat. Mix the egg yolk with the cream and add 2 tablespoons of the hot sauce.

Whisk the egg and cream mixture into the rest of the sauce. Strain the sauce and reheat gently without bringing back to a boil.

Stir in the cheeses and then the whipped cream.

VELOUTÉ

The quantities given here will produce about 3 cups of this velvety smooth sauce.

1 1/2 tablespoons butter
1 shallot, peeled and minced
2 tablespoons flour
2 cups vegetable stock, 1 cup heavy cream
a pinch of salt, freshly ground white peppper

Melt the butter in a saucepan over medium to low heat and cook the shallot until it starts to become translucent. Sprinkle the flour over the shallot and cook 1 to 2 minutes, without browning. Pour on the vegetable stock and simmer 5 minutes, stirring constantly with a whisk. Add the cream and simmer 10 minutes longer. Season to taste with salt and pepper, then strain the sauce.

Fontina is a semifirm yet creamy cheese made from cow's milk. It melts easily and smoothly, and is therefore ideal for cooking. It is used in the traditional fonduta piemontese (Piedmontese cheese fondue), where its slightly sweet, nutty flavor combines remarkably well with the truffles that garnish the dish.

Garlic and olives

These are among the most important ingredients in the cooking of Liguria and are natural partners for pasta

PESTO ALLA GENOVESE

This Genoese basil sauce is internationally famous. There are numerous variations on the theme along the Ligurian Riveria, but they differ only slightly. For example, the pine nuts can be toasted before they are crushed in order to enhance their flavor.

4 garlic cloves, $^1/3$ cup pine nuts
$2^1/2$ cups fresh basil leaves
$^1/2$ cup freshly grated pecorino cheese
$^3/4$ cup freshly grated Parmesan cheese
salt and freshly ground black pepper
$^1/2$ to $^2/3$ cup extra-virgin olive oil

Peel and coarsely chop the garlic. Continue as shown in the picture sequence (a mortar and pestle is traditional, but you could also use a food processor). The finished sauce should have the consistency of mayonnaise. If the pesto is to be used purely as a sauce for pasta, it can be thinned down by stirring in a few spoonfuls of the pasta cooking water.

Dry but still fresh – *that's how the garlic for pesto should be. Garlic that has dried out too much and is sprouting will taste very pungent and sharp, and you will taste that sharpness in the sauce.*

Making pesto:

Using a mortar and pestle, pound the pine nuts with the chopped garlic.

Wash and dry the basil leaves, then chop them coarsely. Add them to the garlic and pine nut mixture and pound to a paste.

Gradually add the finely grated cheeses and mix in well. Season to taste with salt and pepper.

Add the olive oil as when making mayonnaise – little by little and mixing so that it blends with the other ingredients.

Spaghettini with tapenade: Cook 1 pound of pasta in boiling salted water until al dente, drain, tip into a pre-warmed serving dish, and toss with the tapenade.

TAPENADE

This piquant blend of black olives and anchovies comes from Provence. Ready-made tapenade, in jars, is not at all bad, so if you want to prepare a quick olive and pasta dish, then the commercial product offers an alternative to homemade.

²/3 cup black olives, preferably Niçoise olives
2 anchovy fillets, 3 garlic cloves
¹/2 cup cold-pressed extra-virgin olive oil
salt and freshly ground black pepper

Pit and chop the olives. Cut the anchovy fillets in small pieces. Prepare the tapenade as shown in the picture sequence.

Crostini, small rounds of bread rubbed with garlic and then heated in the oven until crisp, are often served with tapenade. But it is equally popular as a sauce for pasta, for example with spaghettini. If the tapenade is too thick to coat the pasta, thin with 1 or 2 tablespoons of the pasta cooking water.

Making tapenade:

Peel and mince the garlic, and sauté in half of the olive oil until golden. Strain this garlic-flavored oil and let cool.

In a mortar and pestle or in a food processor, pound the olives and anchovies with the remaining oil to a fine paste.

Gradually mix in the garlic-flavored oil. Season to taste with salt and pepper.

Garlic and good-quality olive oil

First-class pasta requires ingredients of the best quality — this is particularly true of the oil

WITH GARLIC AND OLIVE OIL

"Spaghetti *aglio e olio*" is one of the standard Italian preparations for pasta, and is a good example of how to conjure up a tasty dish with the minimum of ingredients. This combination also works well with other kinds of long pasta, such as bucatini.

5 garlic cloves
2 hot red chili peppers
$^1/_2$ cup extra-virgin olive oil
$^3/_4$ pound spaghetti or other long, thin pasta
salt and freshly ground black pepper

Peel and mince the garlic. Cut the chili peppers in half, remove the seeds, and cut in very thin strips. Heat the oil in a small pan, add the garlic, and sauté until it begins to brown. (Make sure that the garlic does not brown too much or it will taste bitter.) Add the strips of chili pepper and sauté briefly with the garlic. Remove the pan from the heat. While the sauce is being prepared, cook the pasta in boiling salted water until *al dente*. Drain and place in a pre-warmed serving dish. Pour the sauce over the pasta and mix in thoroughly with two large forks. Season with salt and black pepper and serve immediately.

Top-quality olive oil is essential for this dish because, apart from the pungency of the hot peppers, it is the oil that imparts flavor to the pasta. Indeed it is the quite distinctive flavor of olive oil, particularly cold-pressed extra-virgin oil, that makes this simple dish taste so superb. If you don't like the taste of olive oil you can serve the pasta with butter instead.

Capers preserved in salt, *usually coarse sea salt, are the best to use for this sauce. Capers pickled in vinegar would completely change the character of the dish. Capers in brine could be used, but they must be soaked for an hour beforehand.*

WALNUT AND GARLIC SAUCE

"Alla fornaia" is how the Italians describe this recipe, which means "in baker's style." This distinctive sauce is eaten with long pasta such as spaghetti.

1¼ cups walnut pieces
7 tablespoons extra-virgin olive oil
2 garlic cloves, minced, ¾ cup white breadcrumbs
½ teaspoon salt, freshly ground white pepper
1 pound spaghetti or other long, thin pasta
1 tablespoon chopped fresh parsley

Chop the walnuts into small pieces, removing the bitter membrane if the nuts are freshly shelled. Warm 6 tablespoons of the oil in a saucepan, add the walnuts, garlic, and bread crumbs, and sauté gently, stirring constantly, until the garlic is golden brown. Season to taste with salt and pepper.

While the sauce is being prepared , cook the pasta in boiling salted water until *al dente* . Drain, tip into a pre-warmed serving dish, and mix thoroughly with the remaining oil and the walnut and garlic sauce. Sprinkle with the parsley and serve.

CAPER SAUCE

Capers are much used in pasta sauces in southern Italy, which is where caper bushes grow in profusion.

3 heaping tablespoons capers preserved in salt
½ cup black olives
2 garlic cloves, 2 shallots
12 anchovy fillets, 1 pound ripe plum tomatoes
2 hot red chili peppers
6 tablespoons olive oil
1 pound spaghettini, 2 ounces pecorino romano cheese

Mince the capers and pitted olives. Peel and mince the garlic and shallots. Cut the anchovy fillets in small pieces. Blanch and peel the tomatoes, remove the seeds, and dice. Remove seeds from the chilies, then mince. Heat the oil in a saucepan, add the capers, olives, garlic, shallots, and anchovies and sauté 2 to 3 minutes, stirring constantly. Add the tomatoes and chilies and simmer 15 minutes.

In the meantime, cook the spaghettini in boiling salted water until *al dente*. Drain and mix with the sauce. Garnish with thinly shaved pecorino.

Soups

Pity the poor soup! Once it used to be the main meal of the day, sitting
steaming in its tureen in the middle of the table while the whole family ate
their fill. In our times of plenty, however, soup has been reduced to the
role of first course, and the old deep soup bowls have become little plates
and cups, too small to contain anything more than a tasty appetizer. As a
result, hearty soups have been relegated to snack meals or lunch, and small
pasta shapes designed to be used in soups – such as pretty little stars,
melon-seed or rice shapes, or very thin noodles – have been neglected.
What a shame! Soups with pasta and noodles can be either
robust or elegant, suitable for any dining occasion.

In Italy, *pasta in brodo* (in broth) is eaten as a *primo*, or
first course, served before the meat or fish entrée, or

secondo. Whether ribbon noodles or stuffed pastas are used, the distinctive feature of this dish is that the pasta is not simply tossed, ready cooked, into the hot broth but is actually cooked in it, thereby taking up the flavor of the liquid. If that liquid is just a broth from a can, the culinary effect is not exactly overwhelming, but a homemade stock can make a sublime dish, especially if the pasta has a filling that complements the flavor of the soup.

Soup containing pasta or noodles is extremely popular in Asian cooking. Apart from the indispensable "scallions," a Chinese soup will often contain a cluster of cellophane noodles or the Chinese dumplings known as wonton. Cooks can be seen on every street corner in Hong Kong making wonton, rapidly and with great skill, and then serving them to hungry passers-by in a bowl of clear broth. The solid ingredients are fished out with chopsticks, and the broth is slurped down with much enjoyment.

There seem to be two things on which there is universal agreement. First, pasta should be added only to clear soup, such as a consommé or a bouillon, and not to soups thickened with egg yolks or cream, for example. (Italian minestrone, which usually contains pasta, is actually a clear soup.) And, second, fillings for stuffed pasta should be compatible with the soup: ravioli or tortellini stuffed with salmon have no place in a beef or chicken soup, and beef or game fillings have no place in a fish or seafood soup. Some cooks try too hard to be creative, and the results often do not work. In cases of doubt, remember that simple, unfilled pasta shapes or noodles will blend with just about everything, even the herbs and seasonings that add zest to a soup.

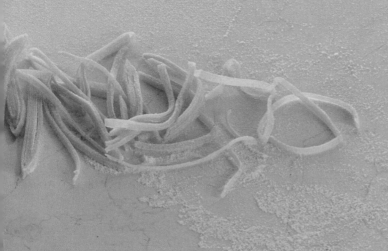

Making beef stock:
Slowly roast the bones, turning them from time to time. As soon as they have all turned golden brown, remove from the oven and drain off the fat. Roast the onion halves until a rich brown.

Pasta in clear broth

From capelli d'angelo to thimbles — hand-cut pasta or the fantastical shapes produced commercially

Chicken soup with homemade noodles used to be a special Sunday dish. But once pasta manufacturers gave free rein to their imaginations, cutting the dough into every imaginable shape and size, from those no bigger than a grain of rice to the alphabet shapes so popular with children, soup-making

changed forever. Ultimately, however, it is not the pasta that gives the soup its flavor; it is the stock, plus the vegetables, meat, and flavorings added. With a little creativity, countless variations on the theme can be produced: flavorsome beef broths, elegant consommés of game or lamb, or chicken soups.

Place the bones in a large stockpot and cover with cold water.

Bring to a boil, skimming off the scum constantly with a ladle.

Add the roasted onion halves, cloves, peppercorns, and bouquet garni. Simmer 1 to 1½ hours.

Line a colander with a linen dish towel and set in a pan. Ladle the stock into the colander.

Let the strained stock cool, refrigerate, then remove the solidified fat from the surface with a perforated skimming spoon.

BEEF STOCK

Rich beef stock is popular as a basis for soups. The recipe here will produce a good clear stock. It can be made even clearer in the traditional manner by "clarifying" with beef and egg white. This also gives the stock a better flavor. Stocks for soup should be prepared without the addition of salt or any other powerful seasonings, since the flavor will become more concentrated when the stock is subsequently reduced and used to make soup. Freshly made stock can be kept a few days in the refrigerator or up to 6 months in the freezer. The ingredients listed here will make about 1½ quarts of stock.

4½ pounds beef bones sawed into chunks
1 pound beef hind-shank bones with marrow, sawed into 2-inch pieces
3 tablespoons vegetable oil
1 onion, unpeeled
2 cloves
6 to 8 white peppercorns
For the bouquet garni:
1 small carrot, ½ small leek
1 thin slice of celery root or 1 celery stalk
½ garlic clove
a few parsley sprigs, 1 bay leaf

Preheat the oven to 350°F. Rinse the bones, and put in a roasting pan with the oil. Put the pan in the oven. Cut the onion in half and put in a small roasting pan, cut-side down, without any oil. Put in the oven. Tie the ingredients for the bouquet garni together in a small piece of cheesecloth. Continue as shown in the picture sequence.

CONSOMMÉ
WITH CAPELLINI AND PEAS

A delicate consommé, whose subtle flavor is perfectly complemented by tender fresh green peas and thin noodles. Cooking the noodles separately keeps the consommé clear.

$^1/_4$ pound capellini
1 $^1/_3$ cups beef stock (see opposite page)
1 cup shelled fresh green peas
salt
freshly ground pepper
2 zucchini flowers (optional)

Cook the capellini in boiling salted water until *al dente*, then drain and rinse briefly with cold water to prevent the noodles sticking together. At the same time, bring the stock to a boil, add the peas, and simmer gently for a few minutes. Add the noodles, season the consommé, and let simmer 2 to 3 minutes longer. Garnish with the zucchini flowers.

CONSOMMÉ
WITH DITALINI AND VEGETABLES

Short pasta tubes, such as tubettini and ditalini (thimbles), are ideal for soups that contain vegetables or meat, since they are easy to eat with a spoon.

$^1/_4$ pound ditalini rigati (about $^3/_4$ cup)
5 ounces kohlrabi, cut in diamond shapes
1 small carrot, cut in rounds
$^1/_2$ zucchini, cut in short strips
1 cup broccoli florets
3 cups beef stock (see opposite page)
$^1/_2$ cup peeled and chopped tomatoes
salt and pepper, 1 tablespoon chopped fresh chives

Cook the pasta in boiling salted water until *al dente*; drain and rinse with cold water. Briefly cook the kohlrabi, carrot, zucchini, and broccoli in 1 cup of the stock. Add the tomatoes and the rest of the stock. Simmer 2 to 3 minutes. Add the pasta, bring back to a boil, and season. Garnish with the chives.

Vegetable soup with pasta and cheese

A popular combination, and not only in Italy

MINESTRONE

This most famous of all Italian soups does not always contain pasta, since it is also made with rice. If pasta is used, then a short variety, such as quadrucci, ditalini, tubettini, or gnocchetti sardi, is best.

3 celery stalks, 2 carrots
3/4 pound waxy potatoes
1/2 pound fresh green peas in the pod
3/4 cup cooked or canned cannellini beans
1 large zucchini
1/2 pound leeks, 4 tomatoes
2 tablespoons butter
1 tablespoon olive oil
1 1/2 cups small broccoli florets
a pinch of salt
freshly ground white pepper
2 quarts chicken stock (see page 86)
1/4 pound tubettini rigati (about 3/4 cup)
1/4 pound thick-cut sliced bacon
1 onion, peeled
2 garlic cloves, peeled
1 tablespoon chopped fresh parsley
For serving:
3/4 cup freshly grated Parmesan cheese

Trim and dice the celery. Peel and thinly slice the carrots. Peel and dice the potatoes. Shell the peas. Put the beans in a strainer, rinse under cold water, and let drain. Cut the zucchini in rounds and then cut the rounds in half. Slice the leeks in thin rings. Blanch and peel the tomatoes, then cut in half, remove seeds, and cut the flesh in strips. Heat the butter and oil in a large pot. Add the celery, carrots, potatoes, peas, broccoli, and beans. Season with salt and pepper, and sauté briefly. Pour on the chicken stock and bring to a boil. Add the pasta. After simmering 5 to 8 minutes, add the zucchini and leeks and stir them in.

Mince the bacon, onion, and garlic, and sauté together in a frying pan over medium heat for 20 minutes. Add to the soup, together with the tomato strips and parsley. Ladle the soup into bowls and serve with the Parmesan.

GREEK TOMATO SOUP WITH ORZO

A real summer soup, made all around the Mediterranean. The preparation is basically the same in the various countries – all that changes is the shape of the pasta added to the soup. In Greece, it usually contains orzo, the tiny pasta shaped like grains of rice. Italian cooks prefer short pasta tubes such as ditalini or *pennini piccoli*, although they sometimes use *risoni*, as one rice-shaped variety is called in Italy. It is vital to use really ripe tomatoes with a fully developed, fruity flavor, otherwise the soup will be dull and insipid. If good fresh tomatoes are not available, use canned rather than making do with unripe fresh ones. The Greek cheeses suggested in the recipe go particularly well with the soup, but you could also use an aged pecorino romano.

1 pound red, ripe tomatoes
1 garlic clove, 1 carrot
1 celery stalk
1/2 bunch of fresh parsley with stems
2 tablespoons extra-virgin olive oil
1/3 cup minced onion
3 cups veal stock, a sprig of thyme
a handful of lovage or celery leaves
salt and freshly ground black pepper
1/2 cup orzo
2 ounces kefalotiri or feta cheese

Wash the tomatoes, cut out the cores, and chop coarsely. Peel and mince the garlic. Peel the carrot and trim the celery; cut both in small pieces. Chop the parsley, including the stems. Heat the oil in a large pot and sauté the onion and garlic until translucent. Add the carrot, celery, and parsley and cook 4 to 5 minutes, stirring constantly. Add the chopped tomatoes and cook 3 to 4 minutes longer, then pour on the veal stock. Add the sprig of thyme and the lovage leaves, and season with salt and pepper. Simmer over low heat about 30 minutes.

Strain the soup into a clean pan, pressing down on the vegetables to extract all the liquid, and bring to a boil again. In the meantime, cook the pasta in boiling salted water until *al dente*. Drain and add to the soup. Sprinkle the crumbled cheese over each serving.

Chicken stock

A good base for many dishes

Good chicken stock is not only the basis for excellent soups but can also be used in vegetable and meat stews, sauces, risottos, and many other dishes. A rich, nutritious stock can be made following the same method as that given for beef stock on page 82. Other kinds of poultry, such as turkey or guinea fowl, could be used instead of chicken.

CHICKEN STOCK

Here, a whole bird is used to make the stock. The meat can be reserved for a soup or for salads or sandwiches. This will yield about 3 quarts of stock.

$4^1/2$- to $5^1/2$-pound stewing fowl, cut in quarters
$2^1/4$ pounds veal bones, chopped in pieces
4 quarts water, 20 black peppercorns
2 garlic cloves, crushed
1 onion, studded with 4 cloves
For the bouquet garni:
1 carrot, $1/2$ leek, 1 celery stalk
2 bay leaves, 2 sprigs of fresh thyme
6 sprigs of parsley

Begin preparation of the stock as shown in the 3-picture sequence left. After skimming off all the scum for the second time, let simmer 3 hours, keeping the liquid just below boiling point. After 2 hours of cooking, add the peppercorns, garlic, onion, and bouquet garni, and add more water if necessary. Continue as in the picture sequence below.

Making chicken stock:
Put the chicken and veal bones in a stockpot and cover with hot water. Bring to a boil, skimming off the scum that rises to the surface. Drain the chicken and bones and rinse with warm water. Return them to the pot, add the measured quantity of water, and bring to a boil, skimming the surface frequently.

After simmering 3 hours on a very low heat, remove the chicken and reserve for later use.

Strain the stock through a colander lined with a linen cloth, letting the liquid run through without pressing.

When the stock has cooled, use a slotted spatula to remove the fat that will have solidified on the surface.

CHICKEN BROTH WITH TAGLIATELLE AND CHICKEN LIVERS

$1/2$ pound tagliatelle, 2 tablespoons vegetable oil
$1/2$ pound chicken livers, carefully cleaned and trimmed
1 tablespoon minced shallot
1 cup peeled and diced tomatoes
1 teaspoon chopped fresh oregano
2 tablespoons chopped fresh parsley
salt and freshly ground black pepper
3 cups boiling chicken stock

Cook the tagliatelle in boiling salted water until *al dente*; drain and rinse briefly with cold water. Heat the oil in a saucepan, add the chicken livers, and brown on all sides. Remove and cut in cubes. Return the chicken livers to the pan, add the shallot and diced tomatoes, and sauté over high heat, stirring, until the livers are just cooked. Stir in the oregano and half of the parsley, and season. Add the noodles. Divide among soup bowls, ladle in the hot stock, and garnish with the remaining parsley.

CHICKEN BROTH WITH CAPELLI D'ANGELO AND VEGETABLES

3 cups chicken stock
$1/2$ cup snow peas cut in diamond shapes
1 small carrot, cut in thin sticks
$1/2$ cup celery root or celery cut in thin sticks
$1/4$ pound capelli d'angelo (angel-hair pasta)
salt and freshly ground black pepper

Bring the chicken stock to a boil, and cook the vegetables until crisp-tender. Cook the snow peas first, adding the carrot and celery-root sticks after 2 to 3 minutes and cooking 1 to 2 minutes more. Add salt and pepper to taste. At the same time, cook the pasta in boiling salted water for 1 to 2 minutes or until *al dente* and drain. Divide the pasta among soup bowls and ladle the stock and vegetables over the top.

BEAN SOUP
WITH PENNETTE RIGATE

"Pasta e fagioli" – pasta and beans – is a combination that is served in many regions of Italy, as well as in Greece. It is most popular in Tuscany, where homemade fettuccine or tagliatelle, cut in small pieces, are used. The soup here can also be made with short pasta such as ditali, lumachine, or pennette (small penne).

1¼ cups dried beans: borlotti, cannellini, navy
2 bay leaves, 6 to 8 fresh sage leaves
1 sprig of fresh savory, 2 garlic cloves
9 tablespoons olive oil, 2 celery stalks
1 each small red and green bell pepper
⅓ cup chopped onion, ½ cup diced carrot
½ cup peeled and chopped tomatoes

1 quart chicken stock (see page 86), salt and pepper
1 teaspoon fresh thyme leaves
2 tablespoons chopped fresh basil
½ pound pennette rigate (about 1½ cups)
freshly grated Parmesan cheese

Soak the beans overnight. Drain and place in a large, shallow pan with the bay leaves, sage leaves, and savory. Crush the unpeeled garlic cloves with the side of a knife and add to the pan. Add 6 tablespoons of the oil and enough water to cover the beans by about 1½ inches. Bring to a boil, then lower the heat and let simmer gently until the beans are very soft, about 1½ hours.

Meanwhile, trim and dice the celery. Cut the bell peppers in half, remove core and seeds, and cut in strips. Heat the remaining oil in a large pot and fry the onions until translucent. Add all the remaining vegetables and sauté 2 to 3 minutes, stirring. Add the stock, bring to a boil, and simmer 30 to 40 minutes.

Remove the herbs and garlic cloves from the beans and discard. Purée half of the beans in a blender or food processor, then press through a strainer. Add the bean purée and the whole beans to the soup and bring it back to a boil. Season with salt and pepper, and add the thyme and basil. Cook the pasta in boiling salted water until *al dente*; drain and add to the soup. Serve Parmesan separately.

MOROCCAN VEGETABLE SOUP
WITH VERMICELLI

The Arabs are one of the peoples who claim the discovery of pasta for themselves, noting that pasta would last longer than flour, and would be easier to transport, on long caravan journeys through the desert. This is a plausible claim, particularly since

there is good evidence that the Arabs introduced pasta into Sicily and southern Italy, and since there are pasta dishes of Arab origin. However, today, pasta is not much eaten in the Arab countries of North Africa, with the exception of soups, which often contain very thin vermicelli. One of these traditional soups is made with lamb or chicken and vegetables (with chickpeas always in evidence). If you prefer, the pasta can be cooked separately, in boiling salted water, but by cooking it in the soup, it absorbs all the spicy flavors.

1 pound boneless shoulder of lamb

1 pound tomatoes, 1 large yellow onion

1 carrot, 1/2 pound zucchini, as small as possible

2 celery stalks, 3 tablespoons olive oil

1/4 teaspoon ground cinnamon

a pinch of cayenne, 2 tablespoons paprika

a pinch of ground saffron, salt and pepper

1 quart lamb stock or chicken stock (see page 86)

2/3 cup cooked or canned chickpeas (garbanzo beans)

1/4 pound zucchini flowers, 1/2 pound vermicelli

For garnish:

small fresh cilantro leaves

Cut the lamb in 5/8-inch cubes. Blanch the tomatoes, peel and cut in half, remove the seeds, and dice. Peel and mince the onion. Cut the carrot in 3/8-inch cubes, and thinly slice the zucchini and celery (use a waffle cutter for the zucchini, if desired). Heat the oil in a large pot and brown the cubes of lamb on all sides; remove from the pot. Sauté the onion in the remaining oil until translucent. Add the carrot and fry 2 minutes longer, stirring constantly. Add the zucchini and celery and sauté briefly. Finally, stir in the diced tomatoes, mixing thoroughly with the other ingredients. Return the lamb to the pot together with the spices and salt and pepper to taste. Add the stock, bring to a boil, and simmer gently about 30 minutes.

After 20 minutes of simmering, add the chickpeas. After a further 7 minutes, add the minced zucchini flowers and the vermicelli. When the soup is done, check the seasoning. Ladle into pre-warmed bowls and garnish with cilantro leaves.

CHINESE NOODLE SOUP
WITH PORK AND VEGETABLES

One of the attractions of this Chinese soup is the contrast between different textures: the soft noodles, the chewy fried pork, and the crisp vegetables.

½ pound pork tenderloin in one piece
2 tablespoons dark soy sauce
2 tablespoons rice wine, 1 tablespoon sugar
2 tablespoons vegetable oil
For the noodle broth:
2 cups chicken stock (see page 86)
¼ pound Chinese egg noodles, 1 cup water
2 tablespoons light soy sauce, 2 tablespoons rice wine
For the vegetables:
2 tablespoons vegetable oil
4 scallions, cut in 1 ½-inch pieces
⅓ cup sliced bamboo shoots
1 hot red chili pepper, seeded and cut in rings
1 cup spinach, well washed and thick stems removed
salt and freshly ground pepper

Season the pork with salt and pepper. Mix together the soy sauce, rice wine, and sugar. Heat the oil in a wok over high heat and brown the pork quickly on all sides. Reduce the heat and cook 15 minutes longer, turning and basting frequently with the soy mixture. Wrap the pork in foil and keep warm.

Wipe the wok clean with paper towels. Cook the noodles in the wok as shown in the picture sequence below. Drain the noodles, reserving the cooking liquid, and set aside. Put the liquid in a saucepan, stir in the soy sauce and rice wine, and season with salt. Let this broth heat gently.

Wipe the wok clean again with paper towels. Heat the oil and briefly stir-fry the scallions. Add the bamboo shoots and chili pepper and stir-fry 1 minute. Finally, add the spinach and stir-fry until the leaves wilt. Season to taste. Cut the pork in thin slices. Divide the noodles among the soup bowls and add the pork, vegetables, and broth.

Cooking egg noodles:
Pour the stock into the wok, bring to a boil, and add the noodles.

Bring the stock back to a boil over high heat, and break up the noodles with chopsticks so that they will cook evenly.

As soon as the stock is boiling again, pour in the water. Cook, stirring occasionally to prevent the noodles from sticking.

CELLOPHANE NOODLE SOUP WITH MEATBALLS AND VEGETABLES

In Asian soups, cellophane noodles, also called bean thread noodles, are used to provide a background for other, more strongly flavored ingredients. They blend well with just about anything, allowing the flavors and texture of ingredients such as meat and vegetables to come to the fore.

1/4 pound cellophane noodles
For the meatballs:
1/2 pound lean ground pork
1 tablespoon fish sauce (nam pla)
1 tablespoon soy sauce
1 teaspoon five-spice powder
salt
For the broth:
1 quart vegetable stock
3 tablespoons fish sauce (nam pla)
For the vegetables:
1 small carrot
2 scallions
1/2 ounce dried tree or wood ear mushrooms, reconstituted in water
1 1/3 cups shredded white cabbage
1 cup thinly sliced leeks
1/4 cup bamboo shoots cut in thin strips
For garnish:
2 garlic cloves, minced
1 tablespoon vegetable oil
fresh cilantro leaves

To make the meatballs, mix the ground pork with the fish sauce, soy sauce, five-spice powder, and some salt. Shape into balls about 1 inch in diameter. Drop into a pan of boiling salted water and cook 3 to 4 minutes; drain.

Mix the vegetable stock with the fish sauce in a large pot and bring to a boil. Cut the carrot in matchstick-sized strips. Slice the scallions. Drain and chop the mushrooms. Add the vegetables to the simmering broth in the following sequence: first the white cabbage; after 2 minutes the carrot; after another 2 minutes the leeks and scallions; and after a further 1 minute the bamboo shoots and mushrooms. Then reduce the heat, add the cellophane noodles to the soup, and cook 2 minutes to soften. Add the meatballs.

Quickly fry the garlic in the oil in a small pan until golden brown. Ladle the soup into bowls, distributing the ingredients as evenly as possible. Sprinkle each serving with the fried garlic and garnish with cilantro leaves.

Chinese cabbage of any kind can be used in Chinese wonton soup.

Crispy wonton soup

Deliciously contrasting textures are one of the delights of Chinese cooking

Wontons are one of the best-known dishes in the southern provinces of China, and may be stuffed with pork or seafood, particularly shrimp, depending on the region. They are now found all over Southeast Asia, wherever Chinese people have settled – they are part of the Nonya cuisine of Malaysia, and of the regional cooking of Indochina. In the Philippines, they are not deep-fried but instead are boiled and served in chicken broth.

Wonton wrappers, which are small squares of paper-thin pasta, are seldom made at home, even in China. In order to make the effort of preparing wontons worthwhile, it is a good idea to make a large quantity. They taste equally good hot or cold, and are an ideal snack and an indispensable part of any selection of dim sum.

NOODLE SOUP

1 tablespoon dried shrimp
1 cup hot water, 1 tablespoon peanut oil
³/4-ounce piece of fresh gingerroot, sliced
1 quart chicken stock (see page 86)
¹/2 pound Cantonese or other Chinese noodles
1 small head of Chinese cabbage (bok choy)
1 tablespoon light soy sauce
salt and freshly ground pepper, 1 tablespoon sugar
fresh cilantro leaves for garnish

Soak the dried shrimp in the hot water about 30 minutes; drain, reserving the water. Heat the oil in a pot large enough to hold the finished soup and add the sliced ginger and shrimp. Stir-fry 1 minute, then add the stock and the water used to soak the shrimp.

Let simmer gently about 30 minutes. Meanwhile, cook the noodles in boiling salted water until *al dente*; drain and rinse with cold water.

Add the green parts of the cabbage leaves to the soup and simmer until wilted. Add the noodles, and season with soy sauce, salt, pepper, and sugar. Ladle into soup bowls and add 3 or 4 deep-fried wontons to each bowl. Garnish with cilantro leaves.

WONTONS

¹/₂ pound fresh pork belly (side pork)
¹/₄ pound peeled raw shrimp
¹/₂ cup minced scallions, 2 tablespoons oriental sesame oil
1 teaspoon salt, freshly ground pepper
1 egg yolk, 40 to 60 wonton wrappers
oil for deep frying

Put the pork and shrimp through the fine blade of a meat grinder, chop in a food processor or, even better, mince very finely with a large knife or a Chinese cleaver. Combine the pork, shrimp, scallions, sesame oil, salt, pepper, and egg yolk in a bowl and mix thoroughly. There are two methods of stuffing the wontons. You can use two wrappers for each, as shown below, or just one wrapper. In the latter case, stuff and fold the wontons but do not pull

Stuffing wontons:

Place 2 wonton wrappers on top of each other on your hand, and put a little stuffing near one corner of the stacked wrappers.

Fold that corner over the stuffing and then roll up, leaving the top third of the wrapper flat.

Brush the two ends of the roll with a little egg white, then fold them up over the roll and press firmly together.

Pull the top corners of the two wrappers apart. Keep the wontons covered with a damp cloth until ready to cook.

apart the two ends; the wontons will look like oversized tortellini. As the wontons are prepared, keep them covered.

Heat oil to about 350°F and fry the wontons until light brown all over. Drain on paper towels.

PANCIT MOLO

This is the Filipino version of Chinese wonton soup. Here, the wontons are boiled rather than deep-fried, and are served in a chicken broth with shrimp.

(not illustrated)
For the stuffing:
¹/₄ pound lean boneless pork
¹/₄ pound peeled raw shrimp
3 tablespoons minced water chestnuts
¹/₄ cup minced scallions
¹/₂ teaspoon salt, 1 tablespoon light soy sauce
freshly ground pepper, 1 egg white, lightly beaten
about 40 wonton wrappers
For the soup:
¹/₂ pound skinless boneless chicken breast
1 quart chicken stock (see page 86)
¹/₂ pound peeled small raw shrimp
¹/₂ cup minced scallions
2 garlic cloves, minced, 1 tablespoon light soy sauce
1 tablespoon fish sauce (nam pla)
fresh cilantro leaves for garnish

Grind or finely mince the pork and shrimp. Mix with the water chestnuts, scallions, salt, soy sauce, pepper, and egg white. Use the mixture to stuff the wonton wrappers, as shown in the picture sequence left. Cook the wontons in boiling salted water for about 4 minutes. Remove with a slotted spoon and place in a bowl of cold water. Drain.

Cut the chicken meat for the soup in thin strips. Bring the stock to a boil, add the chicken, shrimp, and scallions, and season with the garlic, the soy and fish sauces, salt, and pepper. Simmer 3 to 4 minutes. Add the stuffed wontons and let stand, off the heat, for a few minutes. Garnish with cilantro leaves.

With cheese, herbs, and spices

Cheese and pasta have been a successful combination since time immemorial. Virtually all hard or semi-hard cheeses that melt when heated can be used. The best known of these, Parmesan, which comes from northern Italy, is one of the few cheeses that does not form long threads as it melts. As a result, it is the perfect partner for pasta, especially as spaghetti or taglierini coated with grated Parmesan can be eaten more or less decorously.

Perhaps the most sublime dish of pasta and cheese is that created by the legendary Alfredo of Rome. His *fettuccine all'Alfredo* demonstrates most impressively that a world-class pasta dish can be produced with almost nothing other than cheese. The dish certainly merits a brief description here. After cooking the pasta, a little of the boiling-hot cooking water is poured into a warmed gratin dish; some freshly grated *grana padano* (hard grating cheese) and a generous quantity of butter are added to the water and whisked together with a fork until pale and creamy; then the pasta – fresh and homemade of course – is added and stirred with two forks (gold-plated ones in Alfredo's kitchen) until it gleams enticingly. It is recommended that an egg yolk be added to finish off the dish to perfection, but this is optional. However, cream has absolutely no place in this recipe, contrary to the belief still held by many cooks.

There can be no mention of Asian dishes in connection with cheese, since both cheese and butter are wholly alien to that part of the world. Instead, Asian pasta dishes make use of herb and spice mixtures, particularly those containing fiery hot chili peppers. Hot spices can turn a bland plate of pasta into a real challenge for the taste buds and make the sweat pour from diners' foreheads. Garlic, too, can have an impact. In Italy, garlic often plays the starring role in a simple sauce – in combination with olive oil, it makes up the famous *aglio e olio* sauce. Virtually any herb or spice can be combined with pasta or added to the cooking liquid. Saffron is an excellent flavoring, and gives a delicate yellow color, too. One well-respected European chef likes to cook his pasta in coconut milk and season it with fresh cilantro leaves. The imagination knows no bounds.

One of the more recent innovations in the culinary art is sheets of pasta patterned with fresh herb leaves. The result is very decorative. Despite the impressive appearance, the preparation of this herb pasta is not as difficult as you might think.

With butter and cheese

The simplest is also the most elegant

Adding butter is the simplest way of serving pasta. Butter coats pasta in a thin film, making it glisten and imparting a wonderful taste. It is added when the pasta is cooked and drained and still warm. And by using browned butter (*beurre noisette*), or with the addition of a few fresh herbs, you can impart even more flavor. The brief contact with heat allows the flavor of herbs to develop to perfection. A word of warning: pasta tossed with too much butter will become very slippery. This is a problem with dishes to be served with a sauce, since the sauce and pasta will not combine readily.

It is hard to imagine Italian pasta without cheese, and there are so many dishes that make use of this delicious combination. The types of cheese used with pasta range from fontina, which melts readily, to the extra hard, crumbly cheeses of the Parmesan family. Whatever is used, it must be freshly prepared to guarantee the best flavor. Whether chopped in small pieces, sliced, grated, or cut in fine shavings, the cheese is generally mixed into the pasta or sprinkled on top of it just before serving. The melting cheese binds the pasta and gives it a creamy texture, or forms a delicious crust on top of baked pasta dishes or those finished under the broiler. The combination of pasta and cheese is found outside Italy as well, namely in the spätzle of Germany and Switzerland. There, the main types of cheese used are Gruyère and Emmental, which are excellent for grating and melting because of their high fat content.

Emmental cheese, *named for Switzerland's Emmental valley, has a mellow flavor that is sweet and nutty. As it matures, its nutty flavor becomes more intense. Made from cow's milk, Emmental is light golden in color and has marble-size holes.*

Gruyère *Produced in Switzerland and France. Made from cow's milk. Rich, sweet, nutty flavor. Ideal for grating.*

Pecorino romano *Sheeps' milk gives this cheese its distinctive flavor. Aged pecorino is stronger than Parmesan.*

Pecorino sardo *The embossed rind is due to the basket in which it matures. Ideal for strongly flavored pasta dishes.*

Sbrinz *A hard, grating cheese from Switzerland. Has a rich, mellow flavor and melts particularly well.*

Idiazabal *from Spain. Made from sheep's milk. A salty, tangy smoked cheese. Ideal for "country-style" pasta.*

Provolone piccante *This is well-aged provolone, a full-bodied grating cheese. It is preferred by some pasta fans.*

Montasio vecchio *(Montasio piccante) is a flavorful grating cheese. Goes well with bacon and ham.*

Fontina *from the Aosta valley in Italy, made from cow's milk. A mild, slightly sweet flavor. Creamy when melted.*

Taleggio *A semi-hard slicing cheese from Lombardy. Flavor changes from mild to full-bodied as it ages.*

Tyrolean Graukäse *A lightly blue-veined cheese. Has a sharp, slightly sour flavor.*

Browned butter, *or beurre noisette, is the simplest pasta sauce there is. The melted butter should be only very lightly browned (the color of hazelnut shells), so that its flavor will be nutty.*

Ricotta *Moist, slightly grainy cheese made from the whey drained off from making other cheeses.*

Mozzarella di bufala *The traditional mozzarella from Campagna and Lazio, made from waterbuffalo milk.*

Only the freshest

Cheese should always be freshly grated

Whatever kind of cheese is used, it should always be grated fresh, since this is the only way of ensuring the best and fullest flavor. Under no circumstances buy packs of ready-grated cheese, even though it may be more convenient.

Parmesan is the ideal cheese to accompany pasta. Parmigiano-Reggiano, the original Italian Parmesan, plus the two kinds of *grana padano*, the closely grained cheese from the plain of the River Po made by the same method as Parmigiano-Reggiano, and *grana trentino*, from the region of the same name, are the preeminent hard grating cheeses, and not only in Italy. In many other countries, including the U.S., Parmesan imitations are produced in vast quantities, but none can compare with true Parmigiano-Reggiano. One way to ensure that you have the genuine article is always to use freshly grated cheese, so that you can check the rind. As shown in the picture sequence opposite, Parmigiano-Reggiano is produced as a cylindrical block between 25 and 30 kilograms in weight, and with a fat content of at least 32%. It is matured for 2 years before it is brought to market; Parmigiano-Reggianos aged for 3 years are stamped *stravecchio*, and those aged 4 years *stravecchione*. Other good grating cheeses are pecorino – romano, sardo, and toscano – and Sbrinz. And well-aged cheeses for slicing, such as provolone piccante, bring their own excellent flavor to pasta.

A simple metal grater, with a very sharp grating surface and small holes, is fine for grating small quantities of hard cheeses, and when grating the cheese directly onto pasta. For larger quantities, a hand-cranked or electric grater will make the job easier. The traditional Italian grater shown here is ideal. The cheese is held against a roller fitted with sharp spikes, and once grated it falls into the drawer beneath. For softer cheeses, such as Gruyère or Emmental, use a metal grater with larger holes. You can cut wafer-thin slices with a cheese slicing knife, or fine shavings with a vegetable peeler.

Never grate more than will be used that day. This way you will ensure that the pasta dish gets the benefit of the full flavor of the cheese. However, if there is some left over, store it in a jar or container with a tightly fitting top – in the refrigerator if possible.

The storeroom can accommodate up to 100,000 blocks of cheese, neatly stacked on wooden shelves. They will stay in the air-conditioned storage areas until the end of the aging period (2 years).

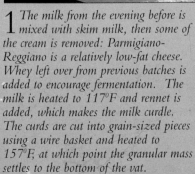

1 The milk from the evening before is mixed with skim milk, then some of the cream is removed: Parmigiano-Reggiano is a relatively low-fat cheese. Whey left over from previous batches is added to encourage fermentation. The milk is heated to 117°F and rennet is added, which makes the milk curdle. The curds are cut into grain-sized pieces using a wire basket and heated to 157°F, at which point the granular mass settles to the bottom of the vat.

2 The cheese is now lifted from the bottom of the vat with a wooden shovel and linen cloth and eased into the cloth – an operation that requires skill and care. As it is rocked to and fro, the cheese gradually forms a ball. The cloth is tied to a wooden pole suspended over the vat, and the ball of cheese is divided up with a large knife. After further processing, each piece will eventually produce a whole block of Parmesan.

3 Still in the linen cloth, the cheese is pressed into a wooden or metal mold; the cloth is folded up over the surface. The mold is covered with a heavy wooden lid, which presses the cheese down. Thus secured, the cheese is immersed in a bath of salted water for 20 to 25 days. After this it is left undisturbed for the next 2 years to age. Finally, the "Parmigiano-Reggiano" brand mark is stamped on the rind, to ensure authenticity.

A fine show

Although extravagant, this makes a real impact

To use half a block of Parmesan as a decorative container for serving pasta might seem just a joke from an eccentric chef, since there are certainly much simpler – and cheaper – ways of adding cheese to pasta. But, in fact, although it is obviously not suitable for a meal for two, it would make a great centerpiece for a pasta party. What is served in the cheese will seem very special indeed, and the half-block of cheese can be used again and again in the same way. If a relatively small amount of pasta is to be served, enough for four or six portions, for example, then the hollow in the cheese does not have to be very big. After repeated use, however, the hollow will become deeper and deeper. Once the pasta has been served, a layer of soft, melted cheese will be left behind and this should be scraped out along with the remaining sauce. Then the half-block of cheese can be kept clean and ready for the next occasion. Spaghetti or tubular pasta such as macaroni, bucatini, ziti, and so on are robust enough for this presentation, since the pasta has to be turned repeatedly in the hollow to coat it in melting cheese.

BUCATINI SERVED IN A BLOCK OF PARMESAN

The following recipe will produce 4 to 6 servings, but the quantities can be increased, depending on the number of guests and the capacity of the block of cheese. The highly concentrated veal stock gives the pasta a particularly hearty flavor. The alcohol used must be high enough proof to burn well.

1 quart veal stock
1 small onion, 1 garlic clove
1 small carrot, 1 celery stalk
1/4 cup extra-virgin olive oil, 3/4 pound tomatoes
2 small hot chili peppers
1/2 teaspoon salt, freshly ground pepper
1 pound bucatini
3 tablespoons alcohol (90 proof), such as grappa

Bring the stock to a boil and let simmer gently until only about 1/2 cup remains. Meanwhile, peel the onion, garlic, and carrot; trim the celery. Mince all these vegetables. Heat the oil in a frying pan and sauté the minced vegetables until they are quite soft. Blanch the tomatoes, peel, remove seeds, and dice. Cut the chili peppers in half lengthwise, remove the seeds and core, and mince. Add the tomatoes and chillies to the pan, and season with salt and pepper. Cook the pasta in boiling salted water until *al dente*; drain and mix immediately with the reduced stock and the sauce.

Just before the pasta has finished cooking, flame the alcohol in the cheese (see picture sequence, right). Transfer the pasta while still hot to the hollow in the half-block of Parmesan, and toss well.

ZITI IN A PIQUANT CREAM AND PANCETTA SAUCE

A combination particularly well suited to "the cheese." Pancetta is unsmoked bacon cured with salt and spices. A dry Lambrusco from the region around Modena would accompany the dish to perfection.

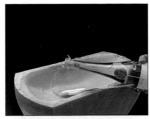

Filling the block of Parmesan:

Pour a generous shot of high-proof alcohol into the hollow cut out of the half-block of cheese.

Brush the alcohol all over the hollow, working quickly.

Flame immediately and let the alcohol burn off completely; the surface of the cheese will heat up and begin to melt.

Pour the hot cooked pasta into the hollow in the cheese.

Stir the pasta with a wooden fork to mix it with the melting cheese.

In Italian restaurants the dish is normally prepared at the table, in huge rounds of Parmesan that have been cut in half crosswise.

(not illustrated)
1/2 pound pancetta, cubed, 3 to 4 tablespoons vegetable oil
1/2 cup chopped onion, 2 garlic cloves, chopped
3/4 cup diced celery
1/2 teaspoon salt, freshly ground pepper
1/2 cup heavy cream
2 hot chili peppers, seeded and minced
a handful of small fresh basil leaves
1 pound ziti

Fry the pancetta, without any additional fat, stirring constantly. Keep warm. Heat the oil in a saucepan and sauté the onion, garlic, and celery (including leaves) until translucent. Add the pancetta, and season with salt and pepper. Pour in the cream and boil to reduce by about half. Add the chili peppers and the basil leaves, whole or coarsely shredded.

In the meantime, cook the pasta in boiling salted water until *al dente*. Drain and mix with the sauce. Transfer to the hollow in the cheese and toss.

Cheese and pasta

Hard cheeses are not the only ones suitable for pasta dishes – soft cheeses also work well

WHOLE-WHEAT PENNE WITH LEEK AND CHEESE SAUCE

Penne rigate is a fairly "rustic" kind of pasta, particularly when made from whole-wheat flour. It is good with this leek sauce, which gets its tangy flavor from pecorino cheese. For an optional finishing touch, place a slice of ripe taleggio on each serving and melt under the broiler.

3/4 pound whole-wheat penne rigate
For the sauce:
1/2 pound leeks, 1/2 garlic clove
6 tablespoons (3/4 stick) butter
1/2 cup meat stock, 1/2 cup cream
1 teaspoon salt, freshly ground pepper
3/4 cup freshly grated pecorino romano cheese
2 tablespoons chopped fresh chives

Cut the leeks in half lengthwise and remove any traces of grit by washing thoroughly in cold water. Cut across in thin strips. Mince the garlic and sauté in the butter with the leek for 2 to 3 minutes. Add the meat stock, bring to a boil, and reduce by about half. Stir in the cream. Season with salt and pepper and, finally, stir in the pecorino. In the meantime, cook the pasta in boiling salted water until *al dente*; drain and mix immediately with the sauce. Transfer to plates and serve garnished with chopped chives.

***Gorgonzola dolce** is a mild variety of this Italian blue-veined cheese. It is less salty than the stronger variety, gorgonzola piccante, and has less blue veining. The most famous blue cheese is the French **Roquefort**. It is made from full-fat sheep's milk and has a rich, creamy texture and pungent flavor. The riper it is, the stronger the flavor will be.*

FRESH TAGLIATELLE WITH GORGONZOLA AND ROQUEFORT

This combination is surprisingly subtle – the sweetish flavor of the gorgonzola contrasts well with the salty tanginess of the Roquefort.

1 recipe of fresh pasta dough no. 4 (see page 40)
For the sauce:
2 tablespoons butter, 1/4 cup minced shallots
1/2 cup heavy cream, 5 ounces sweet gorgonzola (dolce)
To finish:
1/4 pound ripe Roquefort
2/3 cup cherry tomatoes
2 tablespoons butter, 8 fresh sage leaves
salt and freshly ground pepper

Using a knife or a pasta machine, cut the pasta dough into tagliatelle (see pages 52 and 53). Melt the butter in a saucepan and sauté the shallots until translucent. Stir in the cream. Cut the gorgonzola (minus the rind) in cubes and add to the sauce. Let the cheese melt over a low heat, stirring occasionally. Once melted, bring the sauce just to a boil.

*Pasta with cheese
(from left to right):
whole-wheat penne,
tagliatelle, and
cornmeal noodles.*

In the meantime, cook the tagliatelle in boiling
salted water until *al dente*. Drain and mix
immediately with the gorgonzola sauce. Divide the
pasta among 4 plates. Sprinkle each serving with
flakes of Roquefort and place under the broiler to
melt the cheese. Meanwhile, cut the cherry
tomatoes in half and sauté briefly in the hot butter
with the sage. Season and garnish the pasta.

CORNMEAL PASTA WITH TOMATOES AND GOAT CHEESE

The fresh, tangy taste of goat cheese combines
beautifully with the aromatic tomato sauce, while the
cornmeal pasta complements the whole perfectly.

For the pasta dough:
1 cup + 3 tablespoons cornmeal
1 cup + 3 tablespoons all-purpose flour
2 eggs, 2 egg yolks
1 tablespoon olive oil, $^1/2$ tablespoon salt
grated nutmeg

For the sauce:
$^3/4$ pound tomatoes, 2 garlic cloves
$^1/4$ cup extra-virgin olive oil, $^1/4$ cup minced onion
2 tablespoons chopped fresh herbs: thyme, sage, rosemary
$^1/2$ teaspoon salt, freshly ground pepper
6 tablespoons meat stock, 5 to 6 ounces goat cheese, cubed

Make the pasta dough, following the directions on
page 43. Let rest and then cut the dough into thin
noodles with a knife or using a pasta machine (see
pages 52 and 53). Spread out the noodles on a cloth
and let dry a little, so that they will not stick together
during cooking. To make the sauce, blanch the
tomatoes, peel, cut in half, remove the seeds, and
dice. Peel and mince the garlic. Heat the olive oil
and sauté the onion and garlic until translucent. Add
the tomatoes and cook for a few minutes until they
are soft but not completely broken down. Add the
herbs, season with salt and pepper, and stir in the
meat stock. Simmer 1 to 2 minutes. Cook the
noodles in boiling salted water until *al dente*; drain.
Add the cheese to the sauce and mix immediately
with the pasta, so the cubes do not melt completely.

HERB-FLAVORED SPÄTZLE WITH APPENZELLER CHEESE

The tart fruitiness of Appenzeller cheese makes it a particularly good partner for the intense herby flavor of these spätzle; onions fried in butter finish the dish off perfectly. Appenzeller, a Swiss whole-milk cheese, is given a wine or cider wash during curing, which is what makes it slightly fruity in flavor. The choice of herbs and greens will vary according to the season. In spring, you might try a mixture such as dandelion leaves, sorrel, and borage (if available). In summer, use plenty of young spinach leaves mixed with parsley, oregano, basil, and a little lovage or celery leaf.

For the dough:
2 cups chopped mixed fresh herbs and greens (see above)
2 1/3 cups all-purpose flour
6 eggs, 1 teaspoon salt, 1 tablespoon oil
To finish:
5 ounces Appenzeller cheese
1 yellow onion
6 tablespoons (3/4 stick) butter
8 small tomatoes

Put the herbs in a mortar and pestle and pound almost to a paste (or purée in a food processor). Sift the flour into a bowl and add the eggs, salt, oil, and herbs. Continue as shown in the picture sequence below. Cook the spätzle in boiling salted water (see also page 63) until they rise to the surface. Lift them out of the water with a slotted spoon, letting them drain thoroughly as you do so. Shred the Appenzeller. Fill a pre-warmed bowl with alternate layers of spätzle and shredded Appenzeller. Peel the onion and slice thinly. Heat 4 tablespoons of the butter in a frying pan and fry the onions until golden brown. Pour the onions and butter over the spätzle. Serve onto 4 plates and garnish each portion with 2 tomatoes sautéed in the remaining butter.

Preparing herb-flavored spätzle:

Mix all the ingredients thoroughly with a wooden spoon and beat to a smooth, creamy consistency.

Using a knife or metal spatula, scrape the dough, in small portions, from the board into the boiling salted water.

PASTA IN A
PIQUANT CREAM SAUCE

Short tubular pasta, such as mezze penne rigate, ditali rigati, or lumachine, is best suited to this dish. Use the recipe as a starting point, altering it as you wish by using a different type of cheese or adding vegetables, ham, or leftover roast meat. The pungent chili peppers will complement almost any other flavor.

1 garlic clove
2 heaping tablespoons nasturtium leaves and flowers
2 small hot chili peppers
2 tablespoons butter
$^{1}/_{4}$ cup minced shallots
1 pound mezze penne rigate
For the cream sauce:
1 cup heavy cream
3 ounces fontina cheese
$^{1}/_{2}$ cup freshly grated Parmesan cheese
salt
freshly ground white pepper
For garnish:
2 ounces ripe Roquefort
4 nasturtium flowers

Peel and mince the garlic. Cut the nasturtium leaves and flowers in thin strips. Cut the chili peppers in half, remove the core and seeds, and mince. Heat the butter in a frying pan and sauté the shallots and garlic until translucent. Add the nasturtiums and chilies and remove immediately from the heat.

Boil the cream to reduce by about one third. Gradually whisk in the cubed fontina, letting it melt slowly. Remove from the heat and let cool a little, then stir in the grated Parmesan. Cook the pasta in boiling salted water until *al dente*; drain thoroughly, transfer to a pre-warmed bowl, and mix with the cream sauce and the sautéed vegetable mixture. Season with salt and pepper and serve onto pre-warmed plates. Cut the Roquefort in small cubes, sprinkle over the pasta, and place under the broiler until the Roquefort begins to melt, 1 to 2 minutes at most. Garnish each plate with a nasturtium flower and serve immediately.

Pasta with herbs

These pastas can be served with a meat sauce or other highly flavored sauces

BASIL-FLAVORED NOODLES WITH SALAMI SAUCE

Here, the dominant flavor is that of the fresh herbs, even though the dish includes pungent Italian salami. When the pasta is flavored unmistakably with basil and the sauce is seasoned with thyme, rosemary, and parsley, the other flavors take a back seat.

For the pasta dough:
$1/2$ cup fresh basil leaves, 1 garlic clove, $1/2$ teaspoon salt
$2^1/3$ cups all-purpose wheat flour
3 eggs, 3 tablespoons olive oil
For the sauce:
10 ounces well-flavored salami
1 pound tomatoes, peeled and seeded
1 ounce dried porcini or $1/2$ pound fresh porcini (cèpes)
2 tablespoons olive oil, 1 onion, minced
$1/4$ cup red wine
salt and freshly ground pepper
1 tablespoon minced fresh parsley
$1/2$ tablespoon minced fresh thyme
$1/2$ tablespoon minced fresh rosemary

Make the dough as directed in the picture sequence below and on page 41. Cut the salami and tomatoes in dice. If you are using dried porcini, reconstitute them in $1/4$ cup of warm water; fresh ones should be washed and sliced. Heat the oil and sauté the onion until translucent. Add the salami and porcini and sauté 10 minutes, stirring constantly. Stir in the tomatoes and wine (with the strained soaking water if dried porcini were used) and season. Simmer, uncovered, until thick, about 50 minutes. Check the seasoning and stir in the herbs.

Roll the pasta dough thinly and cut maltagliati from it, as shown on page 55. Cook in boiling salted water until *al dente*; drain. Arrange the noodles immediately on plates and pour the sauce over them.

Making the basil-flavored dough:

Put the basil leaves, garlic, and salt in a mortar and pound to a fine purée with the pestle.

Mound the flour on a work surface, form a well, and add the eggs, oil, and the basil and garlic purée.

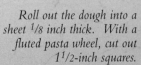

SPRING HERB PASTA

This pasta is made in Liguria and Provence in the spring and is served simply with butter and cheese.

For the pasta dough:

2 cups minced fresh spring herbs (see caption, right)

salt and a little freshly ground pepper

1 tablespoon olive oil

2³/4 cups all-purpose flour

2 eggs, water as required

To finish:

4 seagull eggs (optional), 4 tablespoons butter

1 cup freshly grated Parmesan cheese

Prepare the dough as shown in the picture sequence, kneading it until the flour is evenly colored green by the herbs. Cook the pasta squares in boiling salted water until *al dente*, about 8 minutes. Meanwhile, boil the seagull eggs for 8 minutes, then shell. Arrange the pasta and eggs on pre-warmed plates and serve with foaming browned butter and Parmesan.

Preparing herb pasta:
Using a mortar and pestle, pound the herbs (parsley, sorrel, basil, thyme, marjoram, lemon balm, dandelion leaves), salt, pepper, and oil to a paste.

Sift the flour onto a work surface, form a well in the center, and add the herb mixture and eggs.

Mix and knead to a smooth dough, as described on page 41; add water as required.

Roll out the dough into a sheet ¹/8 inch thick. With a fluted pasta wheel, cut out 1¹/2-inch squares.

With bacon, spinach, and herbs

The simplest combinations are often the best, and this certainly applies to Italian pasta

MALLOREDDUS
WITH SPINACH AND PECORINO

It is its simplicity and the combination of strongly flavored ingredients that make this recipe so satisfying. It uses a traditional Sardinian type of pasta, called malloreddus, sold in cellophane bags in specialty food markets.

1/2 pound fresh spinach leaves
3 slices of bacon, thick-cut
1/2 garlic clove
1 pound malloreddus
2 tablespoons butter
1/4 cup freshly grated pecorino cheese

Wash the spinach well, drain thoroughly, and chop finely. Cut the bacon in small cubes and cook in a large frying pan until it begins to render fat. Peel and mince the garlic and sauté briefly with the bacon. Add the spinach and let it wilt. In the meantime, cook the malloreddus in boiling salted water until *al dente*. Drain the pasta and mix in a pre-warmed bowl with the butter and the bacon-spinach mixture. Sprinkle with the grated pecorino and serve immediately.

MALTAGLIATI
WITH CHIVES AND BACON

This pasta should be made fresh from dough no. 1 (see page 40), cut in irregular shapes as shown on page 55.

2 slices of bacon, thick-cut
about 1 pound maltagliati
4 tablespoons butter
salt and freshly ground pepper
1/4 cup chopped fresh chives
1/4 cup freshly grated Parmesan cheese

Cut the bacon in small pieces and cook in a large frying pan until it begins to render fat. Keep warm. Cook the maltagliati in boiling salted water until *al dente*; drain. Put the pasta in a pre-warmed bowl and add the butter and bacon. Season with salt and pepper. Mix all the ingredients together until the butter has melted. Arrange on pre-warmed plates and sprinkle with the chives and grated cheese.

MEZZE MANICHE RIGATE
WITH SCALLIONS

This short, broad, tubular pasta really demands pungent accompaniments. Plenty of scallions and aromatic herbs are good choices.

12 scallions, 5 tablespoons butter
1/2 bunch of fresh parsley, chopped
2 egg yolks, 1/2 cup freshly grated Parmesan cheese
3/4 pound mezze maniche rigate
freshly ground black pepper
fresh young lovage or celery leaves, 4 cherry tomatoes

Cut the scallions in slices (only the white parts should be used). Melt 4 tablespoons of the butter and cook the scallions over a low heat about 15 minutes. If necessary, add a little water to prevent sticking. Remove from the heat. When the scallions have cooled a little, mix in the parsley and egg yolks and then the Parmesan. In the meantime, cook the pasta in boiling salted water until *al dente*. Drain and toss with the scallion mixture. Arrange on pre-warmed plates and sprinkle with freshly ground pepper and lovage or celery leaves. Garnish with halved cherry tomatoes that have been sautéed in the remaining butter.

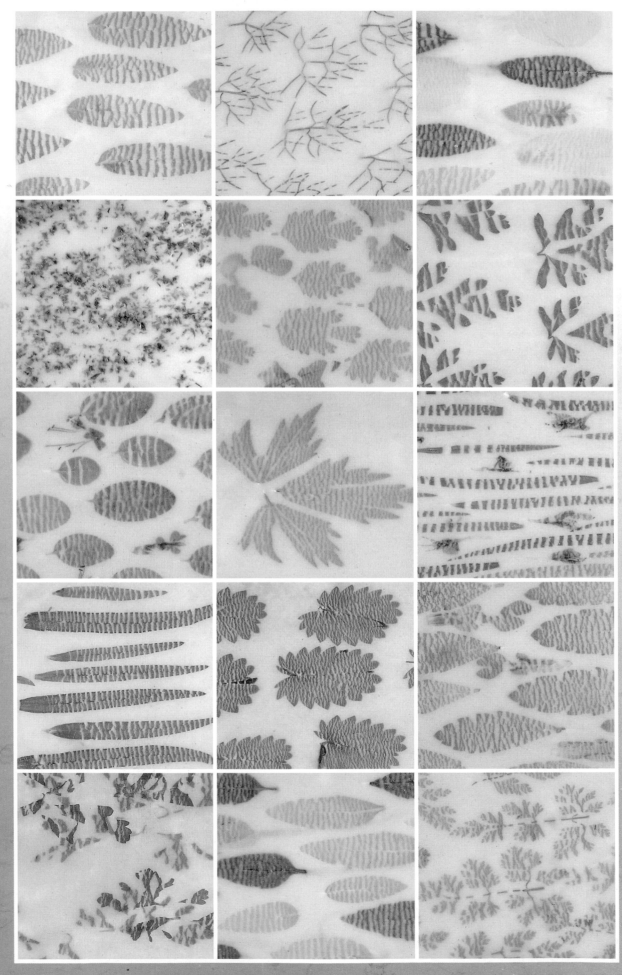

Herb pasta – a delight for creative cooks. Remember, though, that many herbs have an intense flavor, so it is worth giving a little thought to which herbs are best suited to which sauce. The pasta dough can be cut into squares, as shown here, or into pappardelle or thin ribbon noodles.

Herbs in wafer-thin sheets of pasta

Not only does this pasta taste delicious, it looks beautiful, too

1 ³/4 cups + 2 tablespoons all-purpose wheat flour
2 eggs, 1 egg yolk, ¹/2 teaspoon salt
fresh herb leaves

Make the pasta dough as described on page 41. Creating the herb patterns in the pasta dough is actually quite easy: lay the leaves in any arrangement you wish between the thinly rolled out strips of pasta dough and then roll them out again as thinly as possible, as shown in the picture sequence. In this way, the leaves take on quite extraordinary, even bizarre shapes. The rolling can be done in the traditional manner with a rolling pin, or using a pasta machine. The latter method is simpler and easier, although the dough is stretched in only one direction and the leaves will be pulled only relatively small distances apart and stretched to more than twice their length. With a rolling pin, a little more effort is needed of course, but this method gives you an opportunity to modify the pattern in all directions and thus produces a quite different result. You can roll the dough alternately from top to bottom and from left to right, thereby pulling the leaves in several different directions. And depending on how much pressure is applied with the rolling pin, it is possible to vary the size of the tears made in the leaves.

Begin by rolling out a strip of dough to a thickness of between ¹/32 and ¹/16 inch. Arrange the herb leaves on it and then place a second thinly rolled strip of dough on top. In order for the herbs to adhere properly, the dough must be very fresh, so if it begins to dry out, mist it with a little water. Roll out the herb-filled dough to the same thickness as before, either using a pasta machine or by hand.

There is a wide range of patterns you can create, since any herb can be used, provided it has thin, flexible leaves. Rosemary with its stiff needles is obviously unsuitable, as is any other plant with inflexible leaves. Nor should the herb have a very powerful flavor, as is the case with rosemary or savory.

The same principle can be applied to making truffle pasta, which although very expensive is truly a special culinary treat. It must be made with fresh truffles, since those from a can would be squashed into an unsightly mess when rolled between the sheets of pasta. First, carefully clean the truffles (peel black ones first), then cut into wafer-thin slices, preferably with a special truffle slicer. Lay the slices on the thinly rolled sheet of pasta dough, cover with another sheet of dough, and roll thinly again. The rolling-pin method produces a more attractive pattern than a pasta machine. Both black and white truffles can be used – the white ones do not make such a pretty pattern, but their heavenly taste more than compensates. Truffle pasta needs nothing more than freshly melted, foaming butter, perhaps with a little freshly grated Parmesan.

Rolling out herb pasta:

Put the dough through the smooth rollers of the pasta machine in small batches and roll it out in thin strips.

Lay one strip on a work surface, arrange herb leaves over the surface, and place a second strip on top. Press down firmly.

Put the double pasta strip through the machine again and roll out thinly, to more than twice its original length. Cut in large squares or rectangles or wide noodles.

In brodo, *which means in broth, is the perfect way to serve herb pasta. Clear chicken or beef broth will not hide the herb patterns, as a sauce would. Garnish with the same herbs used in the pasta.*

With vegetables and mushrooms

Tomatoes, of course, top the list of vegetables that are combined with pasta. They are indelibly associated not only with spaghetti but with most other kinds of pasta as well, and all other vegetables pale in comparison, even visually. Nevertheless, virtually any vegetable makes a suitable partner for pasta: humble root vegetables, such as carrots and parsnips; many members of the lettuce family, particularly radicchio; fruiting vegetables such as artichokes, bell peppers, and eggplant; and, of course, leeks, onions, and garlic. All impart flavor as well as extra nutritional value to pasta dishes. Some vegetables, particularly spinach and beets, can be worked into the dough to produce pasta of different colors. Nor should we forget the fiery hot chili peppers, so popular in Asian cooking, that can transform the simplest pasta dish when used judiciously.

Whether wild or cultivated, mushrooms are a natural partner for pasta, and often give more flavor than other vegetables, meat, or fish, particularly when used in sauces. In the realm of wild mushrooms and fungi, truffles occupy a special place. Taglierini with thin shavings of fresh white Piedmont truffle is for many gourmets the *ne plus ultra* of pasta dishes – and

also the most expensive. A number of delicious pasta dishes can also be made with black truffles, although these need to be cooked: simmer them for a quarter of an hour in a little port and meat stock before cutting into cubes and mixing in with hot pasta. Truffles should never be combined with other edible fungi or mushrooms: they are too precious and expensive. The same is true of fresh morels, cèpes or porcini, and chanterelles, which have highly individual flavors; they should always be used by themselves.

Pasta is usually cooked as usual in boiling salted water before being combined with vegetables or mushrooms. But creative cooks will know that the flavors of these ingredients can be brought out further and transferred to the pasta by using the vegetable cooking water for cooking the pasta as well. This is not always very effective, but works splendidly with strong-flavored vegetables such as asparagus, celery, and artichokes. Vegetables and pasta can even be cooked together in the same pan of water. And boiling a handful of dried porcini or cèpes in the cooking water before adding the pasta will impart a most distinctive flavor.

With vegetables and prosciutto

Only air-dried prosciutto has the characteristic flavor that combines so splendidly with vegetables

PENNE WITH PEAS AND PROSCIUTTO

Frozen peas can be used for this recipe – they are very convenient, after all – but the dish tastes so much better when made with green peas fresh from the pod.

2 cups veal stock, 1 1/2 pounds fresh green peas in the pod
1/2 pound prosciutto, very thinly sliced
1 small onion, 1 garlic clove
2 small hot chili peppers, 1/4 cup olive oil
2 tablespoons chopped mixed fresh herbs: thyme, parsley, lovage or celery leaves, sage
1/4 teaspoon freshly ground white pepper, salt
1 pound penne
For serving:
freshly grated pecorino or Parmesan cheese

Bring the veal stock to a boil; turn the heat to low and let reduce slowly until only 4 to 5 tablespoons of stock remain. Shell the peas and put to one side. Cut the prosciutto in small squares. Peel and mince the onion. Peel and crush the garlic clove. Cut the chili peppers in half lengthwise, remove the seeds and core, and mince. Heat the olive oil in a suitably large frying pan and sauté the onions and garlic until translucent. Add the prosciutto and fry briefly over a high heat, stirring constantly. Add the peas, herbs, and chili peppers, and pour in the reduced veal stock. Season with pepper and, if necessary, salt. Simmer a few minutes, stirring occasionally. In the meantime, cook the penne in boiling salted water until *al dente*. Drain and mix immediately with the pea and prosciutto mixture. Transfer to 4 pre-warmed plates and sprinkle with grated cheese.

Zucchini flowers and baby zucchini *are a popular accompaniment for pasta in many countries, particularly in the Mediterranean region.*

RIGATONI WITH ZUCCHINI AND PROSCIUTTO

Tender baby zucchini, particularly the very small ones with flowers, work well with a substantial, country-style pasta. Short tubular pasta such as rigatoni or sedanini are particularly suitable.

2 garlic cloves
³/4 pound zucchini
³/4 pound ripe fresh tomatoes or 1 cup canned whole tomatoes, drained
1 small red bell pepper
¹/2 pound prosciutto, very thinly sliced
2 tablespoons butter
¹/2 cup minced shallots
¹/2 teaspoon salt
freshly ground black pepper
1 pound rigatoni
To finish:
1 ¹/2 tablespoons butter
8 to 10 fresh sage leaves
freshly grated Parmesan cheese

Peel and mince the garlic. Wash the zucchini and slice thinly. Blanch fresh tomatoes, peel, cut in half, remove seeds, and chop; chop canned tomatoes. Wash the bell pepper, remove core and seeds, and cut in small cubes. Cut the prosciutto in small squares. Heat the butter in a suitably sized frying pan and sauté the shallots and garlic until translucent. Add the zucchini, tomatoes, and bell pepper. Simmer 2 to 3 minutes, then add the prosciutto. Heat through again, and season with salt and pepper. In the meantime, cook the rigatoni in boiling salted water until *al dente*; drain. Mix with the vegetables and transfer to pre-warmed plates. To finish, heat the butter in a small pan, toss the sage leaves briefly in it, and use to garnish the pasta. Serve with freshly grated Parmesan.

Zucchini flowers with tagliatelle This is a particularly sophisticated variation on the pasta and vegetables theme, particularly if the tagliatelle is freshly made using dough no. 4 (see page 40). Take roughly equal quantities of baby zucchini and flowers; wash, dry, and cut in pieces. Gently sauté minced shallots with a little minced garlic and parsley in plenty of butter, add the zucchini and flowers, and sauté briefly over a high heat. Then pour on a little reduced veal stock as described in the recipe above, and season well with salt and pepper. Cook the tagliatelle in boiling salted water until *al dente*, drain, and mix with the vegetables. Serve with freshly grated Parmesan.

Ribbon noodles with vegetables

Beans, cabbage, and the more bitter-tasting salad leaves can be combined with any shape of pasta, but they go best with ribbon noodles

PAPPARDELLE WITH RADICCHIO AND ARUGULA

Radicchio and arugula are most commonly used in salads. In Italy, however, they are also popular as cooked vegetables, and are often combined successfully with pasta.

1 recipe of fresh pasta dough no. 4 (see page 40)
1 red onion
1/4 pound sliced bacon, thick-cut
5 ounces radicchio, 3 1/2 ounces arugula (about 2 cups)
1/4 cup olive oil, 2 tablespoons dry red wine
salt and freshly ground black pepper
4 nasturtium flowers (optional)

Use a fluted pasta wheel to cut pappardelle from the pasta dough (see page 52), or use dried noodles of a similar size and shape. Peel the onion and chop it coarsely. Cut the bacon slices across in thin strips. Chop the radicchio finely and the arugula coarsely. Heat the oil in a suitably sized pan and gently sauté the bacon and onion until the onion is translucent. Add the wine and boil 1 to 2 minutes. Add the radicchio and let it soften. Season to taste with salt and pepper, and turn the heat down very low. In the meantime, cook the pasta in boiling salted water until *al dente*; drain and transfer to a pre-warmed bowl. Mix the arugula into the sauce, then pour it over the pasta and mix thoroughly. Transfer to pre-warmed plates, garnish each plate with a nasturtium flower, and serve immediately.

TAGLIATELLE WITH BROCCOLI

The broccoli in this recipe is highly spiced, and the result is wonderfully appetizing.

(not illustrated)
1 recipe of fresh pasta dough no. 4 (see page 40)
1 1/4 pounds fresh broccoli
2 garlic cloves
1 to 2 hot chili peppers
6 anchovy fillets, 1/4 cup olive oil
1/2 teaspoon salt
freshly ground black pepper

Use a knife or pasta machine to cut tagliatelle from the pasta dough (see pages 52 and 53). Wash the broccoli and divide in florets. Cook in boiling salted water until just tender; drain and keep warm. Peel and mince the garlic cloves. Cut the chili peppers in half, remove the seeds, and mince. Cut the anchovy fillets in small pieces. Heat the oil in a large frying pan and sauté the garlic, chili

peppers, and anchovy fillets for a few minutes, stirring constantly. Add the broccoli florets, and season with salt and pepper. Cook the tagliatelle in boiling salted water until *al dente*; drain and add to the broccoli mixture. Toss together gently and transfer to pre-warmed plates. If the dish is to be served with cheese, choose an aged pecorino.

FETTUCCINE WITH BEANS AND ARUGULA

Pasta and beans are a combination found in several regions of Italy, particularly in the North. With the addition of arugula, you have an interesting, filling dish.

1 ¼ cups dried beans: borlotti, cannellini, cranberry
1 recipe of fresh pasta dough no. 4 (page 40)
1 garlic clove, 2 tablespoons olive oil
¼ cup minced onion
1 cup canned tomatoes in juice
1 quart veal or chicken stock
½ teaspoon salt
freshly ground black pepper
3½ ounces arugula (about 2 cups)
¾ cup freshly grated Parmesan cheese

Soak the beans overnight; drain. Using a knife or pasta machine, cut fettuccine or tagliatelle from the pasta dough (see pages 52 and 53). Peel and mince the garlic. Heat the oil in a large pan and sauté the onion and garlic until translucent. Add the beans, the tomatoes with their juice, and the stock. Season with salt and pepper. Cover the pan, leaving the lid slightly ajar so the steam can escape, and simmer gently until the beans are soft and the liquid is almost completely gone, 45 to 60 minutes. Add more liquid if necessary. Take out a ladleful of beans and put to one side. Purée everything else in the pan with a hand-held blender (or use a food processor) and then press through a strainer into another pan. Cook the fettuccine in boiling salted water until *al dente*; drain. Add the pasta, the reserved beans, and the arugula leaves to the purée and mix everything together. Transfer to 4 pre-warmed plates, sprinkle with grated Parmesan, and serve immediately.

Tangy tomato sauce
*for orecchiette: fry the
anchovy fillets and then
add the chopped
tomatoes and parsley.
Season well with salt
and pepper.*

TAGLIATELLE WITH ASPARAGUS

A pasta dish for the spring, in which tender young
asparagus is combined with zucchini and their
flowers and fresh herbs.

3/4 recipe of fresh pasta dough no. 4 (see page 40)
1 pound thin asparagus spears
3 tablespoons butter, 1 tablespoon minced shallot
1 zucchini, cut in strips
2 ounces zucchini flowers, cut in strips, plus more for garnish
1/2 teaspoon salt, freshly ground white pepper
1 heaping tablespoon shredded fresh basil leaves
1 tablespoon chopped fresh chives
freshly grated Parmesan cheese for serving

Using a knife or pasta machine, cut tagliatelle from
the fresh pasta dough (see pages 52 and 53), or use
dried tagliatelle. Trim the tough ends of the
asparagus and cut each spear into 1 1/2-inch pieces.
Cook in a large pan of boiling salted water for 3 to 4
minutes. Lift out with a slotted spoon, reserving the
cooking water. Melt the butter in a frying pan and
sauté the shallot until translucent. Add the zucchini
and zucchini flowers and cook 2 to 3 minutes.
Season with salt and pepper. Add the herbs and the
asparagus. In the meantime, cook the tagliatelle in
the boiling asparagus cooking water until *al dente*;
drain and mix with the vegetables. Transfer to pre-
warmed plates, garnish each with a zucchini flower,
and serve with grated Parmesan.

ORECCHIETTE WITH CAULIFLOWER

This simple recipe from southern Italy can also be
made with broccoli.

1 3/4 pounds cauliflower florets, without stems or leaves
2 unpeeled garlic cloves, crushed
2 tablespoons butter, 2 tablespoons vegetable oil
8 anchovy fillets, cut in small pieces
1/2 pound tomatoes, peeled, seeded, and chopped
2 tablespoons chopped fresh parsley, 1/2 teaspoon salt
freshly ground black pepper
1 pound orecchiette (little ears)
freshly grated pecorino romano cheese for serving

Put the cauliflower florets and garlic in a pan of
boiling water and cook 4 to 5 minutes; drain.
Remove the garlic and discard. Heat the butter and
oil in a frying pan and sauté the anchovies briefly.
Add the tomatoes and parsley, and season with salt
and pepper. Let simmer while you cook the
orecchiette in boiling salted water until *al dente*.
Drain the pasta and mix with the tomato sauce and
cauliflower. Transfer to pre-warmed plates and serve
with grated pecorino.

CONCHIGLIE WITH TOMATO SAUCE AND ARUGULA

The arugula could be replaced by another bitter salad
leaf or with wild spring herbs, such as dandelion
leaves and wild herb fennel.

1 pound conchiglie (shells)
14 ounces arugula, coarsely shredded (about 4 cups)
freshly grated Parmesan cheese for serving
For the tomato sauce:
3 tablespoons olive oil, 2/3 cup chopped onion
1/3 cup diced carrot, 2/3 cup chopped celery
1 garlic clove, minced
1 pound tomatoes, fresh or canned
1/2 teaspoon salt, freshly ground pepper
1 small hot chili pepper, seeded and minced

Heat the oil and sauté the onion, carrot,
celery, and garlic at least 5 minutes, stirring
constantly. Press the tomatoes through a
strainer or food mill, and add to the pan.
Season with salt and pepper and add the chili
pepper. Let the sauce simmer while you cook
the pasta in boiling salted water until *al dente*.
After half the pasta cooking time has elapsed, add
the arugula to the boiling water. Drain the
pasta and arugula, and mix with the tomato
sauce. Arrange on pre-warmed plates and
serve with grated Parmesan.

SPAGHETTI IN PARCHMENT

Cooking in paper packages seals in all the flavors and aromas of the ingredients. This recipe will make 12 packages.

1 1/4 pounds fresh ripe tomatoes, 1 pound spaghetti
20 large black olives (Kalamata)
1 bunch of fresh parsley, minced
2 tablespoons olive oil for brushing
12 slices of pancetta
12 anchovy fillets preserved in salt
12 sprigs of fresh parsley
4 tablespoons butter, melted
freshly grated Parmesan cheese for serving
For the tomato sauce:
1 to 2 garlic cloves
1 14-ounce can peeled tomatoes
3 tablespoons olive oil
salt and freshly ground black pepper
1/2 teaspoon dried hot pepper flakes

First make the tomato sauce. Peel the garlic cloves, leaving them whole, and drain the canned tomatoes. Heat the oil in a heavy-based saucepan, sauté the garlic 2 minutes, and then remove and discard it. Add the tomatoes to the garlic-flavored oil and simmer 15 to 20 minutes, stirring occasionally. Season with salt, pepper, and hot pepper flakes. Purée with a hand-held blender (or use a food processor), then simmer 10 minutes.

In the meantime, blanch the fresh tomatoes, peel them, cut each in 8 pieces, remove the seeds, and place in a large bowl. Cook the spaghetti in boiling salted water until almost *al dente*; drain and add to the tomatoes. Add the olives and parsley and mix well.

Cut out 12 pieces of parchment paper, each 10-inches square, and brush them with olive oil. Proceed as shown in the picture sequence below. Bake the packages 15 minutes in an oven preheated to 400°F. Cut the packages open with scissors and drizzle the melted butter over the spaghetti.

Wrapping the packages:

Put the tomatoes and olives on sheets of parchment paper. Wrap some spaghetti around a fork and slide it onto each bed of vegetables.

Flatten the rolled spaghetti into a rectangle and lay a slice of pancetta, an anchovy, and a sprig of parsley on top.

Wrap the parchment paper over the filling, then fold the ends underneath to make a neat package.

PAPPARDELLE WITH A VEGETABLE AND WINE SAUCE

1 recipe of fresh pasta dough no. 4 (see page 40)
1/4 cup extra-virgin olive oil, 1 cup chopped leeks
2 1/3 cups diced zucchini, 3 cups diced eggplant
1 pound ripe tomatoes, peeled, seeded, and chopped
1/2 cup dry white wine, 1 teaspoon salt
freshly ground black pepper, 1/2 teaspoon caraway seeds
1 tablespoon chopped fresh basil
3/4 cup freshly grated provolone piccante or Parmesan cheese

Using a knife or pasta machine, cut pappardelle from the fresh pasta dough (see pages 52 and 53). Heat the oil in a saucepan and cook the leeks, zucchini, and eggplant 6 to 8 minutes, stirring constantly. Add the chopped tomatoes and pour in the wine. Simmer, uncovered, until all excess liquid has evaporated and the sauce is thick. Season with salt, pepper, caraway, and basil. Cook the pasta in boiling salted water until *al dente*; drain and mix with the sauce. Transfer to 4 plates and sprinkle with cheese.

PENNE WITH TOMATOES AND EGGPLANT

9 tablespoons olive oil, 1/3 cup chopped onion
2 garlic cloves, minced
1 3/4 pounds fresh plum tomatoes, peeled and chopped
salt and freshly ground black pepper
1 eggplant, weighing about 1 pound
1 pound penne rigate, fresh basil leaves
3/4 cup freshly grated pecorino cheese

Heat 4 tablespoons of the olive oil in a pan and sauté the onion and garlic until they are translucent. Add the tomatoes, season with salt and pepper, and simmer gently until most of the excess liquid has evaporated and the sauce is thick. Cut the eggplant into slices 3/8 inch thick and season with salt and pepper. Heat the remaining oil in a frying pan and fry the eggplant slices until tender and browned on both sides. Transfer to 4 plates. Cook the pasta in boiling salted water until *al dente*; drain and mix with the tomato sauce. Spoon onto the eggplant, sprinkle with basil, and serve with grated pecorino.

"Pasta alla Norma" – named after Bellini's opera – is how this Sicilian dish of penne with eggplant and tomatoes would be listed on a menu.

Buckwheat noodles are an established tradition

Buckwheat has been used for centuries on the southern side of the Alps, in noodles like spatzlen or pizzoccheri

The pot can never be too big *if Signora Valbuzzi-Gosatti is cooking* pizzoccheri *for diners at "La Gatta." Potatoes, vegetables, and pasta must all have room to float.*

PIZZOCCHERI

The buckwheat dough for these noodles is not rolled out as thinly as pasta for tagliatelle or fettuccine. For authenticity, Tyrolean "mountain" cheeses such as casera should be used, but a good substitute is a mixture of equal quantities of creamy fontina and Gruyère. If chard is not available, spinach can be used instead.

$^1/2$ pound potatoes, $^1/2$ pound Swiss chard leaves
$^3/4$ pound casera cheese, 2 garlic cloves
1 recipe of fresh buckwheat pasta dough (see page 45)
1 cup (2 sticks) butter
8 fresh sage leaves, 1 cup freshly grated Parmesan cheese

Peel the potatoes and cut in $^3/8$-inch cubes; there should be about 2 cups. Cut the chard leaves into strips. Cut the cheese in $^3/8$-inch cubes, and the garlic in thin slices. Roll out the dough into sheets about $^1/16$ inch thick and cut in strips about 2 inches wide. Dust the strips with buckwheat flour, stack them on top of each other, and cut across in noodles about $^1/4$ inch wide. Fill a large pot with water, add salt, and bring to a boil. Add the cubes of potato to the pot. After 10 minutes of cooking, add the noodles. After a further 8 to 10 minutes, add the chard and cook 2 minutes longer. In the meantime, heat the butter in a frying pan and sauté the garlic until translucent, then add the sage leaves. Drain the contents of the pot. Transfer half of the potato-noodle mixture to a pre-warmed bowl, arrange the cubes of cheese on top, and cover with the remaining potato-noodle mixture. Pour over the sage-garlic butter, sprinkle with Parmesan, and serve.

BUCKWHEAT SPÄTZLE

This type of pasta is known as *Schwarzplentene Spatzlen* in the southern Tyrol, *Schwarzplenten* being the Tyrolean term for buckwheat. For a really authentic flavor, use air-dried German speck.

For the spätzle dough:
1 1/2 cups buckwheat flour
3/4 cup + 1 tablespoon all-purpose flour
3 eggs, about 1/2 cup water
1 tablespoon oil, 1/2 teaspoon salt
freshly grated nutmeg
freshly ground white pepper
For the sauce:
1/2 pound fresh spinach
1/4 pound air-dried speck or prosciutto
2 tablespoons vegetable oil
1 teaspoon chopped fresh parsley, 1 cup heavy cream,
4 tablespoons cold butter
For garnish:
2 tablespoons chopped fresh chives
1/2 cup freshly grated Parmesan cheese

Sift the buckwheat and wheat flours together into a suitably sized bowl. (It is important to mix the two types of flour thoroughly.) Whisk the eggs in a bowl, adding half of the water and then the oil. Work this liquid into the flour as quickly as possible, either by hand or with a spoon. If necessary, add the remaining water. The dough should be soft enough to be scraped or easily

pushed through the spätzle press. Season the dough with salt, nutmeg, and pepper.

Wash the spinach and remove the thick stems; chop finely. Cut the speck or prosciutto first in slices and then in small cubes. Heat the oil in a suitably sized pan and fry the speck or prosciutto until the fat is rendered. Add the parsley and cream and cook 3 to 4 minutes. Cut the cold butter in small pieces and whisk in. In the meantime, add the dough to a pan of boiling water, either by scraping it off a board with a knife or by putting it through a spätzle press (see page 63). As soon as the spätzle have all risen to the surface, remove them with a slotted spoon and mix in a bowl with the sauce. Transfer to pre-warmed plates and sprinkle with the chopped chives and grated Parmesan.

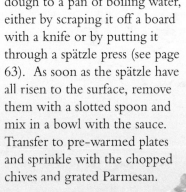

Schupfnudeln and Capuns

Some interesting pasta recipes can be found elsewhere in Europe, other than Italy. The dishes here are representative of traditional frugal Alpine fare

SCHUPFNUDELN

These noodles are simply fashioned by hand into their characteristic shape – thicker in the middle and tapering at both ends – although if the dough contains potato flour it can also be rolled into thin strands or thick noodles. Of humble origin, schupfnudeln are delicious with hearty poultry or game stews, and with vegetables such as cabbage or sauerkraut. The traditional method of cooking them is first to boil them and then to fry them in plenty of butter, so that they remain soft on the inside but have a crisp, buttery crust. The following dough can be made with wheat flour alone, but the addition of rye flour gives a more robust flavor.

1 cup + 3 tablespoons all-purpose flour
3/4 cup rye flour
1 egg, 1 teaspoon salt
about 1/4 cup water, 4 tablespoons butter
1 tablespoon chopped fresh chives

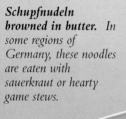

Schupfnudeln browned in butter. *In some regions of Germany, these noodles are eaten with sauerkraut or hearty game stews.*

Put both flours, the egg, salt, and water in a bowl and mix thoroughly together. Turn onto a work surface and knead to a smooth, easily workable dough. Rinse out a bowl with hot water to warm it. Dry the bowl, put in the dough, and let rest 15 minutes. Shape the noodles as shown in the picture sequence. Cook in boiling salted water for 8 to 10 minutes, then drain.

Melt the butter in a frying pan and fry the noodles until they are lightly browned. Arrange on a serving plate, sprinkle with chives, and serve.

Shaping Schupfnudeln:

Remove a small portion of dough, keeping the rest covered by the warm bowl, and pull off a small piece.

Roll thinly on a work surface sprinkled with flour. The noodles should be floured so that they do not stick together.

CAPUNS

A variation on the spätzle theme. These are chard leaves stuffed with spätzle dough and a spicy salami mixture – an unusual but tasty concoction.

40 Swiss chard leaves
4 tablespoons butter
$^1/_2$ cup vegetable stock
$^1/_2$ cup heavy cream
For the spätzle dough:
2$^1/_3$ cups all-purpose flour
3 eggs, 5 tablespoons milk
5 tablespoons water
1 teaspoon salt
For the filling:
2 ounces Canadian bacon
2 ounces salami, preferably German or Swiss
2 ounces dry-cured beef, such as Swiss Bünderfleisch
1 onion
1 tablespoon butter
3 cups white bread cubes
$^1/_2$ tablespoon chopped fresh parsley
1 tablespoon chopped fresh chives
$^1/_8$ teaspoon chopped fresh rosemary
1 tablespoon minced fresh basil

First make the dough. Put the flour, eggs, milk, water, and salt in a bowl and mix to form a smooth, soft dough. Beat with a wooden spoon until blisters form. Cover the bowl and let the dough rest 30 minutes. In the meantime, make the filling. Cut the bacon, salami, and dry-cured beef in small cubes. Peel and mince the onion. Heat the butter in a frying pan, add the meats, onion, bread cubes, and all the herbs and sauté gently, stirring occasionally. Let the mixture cool and then work it into the spätzle dough.

Briefly blanch the chard leaves in boiling water, and spread out on clean dish towels. Put 1 heaping tablespoon of the filling on each leaf and roll up into a tightly sealed package. Melt some of the butter in a large frying pan and lightly brown the packages all over. (There are too many packages to cook at the same time, so work in batches or use two frying pans.) Pour on the stock, add the cream, and simmer gently about 5 minutes. Serve hot.

TRENETTE WITH PESTO AND VEGETABLES

In this pesto, Parmesan is replaced by an aged pecorino romano or fiore sardo. Because the pesto is highly flavored, use it sparingly so that the flavor of the vegetables can be appreciated.

3/4 recipe of fresh pasta dough no. 4 (see page 40)
For the pesto:
2 garlic cloves, 1/4 cup pine nuts
1 cup fresh basil leaves
2 ounces well-aged pecorino romano
salt and freshly ground pepper
5 tablespoons extra-virgin olive oil
For the vegetables:
1/2 pound tomatoes, 1/2 pound zucchini
1 small red bell pepper
2 tablespoons olive oil
salt and freshly ground pepper
freshly grated Parmesan cheese for serving

Using a knife or pasta machine, cut trenette, which are slightly narrower than tagliatelle, from the fresh pasta dough (see pages 52 and 53), or use dried trenette or tagliatelle. Prepare the pesto as described on page 76. Blanch the tomatoes, peel them, cut in half, remove seeds, and dice. Cut the zucchini lengthwise into thin strips. Remove the core and seeds from the bell pepper and dice finely. Heat the olive oil in a frying pan and sauté the prepared vegetables for 2 to 3 minutes, stirring constantly. In the meantime cook the pasta in boiling salted water until *al dente*. Drain, mix with the vegetables and pesto, and season with salt and pepper if necessary. Serve with freshly grated Parmesan.

Spaghetti with pesto and mussels is a Ligurian version of this dish. Allow about $2^{1}/4$ pounds of fresh mussels for 4 people. Scrub the shells thoroughly, then steam open in a little salted water. Remove the mussels from their shells and keep warm. Cook 1 pound of spaghetti in boiling salted water until *al dente*, drain, and mix with the pesto. Add the mussels and heat through briefly, then transfer to 4 pre-warmed plates and serve.

Pasta with pesto and vegetables

A perfect blend of tastes for lovers of pasta, garlic, and vegetables

TROFIE WITH ZUCCHINI AND PEAS

This unusual pasta, which is made from flour, water, and wheat bran, comes from Camogli on the Gulf of Genoa in Liguria. The bran gives the pasta a rich, full-bodied texture, which combines perfectly with the pesto. Trofie are also good with a fresh tomato sauce and plenty of cheese, or *alla carbonara*, that is, with pancetta, eggs, garlic, and cheese.

For the pasta dough:
2^1/3 cups all-purpose flour
1 cup wheat bran
^{1}/2 teaspoon salt, about 1 cup water
For the vegetables:
5 ounces yellow summer squash
3 tablespoons butter or ^{1}/4 cup oil
1 tablespoon minced shallots
1 garlic clove, minced
1^1/3 cups shelled fresh green peas
^{1}/4 cup reduced meat stock
2 ounces squash flowers, minced
salt, ^{1}/2 tablespoon freshly ground black pepper
1 tablespoon chopped fresh parsley
freshly shaved Parmesan cheese for serving

Make the dough as described in the picture sequence. Cut the squash lengthwise in thin slices and then cut the slices across in half. Heat the butter or oil and sauté the shallots and garlic until translucent. Add the squash and peas, pour on the meat stock, and simmer a few minutes over low heat. Finally, add the squash flowers and simmer briefly. In the meantime, cook the trofie in boiling salted water until *al dente*;

remove with a slotted spoon and drain in a colander. Mix the pasta with the vegetables in a pre-warmed bowl, season, and stir in the parsley. Serve sprinkled with Parmesan shavings.

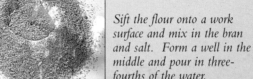

Making trofie:

Sift the flour onto a work surface and mix in the bran and salt. Form a well in the middle and pour in three-fourths of the water.

Mix to a dough, adding the remaining water if needed. Shape into rolls as thick as a finger and cut into pieces ^{3}/8 inch across.

Press out the pieces of dough into a slightly elongated shape and curve gently over the back of a fork.

In spring, *in Liguria, trofie are dressed with fresh herbs — mostly basil, plus some thyme, savory, and rosemary.*

With porcini

One of the finest pasta dishes is pasta con funghi

Pasta cooks should make full use of fresh wild mushrooms whenever they are available. The flavor and texture of wild mushrooms combine particularly well with pasta, whether mixed with butter and herbs, a béchamel sauce, or just cream. Fresh porcini or cèpes (*Boletus edulis*) are by far the best fungi for a pasta dish, and they taste wonderful on their own or in a highly flavored sauce. Truffles and morels are excellent, too. When you cannot find fresh wild mushrooms, dried ones make a very good substitute. They have such a concentrated flavor that they can be used in small quantities as a seasoning, and can even be added to the pasta cooking water to give the pasta a mushroom flavor.

PENNE RIGATE WITH PORCINI IN CREAM

The robust tubular pasta contrasts perfectly with the exquisite flavor of the porcini in a cream sauce.

1 pound fresh porcini (cèpes)
^{1}/4 pound prosciutto, thinly sliced, 1 cup heavy cream
2 tablespoons butter, ^{1}/4 cup minced onion
^{3}/4 cup minced fresh parsley
1 pound penne rigate
salt and freshly ground black pepper

For serving:
freshly grated Parmesan cheese

Clean the porcini thoroughly and trim off the ends of the stems. Slice the porcini lengthwise. Cut the prosciutto slices in ^{3}/8-inch squares. Boil the cream over low heat to reduce to about half of its original volume. Heat the butter, add the onion, and sauté gently until the onion is translucent. Add the porcini and prosciutto and sauté briefly, stirring constantly. Add the reduced cream and the parsley and simmer gently until the porcini are tender. This will take only a few minutes. In the meantime, cook the pasta in boiling salted water until *al dente* and drain. Mix the pasta with the sauce, and season with salt and pepper. Transfer to plates and serve with grated Parmesan.

PAPPARDELLE WITH PORCINI

This recipe calls for a lot of fresh porcini. However, it is also delicious made with a mixture of mushrooms, such as field or meadow mushrooms, Portobello mushrooms, and common cultivated mushrooms. Only the very best pasta, preferably homemade, should be used for this exquisite mushroom dish.

1 recipe of fresh pasta dough no. 4 (see page 40)
about 1 1/2 pounds fresh porcini (cèpes)
1 garlic clove, 3/4 pound ripe tomatoes
4 tablespoons butter, 2/3 cup minced shallots
2/3 cup diced celery
1/2 teaspoon salt, freshly ground black pepper
2 tablespoons vegetable oil
1 tablespoon chopped fresh parsley
1/2 teaspoon chopped fresh thyme
1/4 cup chopped fresh basil

For serving:
freshly grated pecorino or Parmesan cheese

Using a knife or pasta machine, cut pappardelle from the fresh pasta dough (see pages 52 and 53), or use dried pappardelle. Clean the porcini very carefully and trim off the ends of the stems. Slice the porcini lengthwise. Peel and mince the garlic clove. Blanch the tomatoes, peel them, remove seeds, and cut in cubes. Heat the butter in a suitably sized frying pan and sauté the shallots, garlic, and celery gently for a few minutes. Add the porcini and brown over a high heat. Reduce the heat and cook gently for a few more minutes. Season with salt and pepper. Heat the oil in a second frying pan and sauté the diced tomatoes briefly. In the meantime, cook the pappardelle in boiling salted water until *al dente*. Drain and mix immediately with the porcini, tomatoes, and chopped herbs. Check the seasoning, and serve with grated pecorino or Parmesan.

Pasta and truffles

This alliance benefits both parties, both the humble pasta and the aristocratic truffle

Reto Mathis from St. Moritz – a man who knows how to judge the quality of truffles. Many pounds of the "black diamonds" pass through his hands year after year.

The flavor of truffles is best appreciated when there is as little competition as possible from other flavors, so pasta makes an ideal accompaniment for them. Just like a good risotto, pasta provides a simple backdrop against which the truffle can stand out. Truffles also blend well with butter, cream, and mild cheeses, such as the delicately creamy fontina from the Valle d'Aosta. White truffles, from Italy's Piedmont region, are especially favored by pasta lovers. They are used raw, sliced very thinly. White truffles from the area around Alba are considered to be the most fragrant. They are particularly rare and thus very much sought after, so it is no surprise that they change hands at astronomic prices. However, because of their strong flavor, a little truffle goes a long way.

Tagliatelle à la Mathis, a combination that is simple yet sublime. The ribbon noodles are first coated with a cream sauce and then with an equal quantity of sauce Périgord. The finishing touch is black truffle, both sliced and freshly grated.

TAJARIN WITH BUTTER AND TRUFFLES

One of the simplest and quickest pasta dishes of all, but certainly also one of the most expensive, comes from Piedmont. Tajarin, the delicate egg noodles of that region, are simply cooked and drained, then transferred to a large bowl, and tossed with plenty of fresh, melted butter, a little freshly grated Parmesan, and pepper. All this has to be done quickly, before the noodles cool down. They are then served onto pre-warmed plates and fresh white truffle is sliced thinly over the top – the more generously the better.

The celebrated Piedmontese *fonduta* makes a wonderful sauce for tajarin. The *fonduta* is made by melting the delicately creamy fontina cheese from the Valle d'Aosta with milk, butter, and egg yolks. This rich cheese sauce is poured over the noodles and the whole is topped with plenty of freshly sliced white truffle.

White truffles taste finest when sliced fresh and paper-thin. They are particularly exquisite garnishing noodles in a cream or creamy cheese sauce, or noodles simply tossed with brown butter (beurre noisette).

TAGLIERINI WITH SAUTÉED TRUFFLES

A delightful pasta dish that uses black truffles. These taste superb when sliced paper thin and sautéed briefly in hot butter. Combined with thin, homemade ribbon noodles and diced tomatoes, you have a meal ready in no time at all. The trick with this simple dish is to have all three elements – pasta, truffles, and tomatoes – ready more or less simultaneously.

3/4 recipe of fresh pasta dough no. 4 (see page 40)
3 to 5 ounces black truffles (fresh or canned)
2 tablespoons olive oil
3 tablespoons minced shallots
1/2 cup peeled, seeded, and diced ripe tomatoes
4 tablespoons butter
salt and freshly ground white pepper
small fresh basil leaves

Using a knife or pasta machine, cut taglierini from the pasta dough (see pages 52 and 53). Thinly peel the truffles, then cut them into paper-thin slices, using a truffle slicer if you have one. Heat the oil in a small frying pan and cook the shallot until very soft and translucent. Add the diced tomatoes, sauté briefly, and remove the pan from the heat. Melt the butter in a second frying pan, add the sliced truffles, and fry briefly on both sides. Season with salt and pepper. Cook the pasta in boiling salted water until *al dente*; drain and mix immediately with the truffles and tomato. Transfer to 4 pre-warmed plates and garnish with basil leaves.

Truffle lovers *will disapprove, but freshly grated Parmesan makes a perfect accompaniment for this dish.*

Vegetables and noodles Chinese-style

Chinese cooks are such masters of the art of cooking vegetables that meat and fish are hardly missed, even in noodle dishes

NOODLES WITH GINGER AND SCALLIONS

This noodle dish is quick and simple but surprisingly tasty, largely because of the fresh ginger.

1/2 pound dried Chinese egg noodles
For the sauce:
3 ounces fresh gingerroot
5 ounces scallions (8 to 10)
3 tablespoons peanut oil
salt and freshly ground pepper
2 tablespoons oyster sauce
For garnish:
edible flowers (optional)

Peel the ginger, slice finely, and then cut in very thin strips. Trim the scallions and cut in thin strips. Cook the noodles in boiling salted water until *al dente*, 6 to 7 minutes. In the meantime, heat the oil in a wok. Put the strips of ginger into the wok and stir-fry 1 minute. Add the scallions and stir-fry briefly – they should retain a little of their crispness. Season with salt and pepper, and put the wok to one side. Drain the noodles and transfer immediately to the wok. Mix everything together thoroughly. Mix in the oyster sauce, check for seasoning, and transfer to bowls. Garnish with edible flowers and serve immediately.

VEGETABLES WITH RICE NOODLES

Contrast is an important element in Chinese cooking. Here, the crispness of the fried noodles is set against the moist tenderness of the vegetables.

1/2 pound rice noodles, vegetable oil for frying
For the vegetables:
3/4 ounce dried shrimp, 1 small leek
4 scallions, 1 small carrot
1 celery stalk
1/4 each red, green, and yellow bell pepper
2 to 3 tablespoons peanut oil
1/4 cup sliced bamboo shoots, 1/4 cup rice wine
1/2 teaspoon salt, 1 tablespoon sugar
2 tablespoons dark soy sauce
1 cup beansprouts
For garnish:
1 tablespoon chopped fresh cilantro

Rinse the dried shrimp, then let soak in warm water to cover about 1 hour; drain, reserving 2 tablespoons of the soaking water. Cut the leek and scallions into thin rings; dice the carrot; and slice the celery. Remove core and seeds from the bell peppers and cut into more or less evenly sized cubes. Heat some oil in a wok and stir-fry the leek, scallions, carrot, celery, bell peppers, and bamboo shoots briefly in 3 or 4 batches. The vegetables should be crisp-tender. Set the vegetables aside. Put the rice wine, salt, sugar, soy sauce, and reserved shrimp soaking water in the wok and bring to a boil. Return all the vegetables to the wok, together with the beansprouts and shrimp. Heat everything through, tossing well. Check the seasoning. In the meantime, separate the dried noodles and fry in plenty of hot oil until they puff up and are crisp; drain on paper towels. Transfer the noodles to plates or bowls and spoon the vegetables on top, or mix them into the noodles. Sprinkle with chopped cilantro and serve.

Fresh gingerroot often promises more than it delivers. Only really fresh ginger is suitable for such a dish. So when buying ginger, check that it is perfectly fresh: it should be firm to the touch and the skin should not have the slightest fold or wrinkle!

With seafood

Pasta with fish or shellfish is a combination virtually unknown in northern Europe. In Italy, on the other hand, it is very common, particularly in coastal regions. Here the sea and its produce are omnipresent, even in the pasta itself – in noodles colored black with squid ink, which are served with every kind of sea creature imaginable. In other parts of the world, pasta and seafood are a popular partnership, most notably in Asia.

As every cook knows, the cooking of fresh fish is a delicate matter – a few seconds too long and the

fish will be overcooked and dry. The heat of freshly cooked pasta can often be enough on its own: the fish can be cut into very small cubes or strips and then mixed raw into the warm pasta, with a few suitable herbs, such as dill, and some butter or olive oil. The time required to transfer the dish from kitchen to table will be sufficient to cook the fish so that it is hot but still juicy and translucent inside.

Shellfish are common ingredients in pasta dishes, from juicy shrimp to mussels and clams. *Spaghetti alle vongole* (spaghetti with clams) is an Italian classic. Scallops also find their way occasionally into the pasta pot. One unusual specialty from Sicily is *bottarga*, which is pressed and heavily salted tuna roe. It can be grated like cheese over macaroni or spaghetti.

The best of all foods from the sea is lobster, which should always be purchased alive and cooked fresh. Spaghetti or other pasta *all'aragosta* can be cooked in the water used to cook the lobster, or, even better, in a stock in which as much lobster shell as possible has been boiled for half an hour with some white wine and a stick of cinnamon. This lobster-suffused pasta tastes quite extraordinary!

Quick and easy – fish and pasta

Two examples of sophisticated pasta dishes that require little preparation time, using smoked salmon and fresh tuna

Cut the smoked salmon *in 3/8-inch cubes if you are using the middle of a side of salmon. If the piece has been taken from the thinner tail end, it can be cut in thin strips.*

FETTUCCINE AL SALMONE

You need a thick piece of smoked salmon for this recipe, not thin slices.

3/4 recipe fresh pasta dough no. 4 (see page 40)
1 cup heavy cream
1 small hot chili pepper, minced
a pinch of freshly grated nutmeg
some grated lemon zest
1/2 teaspoon salt, freshly ground black pepper
1-pound piece of smoked salmon, skinned
4 tablespoons butter, cut in small pieces
1 tablespoon minced fresh lemon balm or mint

Using a knife or pasta machine, cut fettucine from the pasta dough (see pages 52 and 53), or used dried fettuccine. Put the cream, chili pepper, nutmeg, lemon zest, salt, and pepper in a large saucepan and boil gently to reduce the liquid by a third, about 10 minutes. In the meantime, cut the salmon into 3/8-inch cubes. Cook the fettucine in boiling salted water until *al dente*. Add the butter, piece by piece, to the cream sauce and stir in well. Remove the pan from the heat and add the cubed salmon. Drain the pasta and mix thoroughly with the sauce. Spoon onto pre-warmed plates and garnish with minced lemon balm or mint.

Swordfish *is an excellent alternative to tuna. It has a similar "meaty" texture and a mild flavor, which is why many people esteem it particularly highly.*

GARGANELLI WITH TUNA

Garganelli, homemade from a dough with plenty of egg yolk in it, are excellent with this robust tuna sauce, but dried garganelli or other tubular pasta, such as macaroni, ziti, or bucatini, can be used instead.

3/4 recipe fresh pasta dough no. 4 (see page 40)
3/4-pound fresh tuna steak
salt and freshly ground pepper
about 5 tablespoons olive oil
For the tomato sauce:
1 pound ripe tomatoes
2 garlic cloves
20 black olives, as small as possible
1/2 cup sliced scallions
2/3 cup diced celery, 1/2 cup diced carrot
a pinch of ground ginger
1/2 teaspoon salt
freshly ground pepper
For garnish:
2 tablespoons minced fresh herbs: thyme, rosemary, parsley

Make garganelli from the pasta dough (see page 55). Cut the tuna in 5/8-inch cubes and season with salt and pepper. Heat the oil in a wide pan and fry the tuna just enough to sear it all over. Remove from the pan and put to one side; reserve the oil in the pan. Blanch the tomatoes, peel them, cut in half, remove the seeds, and dice. Peel and mince the garlic. Pit the olives; if large, cut them in half. Reheat the oil in the pan, adding a further 2 tablespoons if necessary, and cook the scallions, celery, carrot, garlic, and olives gently until soft. Stir in the tomatoes with the ginger, salt, and pepper and cook about 10 minutes, uncovered; the pieces of tomatoes should be still just recognizable. In the meantime, cook the pasta in plenty of boiling salted water until *al dente*. Add the tuna to the sauce and heat through. Drain the pasta, mix with the sauce, and spoon onto pre-warmed plates. Sprinkle with the chopped herbs and serve.

With lobster, sardines, and caviar

The ingredients vary enormously, and so do the results — but both these dishes taste wonderful

TAJARIN WITH LOBSTER RAGOUT

This is pasta and seafood cooking at its most elegant and extravagant. Tajarin, a specialty from Italy's Piedmont region, are very narrow tagliatelle-like noodles made from a dough enriched with egg yolks. For a particularly exquisite flavor, cook them in veal stock instead of the court-bouillon suggested here. This delicious pasta combines wonderfully with freshly cooked lobster, champagne sauce, and caviar.

$3/4$ quantity of fresh pasta dough no. 4 (see page 40)
1 whole live lobster, weighing about 1 $3/4$ pounds, or 2 lobsters, each about 1 pound
For the court-bouillon:
1 garlic clove
1 cup each diced leek, carrot, and celery
2 bay leaves, 1 bunch of parsley
2 tablespoons salt, 4 quarts water
For the sauce:
2 cups fish stock, 2 sprigs of fresh tarragon
2 sprigs of parsley, 4 black peppercorns
1 cup heavy cream, $1/2$ cup champagne
1 $1/2$ tablespoons chilled butter, cut in small pieces
To finish:
$1/4$ cup caviar, 4 baby zucchini with flowers
1 $1/2$ tablespoons butter

Using a knife, cut tajarin from the fresh pasta dough (see page 55). For the court-bouillon, lightly crush the unpeeled garlic clove with the side of a knife and put it in a large pot with the leek, carrot, celery, herbs, salt, and water. Bring to a boil and cook about 15 minutes. Quickly slide the lobster headfirst into the bubbling liquid, cover the pot, turn down the heat, and cook 15 minutes. (If you are using 2 smaller lobsters, cook 10 to 12 minutes.) Lift out the lobster and let it cool, then cut it open and remove the meat from the tail and claws. Cut the meat in cubes and keep warm. Strain the court-bouillon and return it to the pot.

Heat the fish stock in a saucepan with the sprigs of tarragon and parsley and the peppercorns, and simmer gently until reduced to about 5 to 6 tablespoons. Strain, add the cream, and simmer a few minutes. Add the champagne and simmer again briefly. Mix thoroughly in the pan with a hand blender or portable electric mixer, and whisk in the butter to thicken the sauce.

In the meantime, cook the tajarin in the boiling court-bouillon until *al dente*; drain and rinse briefly in hot water. Twist portions of noodles around a 2-pronged fork and transfer to 4 pre-warmed plates. Add the lobster and pour the sauce over the top. Garnish generously with caviar and serve, with baby zucchini and their flowers that have been gently stewed in butter.

PASTA WITH SARDINES

This is the most popular pasta dish in Sicily, although its ingredients would suggest it is of Arabic origin. Absolutely fresh sardines and aromatic fennel are essential to create the distinctive flavor of the dish.

1 pound macaroni or bucatini
For the sauce:
1 pound bulb fennel
1/4 cup olive oil
1/2 cup minced onion
2 anchovy fillets, chopped
1 pound fresh sardines
1/2 teaspoon salt, freshly ground pepper
1/2 teaspoon dried saffron threads, crushed
3 tablespoons raisins
1/4 cup pine nuts

Trim the fennel, cut out the hard core, and cook the bulbs whole in boiling salted water until just tender. Drain thoroughly (if necessary, squeeze gently to remove excess water), reserving the cooking water, and then dice finely. Heat the oil in a frying pan and cook the onion with the anchovies until soft. In the meantime, clean and fillet the sardines (or have your fish merchant do this for you) and cut the fish in small pieces. Add the sardines to the pan and cook gently about 5 minutes over a low heat, stirring with a wooden spoon. Season with salt and pepper and stir in the saffron, which in this case is used for its flavor and not for its color. Add the raisins, pine nuts, and fennel, and simmer 4 to 5 minutes longer. In the meantime, cook the pasta in boiling salted water until *al dente*. (For a more pronounced taste of fennel, use the fennel cooking water for the pasta.) Drain the pasta, mix with the sauce, and serve immediately. In Sicily, this dish is not served with cheese, but the addition of a Sicilian pecorino (such as *pecorino pepato*, with peppercorns) or ragusano imparts an interesting flavor.

Wild fennel *grows in the mountainous regions of the Mediterranean countries. In the late spring, it can be found in markets there, such as this one in Agrigento, Sicily.*

Pasta with mussels and clams

There are numerous simple but delicious combinations in Italian pasta cooking

SPAGHETTI WITH MUSSELS, CLAMS, AND COCKLES

Versions of this dish are found everywhere, and not only in Italy. The type of pasta varies, and the choice of bivalves is subject to what is available fresh, since all kinds are suitable.

$3/4$ pound spaghetti
For the seafood:
1 pound fresh mussels
1 pound fresh littleneck or other small hardshell clams
1 pound fresh cockles
1 bunch of parsley
2 garlic cloves
3 tablespoons extra-virgin olive oil
$1/4$ cup minced onion
1 cup dry white wine
For the sauce:
1 pound ripe tomatoes, 2 tablespoons olive oil

1 cup thinly sliced scallions
1 heaping tablespoon coarsely shredded fresh basil leaves
$1/2$ teaspoon salt, freshly ground pepper

Scrub the mussels, clams, and cockles thoroughly under cold, running water, discarding any that are open or damaged. Coarsely chop the parsley. Peel and mince the garlic cloves. Heat the oil in a large pot and sauté the onion, garlic, and parsley over medium heat about 2 minutes. Put the mussels, clams, and cockles in the pot, pour in the white wine, cover, and cook until the shells open, about 8 minutes. (Discard any that remain stubbornly shut.) In the meantime, make the sauce. Blanch the tomatoes, peel them, cut in half, remove the seeds, and dice. Heat the oil in a saucepan and sauté the tomatoes and scallions for a few minutes. Add the basil, salt, and pepper and simmer 3 to 4 minutes longer. Add the sauce to the mussels, clams, and cockles and mix in well. Keep warm. Cook the spaghetti in plenty of boiling salted water until *al dente* and drain. Mix the spaghetti with the mussels, clams, and cockles, and serve immediately.

BUCATINI ALLE VONGOLE

This dish has become famous outside Italy as *spaghetti alle vongole*, although the traditional pasta to use is bucatini, a sort of thin macaroni. The recipe here uses canned tomatoes, but really ripe plum tomatoes would make the dish even better.

³/4 pound bucatini
For the clams:
1³/4 pounds fresh littleneck or other small hardshell clams
¹/2 cup white wine
¹/2 cup water
1 tablespoon olive oil
For the sauce:
2 tablespoons olive oil
¹/3 cup chopped onion
1 garlic clove, minced
1 14-ounce can tomatoes
¹/2 teaspoon salt
freshly ground pepper
For garnish:
2 tablespoons chopped fresh parsley

Scrub the clams under cold, running water, discarding any open or damaged ones. Place them in a large pot, add the white wine, water, and oil, and heat until the shells open. (Discard any that remain stubbornly shut.) Remove the clams from the pan with a slotted spoon. Let the cooking liquid cool a little, so that any grit can settle, then strain the liquid and reserve it. To make the sauce, heat the oil in a suitably large saucepan and sauté the onion and garlic until translucent. Add the canned tomatoes and the liquid in which the clams were cooked. Season with salt and pepper and let the sauce simmer until it is reduced by about half, at least 30 minutes. At this point, the clams can be removed from their shells, making them easier to eat, and added to the sauce. However, the appearance of the dish is enhanced if some are left in their shells. Cook the bucatini in plenty of boiling salted water until *al dente*, drain thoroughly, and mix with the sauce. Transfer to pre-warmed plates, sprinkle with the chopped parsley, and serve immediately.

PAPPARDELLE WITH
SCAMPI AND ASPARAGUS

A successful combination of crustaceans and crunchy fresh vegetables. The dish comes from Sicily, whose waters teem with scampi (which is the Italian name for lobsterettes such as Dublin Bay prawns). Asparagus, too, is found in Sicily, growing wild in the mountainous regions; it is sold at markets on the island in the spring. Only the pasta is not indigenous to Sicily, since pappardelle come from northern Italy. If fresh scampi or Dublin Bay prawns are not available, you can substitute large raw shrimp in shell.

$3/4$ recipe fresh pasta dough no. 4 (see page 40)
1 sachet (or about 1 tablespoon) squid ink
2 tablespoons olive oil
For the sauce:
1 garlic clove
$3/4$ pound ripe plum tomatoes
$1/4$ cup extra-virgin olive oil
$1/4$ cup minced onion
$1/2$ teaspoon salt, freshly ground pepper
1 small hot chili pepper
$1/2$ cup dry white wine
16 medium-sized scampi
$1/2$ pound thin green asparagus

Make the pasta dough as described on page 41. Before kneading, cut the dough in half and add the squid ink and oil to one half to color it black. Using a fluted pasta wheel, cut pappardelle from both the plain and the black doughs (see page 52). Lightly crush the unpeeled garlic clove with the side of a knife. Blanch the tomatoes in boiling water, peel them, and mince. Heat the oil in an appropriately sized pan and sauté the onion until translucent. Add the garlic and the tomatoes and cook 3 to 4 minutes over a high heat. Season with salt and pepper. Cut the chili pepper in half lengthwise, remove the seeds, and cut in fine strips. Add to the pan with the white wine. Cook 2 minutes longer, uncovered. Twist the heads off the scampi, then lay them on their back on a chopping board, and cut in half lengthwise with a sharp knife; devein if necessary. Trim the asparagus and cut in pieces approximately $1^{1}/2$ inches long. Add the asparagus to the sauce and simmer 3 to 4 minutes, then add the scampi and simmer until they are just cooked, about 2 to 3 minutes.

In the meantime, cook the pasta in boiling salted water until *al dente*; drain, mix immediately with the sauce, and serve.

TAGLIATELLE VERDE
WITH SCALLOPS

This dish is particularly good when made with fresh scallops, but frozen ones are a good substitute.

1 recipe fresh green pasta dough (see page 46)
1 garlic clove, $1/2$ pound ripe tomatoes
3 tablespoons vegetable oil
$2/3$ cup minced shallots
$1/3$ cup diced celery
$1/2$ teaspoon salt
freshly ground pepper
$1/2$ teaspoon chopped fresh thyme
1 tablespoon chopped fresh parsley
$1/2$ cup dry white wine
$3/4$ pound sea scallops, with coral if available
$1/4$ pound peeled small raw shrimp

Using a knife or pasta machine, cut tagliatelle from the pasta dough (see pages 52 and 53), or use dried tagliatelle. Peel and mince the garlic clove. Blanch the tomatoes, peel them, cut in half, remove seeds, and chop. Heat the oil in a suitably sized pan and sauté the shallots, garlic, and celery for a few minutes until translucent. Add the tomatoes, season with salt and pepper, sprinkle on the chopped herbs, and pour in the white wine. Simmer gently 2 to 3 minutes. Cut each scallop in half horizontally and add to the sauce with the shrimp. Simmer until the shellfish is just cooked, 3 to 4 minutes. In the meantime, cook the pasta in boiling salted water until *al dente*. Drain, mix immediately with the sauce, and serve.

A delightful variation can be made using only mussels. Steam them open in a little extra fish stock, then remove from their shells. Add the strained cooking liquid to the tomato sauce.

POTATO NOODLES WITH TOMATOES AND SEAFOOD

For the dough:

1 pound baking potatoes

1 cup + 3 tablespoons all-purpose flour

$^1/_2$ cup freshly grated Parmesan cheese

$^3/_4$ teaspoon salt, freshly ground pepper

2 eggs

For the sauce:

1 pound ripe tomatoes

1 garlic clove

$^1/_4$ cup olive oil

$^1/_4$ cup minced onion

$^1/_2$ cup diced carrot, $^1/_2$ cup diced celery

1 anchovy fillet, minced

$^1/_2$ teaspoon salt, freshly ground pepper

1 cup fish stock

$^3/_4$ pound littleneck or other small hardshell clams

$^1/_2$ pound squid

$^1/_4$ pound small peeled shrimp

2 tablespoons chopped mixed fresh herbs: basil, parsley, thyme, and a little rosemary

Make the potato dough following the directions on page 223, then cut and shape the noodles. Dust them with flour, cover with a cloth, and set aside. Blanch the tomatoes, peel them, cut in half, remove seeds, and dice. Peel and mince the garlic. Heat the oil in a large saucepan and sauté the onion and garlic until translucent. Add the carrot and celery and sauté gently 2 to 3 minutes longer. Add the diced tomatoes and anchovy, and season with salt and pepper. Pour on the fish stock and simmer gently about 15 minutes. Scrub the clams and steam them open. Remove the clams from their shells (discard any that remain closed). Clean the squid, cut the tentacles from the body, and cut the cleaned body into rings. Add the clams, squid bodies and tentacles, and shrimp to the tomato sauce and cook 5 minutes more. Cook the potato noodles in a large pot of boiling salted water until they rise to the surface, remove with a slotted spoon, and drain thoroughly. Arrange the noodles on 4 plates, pour the seafood sauce over the noodles, and sprinkle with the chopped herbs.

TRUFFLE FAZZOLETTI WITH SKATE WINGS

"Fazzoletti," which means handkerchiefs, is the Italian name for this pasta dish, in which meat, vegetables, or fish are layered with pasta squares.

1 recipe fresh cornmeal pasta dough (see page 43)
1 large, fresh black truffle
1 1/4 pounds skate wings, 3 tablespoons butter
3/4 cup each finely diced carrots and celery
3/4 cup minced scallions, 1/2 teaspoon salt
freshly ground pepper, truffle oil
fresh chervil leaves for garnish
For the sauce:
1/2 cup each coarsely chopped carrot and sliced leek
2 cups fish stock, 2 tablespoons dry sherry
1/2 cup heavy cream, 1 1/2 tablespoons chilled butter

To make the fazzoletti, roll out the dough very thinly in a pasta machine. Following the directions given for herb pasta on page 111, cover half of the strips of dough with paper-thin slices of fresh black truffle and lay the remaining dough on top. Roll out again, preferably with a rolling pin this time. Cut 12 rectangles, approximately 3 x 4 inches.

Use a sharp knife to remove the skin from the skate wings; take the fish off the bone and cut it in 8 pieces big enough to layer with the pasta rectangles. Brown the fish on both sides in the hot butter, and remove from the frying pan. Using the same butter, sauté the vegetables for 5 to 6 minutes. Season, add a few drops of truffle oil, and return the fish pieces to the pan. Keep warm over a very low heat.

To make the sauce, combine the carrot, leek, and fish stock in a saucepan and boil until only 4 to 5 tablespoons of liquid remain. Add the sherry. After a minute, stir in the cream and simmer over low heat 2 to 3 minutes longer. Strain the sauce and return to the pan, then use a hand blender or portable electric mixer to make the sauce foamy; thicken with the butter. Cook the pasta in boiling salted water until *al dente*; remove with a slotted spatula and drain on a dish towel. Layer the pasta, skate, and vegetables on 4 pre-warmed plates, and spoon the foamy sauce over the top. Garnish with chervil.

With lobster and crayfish

The special flavor of these crustaceans demands pasta out of the ordinary. Ribbon noodles go particularly well with such sophisticated sauces

BLACK NOODLES WITH CRAYFISH IN CREAM SAUCE

This very elegant pasta dish can also be made with scampi (Dublin Bay prawns) or large shrimp, and you can substitute plain egg pasta for the pasta colored black with squid ink. It is up to you how wide you want to cut the ribbon noodles – from the thin taglierini to the much wider pappardelle.

fresh chervil leaves for garnish
1 recipe fresh black pasta dough (see page 48)
24 live crayfish
For the sauce:
1/4 cup vegetable oil
1 cup each coarsely chopped leek, carrot, and celery
1 1/2 tablespoons cognac
1 bay leaf, 1 teaspoon salt
1/2 teaspoon black peppercorns
1/2 cup white wine
1 small carrot, 1 celery stalk
1 cup heavy cream, freshly ground pepper

Using a knife or pasta machine, cut the pasta dough into ribbon noodles (see pages 52 and 53). Lower the crayfish into boiling water and simmer until cooked, about 6 minutes. Drain and rinse in cold water. Pull off the heads and claws, peel the tails, and devein if necessary; set the tail meat aside. If the claws are big enough, remove the meat from them as well. Reserve the heads and shells.

To make the sauce, heat the oil in a large saucepan, add the chopped vegetables, and sauté briefly over high heat. Add the crayfish heads and shells (reserving a few whole heads for garnish) and brown thoroughly over high heat, stirring constantly. Pour in the cognac, and add the bay leaf, salt, and peppercorns. Pour in enough water to cover the crayfish shells and vegetables. Bring to a boil, then simmer gently over low heat about 40 minutes. Skim off any froth that rises to the surface. Strain the liquid into a clean pan (do not press down on the shells and vegetables in the strainer). Bring the strained liquid to a boil and reduce over low heat to about 1/2 cup. Add the white wine and continue to boil until reduced again to about 1/2 cup. Cut the carrot and celery into very fine strips, add to the pan, and pour on the cream. Simmer 3 to 4 minutes longer. Add the crayfish meat and warm through. Check the seasoning. Cook the noodles in boiling salted water until *al dente*, drain thoroughly, and mix with the sauce. Transfer to 4 plates, and garnish each with a crayfish shell with claws and chervil leaves.

LOBSTER WITH TAGLIERINI

A luxurious combination that demands the best and freshest ingredients, including homemade pasta.

1/2 recipe fresh pasta dough no. 4 (see page 40)
small fresh basil leaves for garnish
For the sauce:
1/2 cup white wine, 1 1/2 tablespoons dry white vermouth
3 tablespoons minced shallots
2 cups fish stock
14 tablespoons (1 3/4 sticks) chilled butter, cut in small pieces
salt and freshly ground white pepper
a few drops of lemon juice
For the lobster:
1 carrot, 1 leek, 1 celery stalk
1 garlic clove, salt
2 live lobsters, each weighing 1 to 1 1/4 pounds

Using a knife or pasta machine, cut taglierini from the pasta dough (see pages 52 and 53) and spread out on a clean dish towel. To make the sauce, combine the white wine, vermouth, and shallot in a saucepan and boil to reduce a little. Pour in the fish stock and reduce the liquid by half.

In the meantime, fill a deep pot with water and add the vegetables, peeled garlic clove, and salt. Bring to a boil. Lower the lobsters, head first, one at a time, into the boiling water, ensuring that the liquid has returned to a boil before adding the second lobster. Cook about 10 minutes, then remove the pot from the heat and leave the lobsters in the liquid 5 minutes longer. Remove the lobsters from the pot. Twist the claws from the body and reserve. With a large knife, cut the body in half lengthwise, remove the dark intestinal vein, take the meat from the shell, and cut in pieces; keep warm. Arrange the lobster-shell halves on pre-warmed plates. Cook the taglierini in boiling salted water until *al dente* and drain. Add the butter to the sauce, a few pieces at a time, and whisk in. Season and add lemon juice to taste. Toss the taglierini and lobster meat with the sauce and spoon into the lobster shells. Garnish each plate with a lobster claw and a few basil leaves.

Pizokel are made like spätzle (see page 63), being cut straight from a chopping board into boiling salted water. The only difference is that pizokel are a little thicker.

SPINACH PIZOKEL
WITH SCAMPI IN PROSCIUTTO

Pizokel, a Swiss specialty, look like outsize spätzle, and they are made in the same way.

For the pizokel:

1 cup all-purpose flour, 2 eggs

²/3 cup quark or sour cream, 1 tablespoon melted butter

salt and freshly ground pepper

freshly grated nutmeg

For the port sauce:

1¹/2 tablespoons minced shallots, 1 teaspoon butter

¹/2 cup port wine, 2 tablespoons hollandaise sauce

¹/2 cup heavy cream, whipped

salt and freshly ground pepper, a little lemon juice

For the spinach:

1 cup spinach leaves, 1 tablespoon butter

freshly grated nutmeg

¹/4 cup cream

In addition:

12 peeled scampi (Dublin Bay prawns) or large shrimp

6 thin slices of prosciutto, cut in half

¹/4 cup olive oil for frying

Make a smooth spätzle-type dough from the pizokel ingredients (see page 62) and put to one side. To make the sauce, cook the shallot in the butter until soft. Add the port and reduce until almost all the liquid has evaporated. Remove from the heat and stir in the hollandaise sauce. When ready to serve, stir in the whipped cream and reheat gently. Season with salt, pepper, and lemon juice.

Wash the spinach and chop roughly. Season the scampi with salt and pepper, and wrap each in a half slice of prosciutto. Place the dough on a wooden board and, with a metal spatula, cut it in thin strips straight into a pan of boiling salted water. As the pizokel cook, wilt the spinach in the melted butter in a frying pan. As soon as the pizokel rise to the surface of the water, remove them with a slotted spoon and mix them with the spinach. Season with salt, pepper, and nutmeg, and mix in the cream. Heat through. Fry the scampi in the olive oil until golden brown. Spoon the pizokel and spinach mixture onto pre-warmed plates and arrange the scampi on top. Serve with the port sauce.

More than just a side-dish

Two shellfish dishes, sufficient in themselves, but complemented to perfection by the addition of pasta

SQUID-INK NOODLES AND ZUCCHINI WITH ROCK LOBSTER

3/4 recipe fresh black pasta dough (see page 48)
1 rock lobster tail, weighing 1 pound, or 2 tails, about 10 ounces each, thawed if frozen
For the lobster sauce:
2 cups rock lobster or fish stock
2/3 cup heavy cream
salt and freshly ground pepper
For the zucchini:
1/2 pound baby zucchini
1/4 cup minced shallots, 2 tablespoons olive oil
1 tablespoon balsamic vinegar
For garnish:
fresh chervil leaves

Using a knife or pasta machine, cut ribbon noodles 3/8 inch wide from the pasta dough. Cook the lobster tail in boiling salted water or a court-bouillon for about 15 minutes. Drain and let cool, then remove the meat from the shell. Devein, and cut the meat into slices of even thickness. Put back into the original shape, wrap in foil, and keep warm. Slowly boil the lobster stock to reduce to about a fifth of its original volume. Stir in the cream, season with salt and pepper, and simmer gently 3 to 4 minutes longer. In the meantime, trim the zucchini and cut lengthwise in paper-thin slices. (This is most easily done with a mandoline.) Cut the slices in half lengthwise. Sauté the shallots in the olive oil until translucent. Cook the noodles in boiling salted water until *al dente*; drain. Add the zucchini strips to the shallots and sauté over high heat for 2 to 3 minutes. Add the balsamic vinegar and then the squid-ink noodles and toss well to mix. Arrange on 4 pre-warmed plates with the sliced lobster. Pour on the lobster sauce and garnish with chervil leaves.

From the wok

Stir-frying seafood is an ideal way of preparing it for serving with pasta

Stir-frying is really successful only in a wok because the prepared ingredients can be cooked rapidly over high heat while being constantly moved around at speed, so that all the surfaces of the food come into contact with the hot wok. This cooking method is ideal for vegetables, because they retain their crispy freshness and flavor. The same applies to seafood. The scallop dish below, and the shrimp dishes on pages 152 and 153, are good examples of this Asian cooking technique. The texture of the stir-fried seafood contrasts interestingly with that of the soft noodles.

SCALLOPS WITH EGG NOODLES

1 pound sea scallops
1 green bell pepper, 1 carrot
2 scallions, $^1/_2$-ounce piece of fresh gingerroot
$^1/_4$ pound Chinese egg noodles

3 tablespoons peanut oil
2 teaspoons oyster sauce
salt and freshly ground pepper
2 cups eggplant cut in $^3/_8$-inch cubes
$^2/_3$ cup sliced celery
1 tablespoon light soy sauce
1 hot red chili pepper, cut in rings

Cut the scallops in half horizontally. Cut the bell pepper in half, remove the core and seeds, and cut in diamond shapes. Peel the carrot and cut in sticks. Slice the scallions. Peel and slice the ginger. Cook the noodles in boiling salted water for 4 minutes or until done, drain, and rinse with cold water. Heat 1 tablespoon of oil in a wok and briefly stir-fry the scallops. Add the oyster sauce, and season with salt and pepper. Mix everything together, then remove from the wok and place to one side. Heat the remaining oil in the wok and stir-fry the eggplant until lightly browned. Add the carrot, bell pepper, celery, and scallions and stir-fry until all the vegetables are cooked but still crisp. Add the soy sauce and chili-pepper rings and mix everything together thoroughly. Add the scallops and the noodles, and toss briefly to reheat, then transfer to Chinese soup bowls and serve hot.

FISH WITH
NOODLES AND VEGETABLES

The presentation of food has always been very important in Asia. The stir-fried dishes do not necessarily have to be served in individual serving bowls. An attractive alternative is to pile them on a long serving platter, and then to put the head and tail of the fish at each end, to give the appearance of a whole fish. This recipe will serve 2.

1¹/₂-pound whole fish: tilefish, striped bass, red snapper, white or sea perch, cleaned

salt and freshly ground pepper

1 tablespoon vegetable oil

¹/₂ ounce dried cloud ear mushrooms

1 carrot, 2 scallions, 1 hot red chili pepper

2 tablespoons oriental sesame oil

¹/₂ cup thinly sliced leek, ¹/₂ cup thinly sliced zucchini

³/₄ cup diced red bell pepper

1 tablespoon minced fresh gingerroot

¹/₄ cup canned bamboo shoot cut in strips

1 tablespoon soy sauce

3 to 4 ounces Chinese egg noodles

fresh cilantro for garnish

Season the fish inside with salt and pepper. Lay it in a suitably sized baking dish, brush with vegetable oil, and cook in an oven preheated to 400°F for 20 minutes. In the meantime, soak the mushrooms in cold water. Peel the carrot and cut in thin sticks. Trim the scallions and cut in thin rings. Cut the chili pepper in half, remove the seeds and core, and cut in thin strips. Remove the fish from the oven; neatly cut off the head and tail and reserve. Take the flesh from the fish, discarding skin and bones, and cut in 5/8-inch pieces. Heat the sesame oil in a wok and stir-fry all the prepared vegetables with the drained mushrooms until crisp-tender. Season with the soy sauce, and salt and pepper to taste. Carefully mix in the fish pieces. Cook the noodles in boiling salted water about 5 minutes, drain, and add to the other ingredients. Arrange the fish and noodle mixture on a serving dish, with the fish head and tail placed at the ends so that the fish appears still to be whole. Garnish with cilantro.

A mingling of flavors and textures in the Asian style

Creativity is required when combining ingredients, which in Asia is usually determined by what is available in the market

CANTONESE-STYLE SHRIMP WITH RICE NOODLES

Contrast is a basic feature of the cooking of southern China, and here the crispness of the fried shrimp is countered by the softness of the fresh noodles. This recipe is only one of many ways in which shellfish cooked in a wok can be combined with noodles and vegetables. As well as shrimp of different sizes, lump crabmeat and rock lobster can be used, together with egg or cellophane noodles.

1 pound raw medium shrimp
2 ounces fresh shiitake mushrooms
3/4-ounce piece of fresh gingerroot
1/4 pound Chinese rice noodles
1/4 cup vegetable oil
1/2 cup thinly sliced leek
1/4 cup bamboo shoots cut in strips
1 tablespoon chopped fresh cilantro for garnish
For the sauce:
2 scallions
1 hot red chili pepper
3 tablespoons light soy sauce
2 tablespoons rice wine
1 teaspoon tomato paste
1 teaspoon rice vinegar
1/2 cup chicken stock (see page 86)
salt and freshly ground pepper
1/2 teaspoon palm or raw brown sugar

Peel the shrimp, leaving on the last tail section, and devein. Rinse and dry thoroughly on paper towels. Remove the thick stems from the shiittake mushrooms and cut the caps in half or quarters, depending on size. Peel the ginger and cut in thin slices. Pour boiling water over the noodles and let stand about 3 minutes, then drain and rinse with cold water. Put to one side. For the sauce, trim and mince the scallions; cut the chili pepper in half, remove seeds, and mince. Mix together the rest of the sauce ingredients.

Heat 2 tablespoons of the vegetable oil in a wok. Season the shrimp with salt and pepper and stir-fry until pink and a little crisp. Remove from the wok and put to one side. Heat another tablespoon of oil in the wok and stir-fry the prepared vegetables until crisp-tender – first the mushrooms, then the leek and ginger, and finally the bamboo shoots; remove from the wok. Heat the remaining oil in the wok and stir-fry the scallions and chili briefly. Pour on the prepared sauce liquid and boil to reduce it slightly. Return all the vegetables to the wok and add the noodles. Toss in the sauce for 1 to 2 minutes to reheat. Mix in the shrimp, sprinkle with cilantro, and serve immediately.

In Singapore, freshly cooked lump crabmeat is often used instead of shrimp, and the dish is served in the empty crab body shells.

SEAFOOD WITH EGG NOODLES

While the composition of this dish is flexible – using seafood and vegetables that are the best and freshest in the market – the choice should offer contrasts in both texture and flavor. Cooking in a wok makes it possible to adjust cooking times accordingly. Firm-fleshed fish, such as monkfish or halibut, are the most suitable for stir-frying.

1/2 pound Chinese egg noodles
1/2 pound squid, 1/2 pound raw medium shrimp
1/2 pound firm white fish fillet
4 dried Chinese mushrooms
3 slices of fresh gingerroot
1 garlic clove, 3 tablespoons peanut oil
2/3 cup snow peas, 2 tablespoons water
For the sauce:
1 1/2 cups chicken stock (see page 86)
3 tablespoons light soy sauce, 1/2 teaspoon sugar
2 tablespoons oriental sesame oil
1 teaspoon cornstarch, salt and freshly ground pepper
For garnish:
fresh cilantro leaves

Soak the noodles in boiling water until they separate from each other; drain. Clean the squid, cut off the tentacles, and slit open the squid bodies. Lay the bodies flat and score a diamond pattern in the flesh with a sharp knife; cut in bite-size pieces. Peel the shrimp, leaving on the last tail section, and devein. Cut the fish in bite-size pieces. Soak the mushrooms in hot water. Cut the ginger in fine shreds; peel and mince the garlic. Heat the oil in a wok and brown the ginger and garlic. Add the drained mushrooms and the snow peas together with the water. Stir-fry for 1 minute. Remove the contents of the pan, and briefly stir-fry the fish pieces. Put the mushroom mixture back into the wok, add the shrimp and squid, and stir-fry until the squid pieces curl up. Mix the sauce ingredients together, add to the wok, and stir until the sauce thickens. Season with salt and pepper. Add the drained noodles and simmer until they have soaked up the sauce, 1 to 2 minutes. Arrange on a pre-warmed serving dish and garnish with cilantro leaves.

With meat, poultry, and game

Being quite bland, pasta always cries out for sauces and other accompaniments that will impart flavor. A *ragù,* or rich meat sauce, is one of the best ways to give a pasta dish flavor. But it is important to be judicious: the pasta should not be swimming in the sauce. And the sauce must be thick and concentrated, so that it coats the pasta and does not pool on the plate. The same rules are true for a tomato sauce.

In Italy, a full set of flatware is not provided for the pasta course, just a fork or a fork and a spoon, so any meat to be mixed with pasta is usually cut in small pieces. A *ragù,* then, does not normally contain chunks of meat of the size you might find in a stew, for example, that need to be cut with a knife.

Depending on the meat from which the *ragù* is made, it may be cooked just a few minutes or simmered for an extended period. Some of the most elegant accompaniments for pasta are undoubtedly game birds such as quails. Beef, pork, veal, and chicken are popular in pasta sauces, as are salami, prosciutto, and other preserved meats. Fresh pork sausage, particularly the Italian luganeghe, is wonderful in a sauce for spaghetti or macaroni. In fact, any kind of meat can be used in a *ragu*, mixed with vegetables such as tomatoes, onions, garlic, and bell and chili peppers.

When making a *ragù*, a better texture is achieved by using a knife to mince the meat, rather than putting it through a meat grinder. This is particularly important for delicate meat, such as quail or squab, which always suffers a certain degree of damage when ground.

An Italian-style *ragù* is not the only way of serving meat with pasta. Spicy Asian dishes can also lift pasta out of its bland neutrality – whether it be a wholly inauthentic meat curry, or a Chinese duck or chicken stew, seasoned with soy sauce and a little five-spice powder, the widely used Chinese seasoning that tastes of anise and cinnamon. Pasta provides a flexible basis for many different blends of ingredients. It also offers the imagination plenty of scope, and is a splendid vehicle for the latest creations of those who like to experiment in the kitchen. How else would the myriad combinations that surprise and delight our palates at the dinner table have come into being?

SPAGHETTI ALLA CARBONARA

This spaghetti dish, with its combination of eggs and bacon, is a simple but classic one. You have the choice between the distinctive taste of Italian pancetta (traditionally used in this recipe) and ordinary bacon.

¹/2 pound pancetta or smoked bacon
1 garlic clove, 1 pound spaghetti
2 tablespoons vegetable oil, 4 eggs
³/4 cup freshly grated Parmesan cheese
salt and freshly ground pepper

Cut the pancetta or bacon in strips. Lightly bruise the unpeeled garlic clove. Cook the pasta in boiling salted water until *al dente*. In the meantime, continue as shown in the picture sequence below.

Preparing spaghetti alla carbonara:

Heat the oil in a large saucepan and fry the pancetta and garlic until the pancetta starts to become crisp.

Break the eggs into a bowl. Add the cheese and whisk thoroughly. Season to taste with salt and pepper.

Add the drained spaghetti to the pan and mix with the pancetta. Remove the pan from the heat, add the egg and cheese mixture, and stir in well.

CHESTNUT NOODLES WITH PANCETTA

A very simple dish that requires the best possible ingredients. Pancetta must be used because it is essential to the flavor. Only pancetta has the distinctive taste that combines so well with the chestnut noodles and cheese.

For the dough:
2 cups all-purpose flour
1 cup + 3 tablespoons chestnut flour
3 eggs
2 egg yolks
¹/2 teaspoon salt
For the sauce:
¹/2 pound pancetta, sliced thin
1 tablespoon vegetable oil, 1 cup heavy cream
³/4 cup freshly grated Parmesan cheese
salt and freshly ground pepper
For garnish:
2 tablespoons chopped fresh chives

Make the dough following the directions on page 43, and cut it in noodles about ¹/4 inch wide. Cut the pancetta in strips. Heat the oil in a frying pan, fry the pancetta until crisp, and put to one side. Put the cream in a saucepan and boil to reduce by half; let cool. Add the Parmesan to the cream, season to taste with salt and pepper, and mix in the pancetta. Cook the noodles in boiling salted water until *al dente*, drain, and mix immediately with the sauce.

Sprinkle with the chopped chives and serve on pre-warmed plates.

FARFALLE WITH
MEAT SAUCE AND YOGURT

In Turkey, where it is known as "*mankarna mantisi*," this dish is made just with beef, but the addition of pork improves the taste considerably. The quantity of garlic can, of course, be reduced to suit individual tastes.

1 recipe fresh pasta dough no. 1 (see page 40)
For the meat sauce:
7 tablespoons vegetable oil, 1 cup minced onions
1/3 cup diced parsley root (optional)
1/3 cup diced celery, 2 cups diced red bell pepper
1/2 pound ground round, 1/2 pound ground pork
1 teaspoon salt, freshly ground black pepper
1 tablespoon paprika
1/2 tablespoon chopped fresh mint, 1 cup beef stock
For the yogurt sauce:
6 garlic cloves
1 cup plain yogurt, 1/2 teaspoon salt
For garnish:
fresh mint leaves

Cut farfalle from the pasta dough (see page 55), or use dried pasta. Heat 4 tablespoons of the oil in a large pan and fry the onions until soft and translucent; add the parsley root, if using, the celery, and bell pepper and cook 5 minutes longer. Heat the remaining oil in a second pan and brown the ground meats, stirring with a wooden spoon to break them up. Mix the meat with the vegetables. Season with salt, pepper, paprika, and mint. Pour in the stock and simmer 10 to 15 minutes. The liquid should be reduced by about half.

Peel and mince the garlic, and stir into the yogurt with the salt. Cook the pasta in boiling salted water until *al dente*, drain, and divide among 4 pre-warmed plates. Spoon off about half of the liquid from the meat sauce and reserve; pour the rest of the sauce over the pasta. Add the yogurt sauce and pour the reserved cooking liquid over the top. Garnish each serving with mint leaves.

Simple pasta dishes

Bacon, ham, and cheese make it easy to add flavor to pasta

The "chitarra" *is a wooden frame on which pasta can be cut. The top and bottom of the frame are strung with wires, like the strings of a guitar. The sheet of dough is laid across the wires and rolled out with a rolling pin. The cut noodles drop into the inside of the frame where they collect on a board.*

SPAGHETTI ALLA CHITARRA

This spaghetti, with its square cross section, is made on a special cutting device known as a *chitarra* (guitar), from which it takes its name. The spaghetti cutters on a pasta machine will give much the same effect or you can use ordinary spaghetti.

1 pound spaghetti alla chitarra
For the sauce:
2 1/4 pounds ripe plum tomatoes
1/2 pound pancetta
1 onion
1/4 cup olive oil
salt and freshly ground pepper
For serving:
1 cup freshly grated pecorino cheese
30 fresh basil leaves

Blanch the tomatoes, peel them, remove the seeds, and dice. Cut the pancetta first in slices and then in short strips. Peel the onion and cut in rings. Heat the oil in a pan and lightly brown the pancetta and onion. Add the diced tomatoes and season lightly with salt. Turn the heat down very low, cover the pan, and simmer 15 minutes. Remove the lid and simmer gently 45 minutes longer, checking periodically to ensure that all the liquid does not evaporate. Shortly before the end of the cooking time, season the sauce with salt and pepper. Cook the spaghetti in boiling salted water until *al dente* and drain. Immediately mix with some of the sauce. Serve the pasta onto pre-warmed plates and spoon on the rest of the sauce. Sprinkle with cheese and garnish with basil leaves.

Pancetta *is Italian bacon cured with salt and spices (not smoked) and then rolled up into a sausage shape. Its flavor is different from ordinary bacon.*

TAGLIATELLE WITH HAM AND CREAM SAUCE

This ham and cream sauce, from the Italian province of Parma, has a quite extraordinary flavor. Prosciutto can be very salty, so taste the sauce before adding any additional seasoning.

1 recipe fresh pasta dough no. 4 (see page 40)
For the sauce:
1/4 pound prosciutto, preferably prosciutto di Parma
1/4 pound cooked ham
6 tablespoons (3/4 stick) butter
1 cup heavy cream
a pinch of freshly grated nutmeg
1 cup freshly grated Parmesan cheese
freshly ground pepper
For garnish:
1 tablespoon chopped fresh parsley
1 tablespoon chopped fresh chives

Using a knife or pasta machine, cut tagliatelle from the pasta dough (see pages 52 and 53), or used dried tagliatelle. Cut the prosciutto and ham in small pieces. Melt the butter in a saucepan, add the prosciutto and ham, and cook a few minutes. Pour in the cream, season with grated nutmeg, and stir in half the Parmesan. Simmer over a low heat about 10 minutes. Season the sauce with pepper. In the meantime, cook the tagliatelle in boiling salted water until *al dente*. Drain and mix immediately with the sauce. Transfer to pre-warmed plates and sprinkle with the remaining Parmesan and the chopped parsley and chives.

Penne with prosciutto and peas is an excellent variation of this dish, to make when fresh green peas are available in the summer. Replace the cooked ham with 2 cups of freshly shelled green peas. Add them to the sauce halfway through the cooking time, so that they simmer only 5 minutes. Cook the penne in boiling salted water until *al dente*, mix with the sauce, and garnish just with chopped parsley, omitting the chives.

Prosciutto di Parma *gives this dish its characteristic flavor. This salt-cured and air-dried Italian ham can be bought in gourmet markets and many supermarkets.*

Pasta with variety meats

Chicken livers are particularly good in pasta sauces, but variety meats from veal and other animals can also be used

TAGLIATELLE WITH RICH RABBIT SAUCE

Tender white meat of rabbit combined with flavorful variety meats makes a delicious and quick-to-prepare pasta sauce. Tubular pasta such as penne rigate go well with the sauce, but ribbon noodles with plenty of egg yolk are even better.

³/4 recipe fresh pasta dough no. 4 (see page 40)
For the rabbit sauce:
1 pound boneless rabbit meat
¹/4 pound rabbit liver (or chicken livers)
8 rabbit kidneys (optional)
2 teaspoons paprika, 1 tablespoon olive oil
1 thick-cut slice of smoked bacon, chopped
¹/2 cup chopped onion, ¹/2 garlic clove, crushed
¹/2 cup diced carrot
1 pound tomatoes, peeled, seeded, and chopped
3 sprigs of fresh thyme, 1 small sprig of fresh rosemary
salt and freshly ground pepper
1 cup dry white wine
¹/4 cup vegetable oil

To finish:
2 heaping tablespoons freshly grated Parmesan cheese
1 heaping tablespoon white bread crumbs
4 tablespoons butter, cut in small pieces

Using a knife or pasta machine, cut tagliatelle from the pasta dough (see pages 52 and 53), or use dried tagliatelle. Cut the rabbit meat and liver in small cubes. Trim the kidneys and cut in half lengthwise. Sprinkle the meats with the paprika and leave about 15 minutes for the flavor to soak in. Heat the olive oil in a wide saucepan, add the bacon, and brown quickly. Add the onion, garlic, and carrot and saute 3 to 4 minutes. Stir in the chopped tomatoes and herbs, season with salt and pepper, and pour in the white wine. Simmer 10 to 15 minutes longer. Heat the vegetable oil in a frying pan and quickly brown the rabbit meat, liver, and kidneys over medium-high heat. Season with salt and pepper, and fry 1 to 2 minutes more. Add to the tomato sauce and cook 2 to 3 minutes over high heat. In the meantime, cook the tagliatelle in boiling salted water until *al dente*. Drain and mix with the rabbit sauce. Arrange on 4 heatproof serving plates. Mix the Parmesan with the bread crumbs, sprinkle over the pasta, and dot with the pieces of butter. Brown under the broiler, and serve immediately.

TAGLIERINI
WITH CHICKEN LIVERS

Livers can be used to make marvelous pasta sauces, from inexpensive chicken livers to *foie gras*, the liver of specially fattened geese or ducks. The latter is, of course, expensive, but lightly cooked fresh *foie gras*, with a little pan juice or truffle sauce dribbled over, is indescribably delicious with ribbon noodles.

1 recipe fresh pasta dough no. 4 (see page 40)
For the sauce:
2 cups chicken stock, 1 small garlic clove
4 tablespoons butter, 2/3 cup minced shallots
1/2 pound chicken livers
2 tablespoons port wine, 1/2 teaspoon salt
freshly ground pepper
1 tablespoon paprika
For garnish:
1 fresh truffle (optional)
2 baby zucchini with flowers, 2 tablespoons butter

With a knife or pasta machine, cut taglierini from the pasta dough (see pages 52 and 53), or use dried ribbon noodles. Boil the chicken stock over a low heat until reduced to just under 1/2 cup. Peel and mince the garlic. Melt the butter in a suitably sized pan and gently fry the shallots and garlic until translucent, stirring frequently. Trim the chicken livers and cut in small pieces. Add to the shallots and brown over medium-high heat, stirring constantly. Add the port, stir in the reduced chicken stock, and season with salt, pepper, and paprika. Simmer 2 to 3 minutes more over a low heat. In the meantime, cook the taglierini in boiling salted water until *al dente*. Drain and mix with the sauce. Clean or peel the truffle and slice thinly. Cut the two zucchini, including the flowers, in half lengthwise. Heat the butter in a pan and brown the truffle slices on both sides, then add the zucchini and brown on both sides as well. Arrange with the pasta on pre-warmed plates. If cheese is to be served with this dish, it should be a freshly grated, aged Parmesan.

PASTA SQUARES WITH DUCK

This Greek dish is called "*hilopites me papia*," which translates roughly as "a thousand pies." Virtually identical recipes for pasta with duck are found along Italy's Adriatic coast, the only differences being that in the South the duck sauce is served with orecchiette and in the Veneto with bigoli, the Venetian whole-wheat spaghetti.

1 recipe fresh pasta dough no. 1 (see page 40)
For the duck:
1 duck, weighing about 4^1/2 pounds
2 garlic cloves
3 celery stalks
1 cup coarsely chopped onions
1 sprig of fresh thyme
1 bay leaf
a few sprigs of fresh flat-leaf parsley
^{1}/4 lemon
10 black peppercorns
salt
For the sauce:
thinly pared zest and juice of 1 lemon
2 teaspoons honey
^{1}/2 teaspoon salt
freshly ground pepper
For garnish:
2 tablespoons toasted sesame seeds
1 tablespoon minced fresh parsley

Roll out the pasta dough very thinly on a floured work surface and cut into 1-inch squares. Lay the squares on cloths to dry. Rinse the duck inside and out, remove all visible fat, and pat dry. Place in a large pot, cover with cold water, and bring slowly to a boil, skimming off any scum that comes to the surface. Peel and bruise the garlic; coarsely chop the celery. Add these to the pot with the onions and all the herbs and seasonings. Simmer until the duck is cooked, about 1 hour. Remove the duck from the pot and keep warm. Strain the cooking liquid, skim off the fat, return to the pot, and bring back to a boil. Cook the pasta squares in it until *al dente*. Drain the pasta in a colander set in a bowl and keep warm. Return the cooking liquid to the pot. Add the lemon zest, cut in thin strips, and the honey, and season with salt and pepper. Boil over high heat until reduced by half, then add the lemon juice. Take the meat off the duck, discard the skin, and cut the meat in ^{1}/2-inch cubes. Mix with the pasta squares. Pour on the lemon sauce, and sprinkle with the sesame seeds and parsley.

FUSILLI WITH A RAGOUT OF WILD DUCK

A coarse-textured meat sauce goes particularly well with curly pasta such as fusilli, which soaks up the sauce splendidly.

1 pound fusilli
For the duck ragout:
1 wild duck, weighing about 1 ^{1}/$_2$ pounds
2 thick-cut slices of bacon
1 celery stalk, 1 small carrot
^{1}/$_2$ onion
2 tablespoons vegetable oil
1 cup red wine (Merlot)
1 tablespoon tomato paste
^{1}/$_2$ tablespoon salt
freshly ground white pepper
1 bay leaf
1 sprig each of fresh thyme and rosemary
1 cup duck or chicken stock
1 tablespoon chopped fresh parsley

Take all the meat off the duck and discard the skin. Mince the meat with a knife or grind as coarsely as possible in a meat grinder. Cut the bacon in thin strips. Cut the celery and carrot in julienne strips. Thinly slice the onion. Continue as shown in the picture sequence. Cook the fusilli in boiling salted water until *al dente*, drain, and transfer to a pre-warmed bowl. Mix the pasta with the duck ragout and serve immediately.

Preparing the duck ragout:
Heat the oil in a large pan and sauté the bacon until crisp. Add the vegetables and fry briefly, then add the meat from the duck.

Pour in the red wine, stir in the tomato paste, and season. Bring to a boil, then reduce the heat to a simmer.

Add the bay leaf, thyme, rosemary, and stock, and let simmer, stirring from time to time.

Cook until the meat is tender and the ragout is thick and rich. Add the parsley.

SWEETBREADS ON MACARONI AU GRATIN

Sweetbreads blend very agreeably with pasta and melted cheese. Be sure to use balsamic vinegar that is at least 10 years old.

2 cups veal stock

1 pound veal sweetbreads

3 tablespoons extra-virgin olive oil

2/3 cup chopped shallots

1/3 cup diced carrot

1/3 cup diced celery, 1/2 garlic clove, minced

2 tablespoons balsamic vinegar

1/2 teaspoon salt, freshly ground white pepper

1/2 teaspoon paprika

2 tablespoons butter, 1/2 cup snow peas

4 nasturtium flowers for garnish (optional)

For the macaroni au gratin:

3/4 pound long macaroni, 4 tablespoons butter

1/2 cup freshly grated Parmesan cheese

2 tablespoons minced fresh herbs: parsley, thyme

Bring the veal stock to a boil and let reduce slowly over low heat to just under 1/2 cup. In the meantime, briefly blanch the sweetbreads in boiling water, remove the membrane as carefully as possible, and cut in slices about 3/8 inch thick; set aside. To prepare the macaroni au gratin, cook the macaroni in boiling salted water until *al dente*; drain. Melt the butter and use some to grease 4 individual serving plates (they should be deep and heatproof). Arrange the macaroni in a single layer on the plates, starting at the outside edge and spiraling in, curving to fit. Dribble the remaining melted butter over the pasta. Mix the grated Parmesan with the minced herbs and sprinkle over the pasta. To make the sauce, heat the oil in a saucepan and sauté the shallots until soft. Add the carrot, celery, and garlic and sauté a few minutes more. Pour on the balsamic vinegar. Add the reduced veal stock and simmer gently until the liquid is reduced to about half its original volume. Remove the pan from the heat. Season the sliced sweetbreads with salt, pepper, and a little paprika. Heat the butter in a frying pan and fry the sliced sweetbreads over high heat for 2 to 3 minutes on each side. In the meantime, place the plates of macaroni under the broiler to brown. Add the fried sweetbreads to the sauce, together with the snow peas, cut in strips. Heat through, then spoon on top of the macaroni au gratin. Decorate each plate with a nasturtium flower.

Pasta and Roquefort gratin For this variation, use penne, penne rigate, or medium-sized conchiglie. Cook in boiling salted water until *al dente* and drain. Grease the plates with melted butter and make a layer of pasta on each one. Lightly whip 1/2 cup cream with 1/2 cup freshly grated Parmesan, season with a little pepper and nutmeg, and pour over the pasta. Cut 1 1/2 to 2 ounces of Roquefort in small cubes and dot the pasta with it. Warm under the broiler until the surface is light brown and crispy. The Roquefort imparts a very distinctive flavor.

BRAISED QUAILS
WITH PARSLEY PASTA

The fresh flavor of parsley is a perfect match for both the quails and the chanterelles in this dish. Whole parsley leaves encased in sheets of pasta, known in Italy as *fazzoletti*, add to the subtle flavor.

12 large squares of pasta with parsley leaves (see page 111)	
For the quail ragout:	
4 6-ounce quails	
salt and freshly ground pepper	
2 tablespoons vegetable oil	
1/2 cup each minced shallots and celery	
1/4 cup each finely diced carrot and parsley root (optional)	
1/4 cup finely diced smoked bacon, 2 garlic cloves	
1 teaspoon flour, 1 cup chicken stock	
2 tablespoons chopped fresh parsley	
To finish:	
1 1/2 tablespoons butter	
1/4 pound small fresh chanterelles	

Put the pasta squares between damp cloths to prevent them from drying out. Cut the quails in half lengthwise. Cut off the legs and wings. Season all the pieces of meat lightly with salt and pepper and put to one side. Heat the oil in a large pan and sauté the shallots until translucent. Add the celery, carrot, and parsley root (if using) and sauté briskly for 2 to 3 minutes; remove the vegetables from the pan with a slotted spoon and keep warm. Add the bacon to the pan and cook until the fat is rendered. Add the pieces of quail and brown over high heat. Bruise the unpeeled garlic cloves with the side of a knife and add to the pan with the sautéed vegetables. Sprinkle with the flour and cook 3 to 4 minutes, stirring well. Add the chicken stock and simmer until the meat is cooked and the liquid has reduced by more than half. Add the parsley, and adjust the seasoning if necessary. Cook the pasta squares in boiling salted water until *al dente*; remove with a slotted spatula and drain thoroughly. Melt the butter in a small pan and sauté the chanterelles, adding salt and pepper to taste. For each serving, layer some quail ragout between 3 squares of pasta. Garnish with sautéed chanterelles.

Squab and wild boar

The meat of game animals and game birds is a popular accompaniment for pasta, and these dishes are some of the finest that pasta cooking has to offer

LINGUINE WITH SQUAB

This dish is traditionally made with wild pigeons, which have a much stronger flavor than the plump farm-reared squab. However, squabs, with their light, delicate meat, impart a subtle flavor to the dish, and are well worth trying. The flavor is further enhanced by the addition of Italian prosciutto.

$3/4$ recipe fresh pasta dough no. 4 (see page 40)
2 squabs, weighing about 10 $1/2$ ounces each
$1/2$ carrot, 1 small celery stalk
$3/4$ pound plum tomatoes, peeled and seeded
$1/4$ pound prosciutto, 2 scallions
2 to 3 tablespoons olive oil
$1/4$ cup chopped onion, 1 tablespoon minced fresh parsley

Cut noodles $1/16$ to $1/8$ inch wide from the pasta dough (see pages 52 and 53), or use dried linguine. Cut each squab in quarters. Cut the carrot in thin strips, and thinly slice the celery. Chop the tomatoes coarsely. Cut the prosciutto in small cubes, and chop the scallions in rings. Heat the oil in a large pan and sauté the onion, carrot, and celery about 5 minutes, stirring constantly. Add the pieces of squab and brown evenly all over. Stir in the tomatoes, cover the pan, and simmer 1 hour. Add a little water from time to time if necessary. Lift out the squab, take the meat off the bone, and return it to the pan. Add the prosciutto and scallions to the sauce and warm through. Cook the linguine in boiling salted water until *al dente*, drain, and mix with the sauce. Serve sprinkled with parsley.

PAPPARDELLE AL CINGHIALE

Ribbon noodles with a stew of wild boar is a classic dish in Tuscany and the Marches, and there are very similar dishes that use rabbit instead of wild boar. True, the recipe does take time to prepare, but if you are (or know) a hunter it is also fairly cheap.

$3/4$ recipe fresh pasta dough no. 4 (see page 40)
1 pound boneless shoulder of wild boar (or substitute pork)
$1/4$ cup olive oil, 1 tablespoon flour
$3/4$ pound tomatoes, peeled and chopped
salt and freshly ground pepper
For the marinade:
1 small onion, 1 garlic clove
$2/3$ cup diced carrot, 1 $1/2$ cups red wine (Chianti classico)
12 juniper berries
1 teaspoon black peppercorns
1 piece of pared lemon zest
1 bay leaf, 1 sprig of fresh rosemary

Cut pappardelle from the pasta dough (see pages 52 and 53), or use dried ribbon noodles. Cut the meat in $3/8$-inch cubes and place in a deep bowl. To make the marinade, peel and slice the onion. Crush the unpeeled garlic clove with the side of a knife. Add the onion and garlic to the meat, together with the remaining marinade ingredients. Cover the bowl and let marinate in a cool place for at least 12 hours. Remove the meat and pat dry with paper towels. Strain the marinade and reserve. Heat the oil in a heavy pan over medium heat and brown the cubes of meat on all sides. Sprinkle with the flour and stir thoroughly. Add the chopped tomatoes and pour in the reserved marinade. Turn up the heat and bring to a boil, stirring to mix in the browned bits on the bottom of the pan. Reduce the heat, cover the pan, and simmer until the meat is cooked, about 2 hours (less for domestic pork). Remove the lid and continue simmering to reduce the sauce by about half. Season to taste with salt and pepper. Cook the noodles in boiling salted water until *al dente*, drain, and transfer to a pre-warmed bowl. Mix with the boar ragout and serve immediately.

NOODLES WITH CHICKEN AND ASPARAGUS

The crispy vegetables, stir-fried in a wok, are a perfect accompaniment for the chicken and noodles.

3/4 pound Chinese egg noodles
For the chicken:
1/2 pound skinless boneless chicken breast
2 tablespoons rice wine, 1 tablespoon light soy sauce
2 teaspoons cornstarch, 1/2 teaspoon sugar
salt and freshly ground pepper
a pinch of ground ginger
For the vegetables:
2 ounces sliced cooked ham (preferably Smithfield or similar country ham)
4 dried Chinese mushrooms, reconstituted in water
1/2 pound thin green asparagus, 1/4 cup peanut oil
3/4 cup thinly sliced leek
1/2 cup thinly sliced canned bamboo shoots
In addition:
1/2 cup chicken stock (see page 86)
1 tablespoon dark soy sauce
1 tablespoon chopped fresh cilantro

Cut the chicken breast diagonally in thin slices and place in a bowl. Mix the rice wine and soy sauce together, stir in the cornstarch, and pour over the chicken. Sprinkle with the sugar, salt, pepper, and ground ginger, mix well, cover, and let marinate about 1 hour. Cut the cooked ham in strips about 1/4 inch wide. Drain the soaked mushrooms, squeeze dry, and slice. Trim the woody ends from the asparagus stalks, then cut in pieces 1 1/2 to 2 inches long. Heat the oil in a wok and quickly brown the ham and mushrooms, stirring; remove from the wok and keep warm. Put the leek, bamboo shoots, and asparagus in the wok and stir-fry until the asparagus is tender. Remove and keep warm. In the meantime, cook the noodles in plenty of boiling salted water until *al dente* and drain well. Take the chicken from the marinade and drain well, reserving the liquid. Heat the oil remaining in the wok and stir-fry the chicken until lightly browned. Add all the vegetables, pour on the reserved marinade and the chicken stock, and toss everything together until piping hot. Add the dark soy sauce and, if necessary, a little more salt and pepper. Add the noodles, mix in, and transfer to bowls. Sprinkle with chopped cilantro.

FRIED EGG NOODLES WITH PORK

The crispy fried noodles and crunchy vegetables contrast perfectly with the moist, tender meat.

3/4 pound lean boneless pork, diced
2 teaspoons dark soy sauce, 1 tablespoon rice wine
1/2 teaspoon cornstarch
1/2 teaspoon each salt, sugar, and freshly ground pepper, all mixed together
4 dried tree or wood ear mushrooms, reconstituted in water
1/2 red bell pepper, 1/2 carrot
1 bunch of scallions, 2 garlic cloves
1/2 pound dried thin egg noodles
about 1/2 cup peanut oil, 1/2 cup bean sprouts
1/4 pound peeled shrimp, 4 to 6 tablespoons chicken stock
2 tablespoons light soy sauce, 1 tablespoon oyster sauce

Put the pork in a bowl. Mix together the dark soy sauce, rice wine, cornstarch, and seasoning mixture and add to the pork. Cover and let marinate about 1 hour. Cut the drained mushrooms, bell pepper, and carrot in thin strips. Slice the scallions. Peel and mince the garlic. Cook the noodles in boiling salted water until *al dente* and drain well. Let dry and then make 4 noodle cakes, as shown in the picture sequence below; keep warm. Heat 1 1/2 tablespoons oil in a wok and stir-fry the garlic briefly. Add the pork with its marinade and stir-fry over high heat until browned; remove from the wok and keep warm. Put the vegetables, bean sprouts, and shrimp in the wok and stir-fry vigorously. Return the pork to the wok and mix in the stock, light soy sauce, and oyster sauce. Taste and add salt if necessary. Spoon onto the noodle cakes.

Spread out the noodles in a dish lined with paper towels and let dry completely.

Heat the oil in a large frying pan over medium heat. Divide the noodles in 4 portions and add one portion to the oil.

Fry until golden brown and crisp, then carefully turn the noodle cake and fry until the other side is lightly browned.

Meat with noodles in the Sichuan style

The cuisine of this Chinese province is renowned for its hearty, pungently flavored meat dishes as well as for its noodles

SICHUAN PASTE

This spicy mixture is a popular seasoning in Chinese cooking and can be easily made at home. The only unusual ingredient required is fermented black beans, which can be bought in Asian markets.

2 garlic cloves, minced
2 tablespoons fermented black beans
1 teaspoon chopped hot red chili peppers
1 teaspoon chopped fresh gingerroot, 1 teaspoon sugar

Using a mortar and pestle, pound all the ingredients together into a paste.

NOODLES WITH SICHUAN MEAT SAUCE

Here is a good example of a pungently spiced meat sauce from the southern part of China, using Sichuan paste.

1 $1/2$ ounces dried Chinese mushrooms
2 tablespoons peanut oil
$1/2$ pound flat Chinese noodles, 2 cups bean sprouts
1 tablespoon chopped scallions
4 hot red chili peppers for garnish
For the Sichuan meat sauce:
2 garlic cloves, 1 tablespoon peanut oil
$1/3$ cup minced shallots, 2 teaspoons Sichuan paste
$1/2$ pound lean ground pork

Soak the mushrooms in 1 cup hot water for about 30 minutes. Press dry and slice thinly. Reserve the soaking water. Heat the peanut oil in a wok and stir-fry the mushrooms 2 minutes; remove and keep warm. Peel and mince the garlic. Add the 1 tablespoon peanut oil to the oil already in the wok, heat, and stir-fry the garlic and shallots until translucent. Add the Sichuan paste and stir-fry 2 minutes over low heat. Add the pork and stir-fry 2 minutes more, then pour in about $1/2$ cup of the mushroom soaking water. Continue to stir-fry until the liquid has evaporated. Remove from the heat and keep warm. Cook the noodles with the bean sprouts in boiling water for about 3 minutes; drain, reserving the cooking liquid. Rinse the noodles in cold water, then return to the cooking water and boil 1 minute to heat through.

Transfer the noodles and bean sprouts to 4 bowls and top with the mushrooms and the pork mixture. Sprinkle with the scallions, and garnish each bowl with a red chili "flower."

Marinades *containing soy sauce, fish sauce (nam pla), or oyster sauce may not need additional salt as these ingredients are very salty. Wait until the very end, when all the ingredients are mixed together, then check the seasoning.*

FRIED RICE NOODLES WITH BEEF

1/2 pound flat rice noodles (see page 36)

1/2 pound flank steak or other lean tender beef

3 slices of fresh gingerroot, 1 small garlic clove

1 teaspoon fermented black beans

1 green bell pepper

4 tablespoons peanut oil

1 cup bean sprouts, 1 tablespoon dark soy sauce

freshly ground black pepper

For the marinade:

2 teaspoons light soy sauce, 2 tablespoons dark soy sauce

1 tablespoon cornstarch

2 tablespoons rice wine, 1 teaspoon sugar

Cook the noodles in boiling water until almost *al dente*, drain, rinse with cold water, and set aside. Slice the meat thinly. Peel and grate the ginger. Mince the garlic and fermented black beans.

Remove the seeds and core from the bell pepper, and cut in pieces about $^5/8$ x $^3/4$ inch. Mix all the ingredients for the marinade in a bowl, add the meat, and let marinate 20 minutes. Heat a wok and pour in 3 tablespoons of peanut oil. As soon as the oil is smoking, pull the noodles apart, put them in the wok, and stir-fry 1 minute. Add the bean sprouts and stir-fry 1 minute longer. Remove the noodles and bean sprouts from the wok and set aside. Pour the remaining oil into the wok and stir-fry the ginger and garlic. Add the black beans and bell pepper and stir-fry 1 minute. Drain the meat, add to the wok, and stir-fry until cooked. Put the noodle mixture back into the wok, with a little more oil if necessary, and toss until piping hot. Stir in the dark soy sauce, season with pepper, and serve.

Noodles with meat and shrimp

The cooks of Southeast Asia are particularly skilled in creating such combinations

RICE NOODLES WITH PORK AND TOFU

Noodles and meat are often used together in noodle dishes, but the addition of shrimp, which rounds off the flavor of this dish perfectly, is most characteristic of Thai cooking. Small quantities of dried shrimp are usually used as a seasoning; fresh shrimp are added in more or less equal proportion to the meat.

$^1/2$ pound tomatoes, 1 pound boneless pork
5 ounces firm tofu, $^1/4$ pound shallots
$^1/4$ cup oriental sesame oil
1 pound thin rice noodles (vermicelli), pulled apart
$^3/4$ pound raw shrimp, peeled and deveined
3 cups fresh bean sprouts, 3 cups coconut milk
$^1/4$ cup Chinese bean sauce
2 tablespoons fish sauce (nam pla), 1 teaspoon sugar, salt
2 tablespoons chopped fresh chives

Blanch the tomatoes, peel them, cut in eighths, and remove the seeds. Cut the tomatoes in strips about $^5/8$ inch wide. Cut the pork in strips. Cut the tofu in 1-inch cubes, and cut the shallots in thin strips. Heat 2 tablespoons sesame oil in a wok. Add the noodles and stir-fry until they are light brown and crisp. Add the tomatoes and stir-fry briefly. Remove the noodle and tomato mixture from the wok and put on one side. Clean out the wok with paper towels. Heat the remaining oil in the wok and stir-fry the pork. Add the shrimp, tofu, bean sprouts, and shallots and stir-fry 3 to 4 minutes. Pour on the coconut milk, and add the bean sauce, fish sauce, and sugar. Add the fried noodles, mix everything together thoroughly, and season with salt. Garnish with chopped chives and serve.

BAMI GORENG

This fried noodle dish is the counterpart to the popular rice dish known as Nasi Goreng, and is equally popular, not only in Indonesia. It is now part of the fast-food repertoire in many European countries. Prepared properly, with fresh ingredients, it remains a dish worth eating.

5 ounces each boneless chicken breast and pork
$^3/4$ pound thin Asian egg noodles
$^1/2$ cup peanut oil
1 $^1/4$ cups chopped scallions
$^1/2$ cup minced onion
3 garlic cloves, minced
2 cups shredded Chinese cabbage or Napa cabbage
2 hot chili peppers, seeded and minced
1 tablespoon minced fresh gingerroot
$^1/4$ pound small peeled shrimp
1 teaspoon salt
1 teaspoon sugar
2 tablespoons light soy sauce
For garnish:
strips of very thin omelet (optional)
fresh cilantro leaves

Cut the chicken and pork in thin strips. Continue as shown in the picture sequence. It is important that the oil should always be sizzling hot and that cooking times be as short as possible. When everything is ready, check the seasoning and if necessary add a little more salt and soy sauce.

Transfer to plates or bowls and sprinkle with the strips of omelet and cilantro.

Making Bami Goreng:
Add the noodles to a pan of boiling salted water and separate them with a fork. Simmer 1 minute, then drain in a colander, and rinse with cold water.

Heat the oil in a wok until it begins to smoke. Stir-fry the noodles until crisp; remove and put to one side.

Add the meat to the wok with the scallions, onion, and garlic, and stir-fry until lightly browned.

Add the Chinese cabbage and stir-fry briefly. Add the chilies, ginger, and shrimp and stir-fry 1 to 2 minutes more.

Season with salt, sugar, and soy sauce. Return the fried noodles to the wok and toss to mix with the other ingredients.

Salads – pasta with meat and vegetables

Good examples of how delicious pasta salads can be

Too many recipes for pasta salads use mayonnaise as a dressing, which coats and disguises all the ingredients, and makes one pasta salad indistinguishable from another. However, the recipes on this page are proof not only that pasta can taste excellent in cold dishes but that it can provide a feast for the eyes as well. Because of its neutral taste and soft texture, pasta generally takes a subordinate role in a dish. It is these qualities that make it ideal for salads, where tangy dressings and ingredients with more assertive flavors can be appreciated. For added interest, try serving ingredients such as meat warm, to contrast with cool pasta and vegetables.

WARM SWEETBREADS WITH ASPARAGUS AND NOODLES

Use half plain wheat noodles and half green wheat noodles (colored with green tea) for added interest in this unusual salad.

1/4 pound Japanese wheat noodles

For the salad:

1/2 pound veal sweetbreads, 1/4 pound asparagus tips

1 crisp lettuce heart, 1/2 cup snow peas or sugar-snap peas

8 cherry tomatoes

salt and freshly ground pepper, 1 tablespoon butter

11/2 cups thinly sliced mushrooms

For the dressing:

1/4 cup minced red onion, 2 tablespoons garlic vinegar

1 tablespoon truffle oil, 1 tablespoon neutral vegetable oil

salt and freshly ground pepper

For garnish:

1/2 teaspoon pink peppercorns, crushed

8 nasturtium leaves and 4 flowers (optional)

Blanch the sweetbreads for 2 minutes, then remove the membrane and sinews, and slice; put to one side. Cook the asparagus tips in boiling water until tender, about 4 minutes; drain and refresh in cold water so that they retain their color. Tear the lettuce heart into pieces. Cut the snow peas in diamond shapes, blanch briefly, and refresh. Cut the cherry tomatoes in half. Cook the noodles in boiling salted water for 1 to 2 minutes; drain. Season the sweetbreads with salt and pepper, and fry in the butter for 2 minutes on each side. Mix together the ingredients for the dressing. Put all the salad ingredients in a bowl with the warm sweetbreads and toss together gently. Serve onto plates and drizzle with the dressing. Sprinkle with the peppercorns and garnish with the nasturtium leaves and flowers.

SALAD OF JAPANESE WHEAT NOODLES WITH QUAILS

¹/4 pound thin Japanese wheat noodles

For the salad:

2 quails

salt and freshly ground pepper, paprika

2 tablespoons vegetable oil, 4 small handfuls of curly endive

¹/2 cup each finely diced red, yellow, and green bell pepper

For the salad dressing:

2 tablespoons sherry vinegar, 2 tablespoons walnut oil

salt and freshly ground pepper, a pinch of sugar

1 scallion, cut in thin rings

1 tablespoon chopped fresh chives

fresh herb leaves for garnish

Cut the quails in half and season with salt, pepper, and paprika. Heat the oil in a roasting pan and brown the quails all over. Transfer the pan to the oven preheated to 400°F and roast until cooked, about 10 minutes, basting occasionally with the oil in the pan. Mix together the vinegar, oil, salt, pepper, and sugar for the dressing. Add the scallions and chopped chives, and check the seasoning. Cook the noodles in boiling salted water for 1 to 2 minutes, drain, and rinse with cold water. Cut the warm quail pieces in half again and arrange on plates with the noodles, curly endive, and bell pepper. Pour the dressing over and garnish with herb leaves.

RABBIT, EGGPLANT, AND NOODLE SALAD

5 ounces boneless rabbit, 8 rabbit kidneys (optional)

salt and freshly ground pepper, 1¹/2 tablespoons butter

paprika, 4 baby eggplants, 2 tablespoons vegetable oil

¹/4 pound Japanese wheat noodles with red shiso

8 yellow tomatoes, quartered

2 small handfuls of lamb's lettuce (mâche)

For the dressing:

4 tablespoons vegetable oil, 1 garlic clove, minced

2 shallots, minced, 3 tablespoons light soy sauce

2 tablespoons balsamic vinegar

1 small hot red chili pepper, seeded and cut in rings

salt, 1 teaspoon palm or light brown sugar

Cut the rabbit meat in thin strips, and cut the kidneys in half. Season both with salt and pepper. Brown the rabbit and then the kidneys in the butter. Sprinkle with paprika and fry until cooked, 2 to 3 minutes longer. Slice the eggplants thinly lengthwise, sprinkle with salt, and let drain 10 minutes. Heat the oil and fry the eggplants until golden brown on both sides. Cook the noodles in boiling salted water for 3 to 4 minutes, drain, and rinse with cold water. To make the dressing, heat 1 tablespoon oil in a small pan and sauté the garlic and shallots until soft. Mix the remaining dressing ingredients. Arrange the salad components on plates. Pour the dressing over.

Unusual pasta salads can be made by combining thin Japanese noodles with quails and salad leaves, or rabbit, eggplant, and tomatoes.

Stuffed pasta

It is said that stuffed pasta was invented by monks as a means of presenting meat in the guise of vegetables during periods of fasting. However, since stuffed pasta is also found in Chinese cooking, we cannot take any of this too seriously. Whatever the origins, the variously shaped packages and parcels, encasing the most delicious stuffings, mark a high point in the art of pasta making. Inventive cooks are proving daily that virtually anything that can be minced or that is naturally soft and tender can be used as a stuffing for pasta. In northern Italy, which is widely assumed to be the home of ravioli, tortellini, and agnolotti, there is a long tradition of wrapping all kinds of leftovers in pasta dough.

Cutting, stuffing, and sealing pasta to achieve the desired shape is one of the most time-consuming of all kitchen tasks, but it is also extremely rewarding. Anyone wishing to serve a plate of delicious ravioli for dinner needs a rainy afternoon and a whole army of assistants. Fresh, handmade stuffed pasta is, of course, a unique pleasure, and the only enhancement it requires is a little butter and, perhaps, some freshly grated cheese. There is nothing wrong with tomato sauce, but good ravioli do not need it.

French chefs, who otherwise have little time for pasta, probably came to experiment with stuffed pasta through the influence of Asian cuisines. They were aided in their efforts by the availability of frozen wonton wrappers. These are stuffed and then often sealed at the top with a thin strand of chive or leek, to make little coin purses. Chinese dumplings are steamed or fried in oil, or deep fried, to be served as part of a selection of appetizers called *dim sum.*

A great deal of commercially made stuffed pasta is available today. Some of it is fresh and is of acceptable quality, but too much is uneatable – the dough is too thick, the stuffing is insipid, or the sauce tastes synthetic. Because making pasta at home is very laborious, many cooks resort to the commercial product. But it just cannot compare with fresh, handmade stuffed pasta, and will be a disappointment to those who have tasted the real thing.

so fast that the eye does not have time to register it. The reason why pasta cooks in Bologna do not entrust the entire operation to machines, which can, of course, do everything much more quickly, is that they are concerned not only about maintaining quality but also want to keep alive a splendid culinary tradition. The cost of enjoying a handmade product is accepted by diners, who recognize that they are paying for craft and skill. However, this is not limited to gourmets dining in luxury restaurants – in Bologna, handmade tortellini are regarded as good plain cooking.

Paper-thin is how the pasta dough is when rolled out by skilled hands, such as those of the pastaie, or pasta cooks, in Bologna. The dough acquires its silky, smooth texture as a result of long kneading and even rolling with a long wooden rolling pin. Once rolled out, it is fashioned with incredible speed into vast quantities of tortellini.

Tortellini

Dexterity is needed to shape these little stuffed rings

A maximum of stuffing in a minimum of dough is the secret of handmade tortellini from Bologna. Hundreds and hundreds of these tiny rings of stuffed pasta are freshly prepared every day, by *pastaie* in family businesses. This requires great skill, starting with rolling out the dough as thinly as possible, thin enough to read a newspaper through it. The small pasta squares are cut out quite simply with a knife, without the aid of a ruler, and yet they all turn out the same size, which also applies to the quantity of stuffing used for each one. All hands are then required to fold the squares into triangles and roll them into shape over the index finger. The whole process of pressing them together, turning over the ends, and pulling them off the finger again happens

TORTELLINI ALLA BOLOGNESE

As with all classic recipes, the search for the original will turn up quite a number of versions claiming to be the authentic one. Ingredients change over time, and the proportions are also determined to a certain extent by cost. However, the basis for the stuffing is usually veal or pork, or possibly chicken or turkey. Mortadella also plays a part in a genuine Bolognese stuffing, not only for the flavor it imparts but also because its fat serves to bind the stuffing together. The addition of veal or lamb brains makes the meat stuffing particularly rich and smooth, and prosciutto can add a distinctively different flavor.

1 recipe fresh pasta dough no. 3 (see page 40)
For the stuffing:
1/4 pound each boneless pork and veal
3 ounces skinless boneless chicken breast
4 tablespoons butter
2 ounces veal brains (optional)
1/4 pound mortadella
2 ounces prosciutto
3 egg yolks
1 cup freshly grated Parmesan cheese

salt and freshly ground pepper
freshly grated nutmeg
For serving:
1 recipe fresh tomato sauce (see page 69)
freshly grated Parmesan cheese

Cut the pork, veal, and chicken in cubes. Heat the butter in a pan over medium heat and lightly brown the cubes of meat. Continue frying until the meat is cooked, about 10 minutes longer. Remove the meat and set aside. Quickly brown the brains and mortadella in the pan. Now grind all the meats, together with the prosciutto, in a meat grinder. Add the egg yolks and Parmesan and blend to form a smooth paste. Season with salt, pepper, and nutmeg, cover, and refrigerate 2 to 3 hours. Roll out the pasta dough as thinly as possible and cut in 1 1/2-inch squares. Take balls of stuffing about as big as a hazelnut and put one in the middle of each square. Form the tortellini as shown in the picture sequence. (The edges of the squares do not need to be sealed with water or egg white, as is advisable with ravioli, since with tortellini it is the folded-over ends that prevent the filling from bursting out.) Spread out the stuffed pasta on a well-floured surface and let dry briefly before cooking it in boiling salted water. Tortellini can be served *in brodo*, that is in a clear chicken or beef broth. They can also be served with nothing more complicated than melted butter and minced fresh herbs or, as in the picture below, with fresh tomato sauce and freshly grated Parmesan.

Shaping tortellini:

Fold the pasta square over into a triangle, enclosing the ball of stuffing, and press the edges together to seal. Do not press too hard or the tortellino will lose its neat shape.

Wrap the triangle, apex down, around the index finger and press the ends together tightly so that they stick firmly to each other.

With the fingers of the other hand, fold down the points forming the apex of the triangle. In the same movement, slide the tortellino off the finger.

Stuffed with ricotta

Di magro (lean) is the Italian name for the classic combination of ricotta and spinach, or another leafy vegetable or herb

RAVIOLI WITH RICOTTA AND SPINACH

Pasta stuffed with this mix of ingredients is called *agnolotti* in Piedmont and *ravioli* in Bologna and the surrounding area. The ricotta mixture is used to stuff both the large ravioli and the tiny raviolini. It is also found in tortellini and tortelli, proving that the same stuffing can be used in many different pasta shapes.

1 recipe fresh pasta dough no. 3 (see page 40)
1 egg white, lightly whisked with a fork
For the stuffing:
3/4 pound young spinach leaves, 1 cup ricotta cheese
1/2 teaspoon salt, freshly ground pepper
freshly grated nutmeg
1 cup freshly grated Parmesan cheese, 2 egg yolks
To finish:
6 tablespoons (3/4 stick) butter, 6 fresh sage leaves
freshly grated Parmesan cheese for serving

Put the spinach in a large pan of lightly salted boiling water and cook until starting to wilt, 2 minutes at most. Drain and plunge into ice-cold water, then drain thoroughly and press out as much of the remaining water as possible. Chop the spinach coarsely and mix with the ricotta. Season with salt, pepper, and nutmeg, and stir in the grated Parmesan and egg yolks.

If the ravioli are to be stuffed without the aid of special molds (see pictures), proceed as follows: roll out the dough as thinly as possible and cut into 2 sheets, each about 20 x 12 inches. Using the back of a knife and a ruler, score a grid of 2-inch squares on one of the sheets. Put an equal amount of stuffing on each of the squares. If this process takes a long time, the dough will start to dry out, so you will need to brush a little egg white around each bit of stuffing, so that the second sheet of dough will stick. Lay the second sheet loosely over the first one and press down lightly around the stuffing, so that the edges are well sealed. Using a ruler and a fluted pastry wheel, cut out the squares and lay them on a lightly floured cloth. Cook the stuffed pasta in boiling salted water for 4 to 5 minutes, remove with a slotted spoon, and arrange on plates. Melt the butter until clear, briefly toss the shredded sage leaves in it, and pour over the pasta. Sprinkle with Parmesan and serve.

Making ravioli in a mold:

Put all the ingredients for the stuffing into a bowl and mix together to a smooth paste.

Lay one thin sheet of dough on the ravioli mold and put a little stuffing in each indentation. If necessary, moisten the dough around the stuffing with a little egg white.

Lay a second sheet of dough over the top. Roll lightly with a rolling pin to cut the pasta squares and seal the edges. Lift the ravioli from the mold.

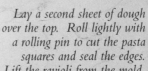

Ricotta cheese has a moist, slightly grainy texture. In Italy, it is made from the whey drained off while making other cheeses, and is set either in the traditional baskets or, more usually nowadays, in plastic or stainless steel molds.

TORTELLONI WITH RICOTTA AND HERBS

1 recipe fresh pasta dough no. 3 (see page 40)

For the stuffing:

1 cup ricotta cheese, 1 egg, 1/2 teaspoon salt

freshly ground pepper

1 tablespoon chopped fresh parsley

1 teaspoon each chopped fresh lovage or celery leaves, thyme, and sage

a few rosemary needles

3/4 cup freshly grated Parmesan cheese

For the sauce:

1 pound ripe tomatoes, 1 garlic clove, 1 hot red chili pepper

3 tablespoons extra-virgin olive oil, 1/4 cup minced onion

1/2 teaspoon salt, 1/2 teaspoon sugar

For garnish:

freshly pared Parmesan cheese

Thoroughly mix together all the ingredients for the stuffing. To make the sauce, first blanch the tomatoes, peel them, remove the seeds, and dice. Mince the garlic. Remove seeds from the chili pepper and mince. Heat the olive oil in a saucepan and sauté the onion and garlic until translucent. Add the diced tomatoes and the chili, and season with salt and sugar. Simmer gently until the tomatoes have

broken down and the sauce is thick, 10 to 15 minutes. Cut out and stuff the tortelloni as shown in the picture sequence. Cook in boiling salted water for 8 to 10 minutes, then remove with a slotted spoon, and transfer to plates. Pour the sauce over and sprinkle with Parmesan shavings.

Preparing the tortelloni:

Roll out the dough thinly and use a fluted cutter to cut out disks 2 1/2 to 2 3/4 inches in diameter.

Put 1 teaspoon of stuffing on each disk of dough, positioning the stuffing exactly in the center.

Fold each disk over into a half-moon shape and press the edges together to seal (moisten the edges with a little water, if necessary).

RAVIOLI WITH BEET STUFFING

Beets are a popular vegetable in northern Italy, and here they are used in a stuffing for ravioli, which are called *casonsei*. In Lombardy, these ravioli are also stuffed with ricotta and pumpkin.

1 recipe fresh pasta dough no. 3 (see page 40)
1 egg white, lightly whisked with a fork
For the beet stuffing:
1 pound fresh beets 1 teaspoon fennel seeds
1 teaspoon salt, 6 tablespoons (³/4 stick) butter
¹/4 cup minced shallots, ³/4 cup white bread crumbs
¹/2 teaspoon salt, freshly ground pepper
¹/8 teaspoon ground ginger, 1 egg yolk
To finish:
6 tablespoons (³/4 stick) butter, ¹/4 cup ground poppy seeds
¹/2 cup freshly grated Parmesan cheese

Carefully peel the beets, cut in quarters, and put in a pan of water with the fennel seeds and salt. Cook until tender, then drain. Put through a meat grinder, or purée in a food processor. Let cool. Heat the butter and sauté the shallots until translucent. Add the bread crumbs and fry until golden, stirring constantly. Combine this mixture with the beet purée and season with salt, pepper, and ginger. Finally, mix in the egg yolk. Roll out the pasta dough thinly and cut out disks about 2 ¹/4 inches in diameter. Put a little stuffing in the middle of each disk and brush the edge with egg white or water. Fold each disk over into a half-moon shape and press the edges firmly together to seal. Cook the ravioli in boiling salted water until they rise to the surface. In the meantime, heat the butter in a small pan and stir in the ground poppy seeds. As soon as the ravioli are done, remove them with a slotted spoon to pre-warmed plates. Pour the poppy-seed butter over them and sprinkle with grated Parmesan.

RAVIOLI STUFFED WITH LAMB

1 recipe fresh pasta dough no. 3 (see page 40)
1 egg white, lightly whisked with a fork
For the stuffing:
³/4 pound lean boneless lamb, trimmed
3 tablespoons olive oil, ¹/2 garlic clove, minced
1 onion, minced, ¹/2 cup lamb stock
¹/2 teaspoon salt, freshly ground black pepper
a pinch of freshly grated nutmeg
4 to 6 fresh sage leaves, chopped
¹/2 teaspoon each chopped fresh rosemary and thyme
To finish:
6 tablespoons (³/4 stick) butter
³/4 cup freshly grated Parmesan cheese
black olives for garnish

Grind the lamb using a meat grinder or food processor. Heat the oil in a pan and sauté the garlic and onion until soft. Add the lamb and brown over high heat, stirring to break it up. Pour in the stock and season with salt, pepper, and nutmeg. Simmer over medium heat about 20 minutes. If necessary, add a little more stock. Stir in the herbs, and let the stuffing cool. Roll out the pasta dough into two thin sheets. Mark 1 ¹/2-inch squares on one sheet. Place a little stuffing in the center of each square, and brush

the pasta around the stuffing with egg white. Lay the second sheet loosely over the first one and press down lightly around the stuffing, so that the edges are well sealed. Using a ruler and a fluted pastry wheel, cut out the squares and lay them on a lightly floured cloth. Let dry 1 to 2 hours. Cook in boiling salted water until *al dente* and remove with a slotted spoon to drain. Melt the butter in a large pan and toss the ravioli in it. Sprinkle with Parmesan and garnish with olives.

RICOTTA TORTELLINI WITH SAVOY CABBAGE

The texture and flavor of crunchy cabbage offer a pleasant contrast to the tortellini.

1 recipe fresh pasta dough no. 3 (see page 40)
For the ricotta stuffing:
$1/3$ cup minced shallots, 2 tablespoons butter
1 cup ricotta cheese, 4 egg yolks
$1/2$ cup fine white bread crumbs
1 tablespoon chopped fresh basil
salt and freshly ground pepper
freshly grated nutmeg
For the vegetables:
$1/2$ carrot, 1 small celery stalk, $1^1/2$-inch piece of leek
$1^1/2$ cups chopped Savoy cabbage
$1/2$ cup (1 stick) cold butter

Sauté the shallots in the hot butter until translucent; let cool. Mix the ricotta, egg yolks, and bread crumbs in a bowl. Add the sautéed shallots and basil, and season with salt, pepper, and nutmeg. Roll out the pasta dough as thinly as possible and cut in 1 $1/2$-inch squares. Place a little stuffing on each square and shape into tortellini, as described on page 179. If possible, they should be left to dry 1 to 2 hours before they are cooked. Cut the carrot, celery, and leek in fine strips (julienne). Blanch the vegetables, including the cabbage, in succession in boiling water; drain and keep warm. Cook the tortellini in boiling salted water until they rise to the surface; remove with a slotted spoon and keep warm. Thicken $1/2$ cup of the cooking liquid with the cold butter and toss the vegetables and tortellini in it. Check the seasoning, and transfer to pre-warmed plates.

CIALZONS

In this version of an Italian dish, traditional in Friuli-Venezia Giulia and Trentino-Alto Adige, pasta half-moons are stuffed with a mixture of rye bread crumbs, spices, and chard. The recipe will make 36 to 40 stuffed pasta shapes.

For the pasta dough:

$1^2/3$ cups all-purpose flour

2 eggs, salt

For the chard stuffing:

$1/2$ pound Swiss chard leaves

$1/3$ cup dry rye bread crumbs

2 tablespoons milk, 1 egg

a pinch each of ground cinnamon and cloves

1 tablespoon each chopped fresh thyme and parsley

1 tablespoon ground juniper berries

salt and freshly ground pepper

In addition:

1 egg white, lightly whisked with a fork

$1/2$ cup (1 stick) butter, melted

freshly pared Parmesan

1 tablespoon minced fresh parsley

Sift the flour onto a work surface, form a well in the middle, and add the eggs and a little salt. Mix the ingredients together, starting from the middle and working out, and knead to a smooth, pliable dough. Wrap in plastic wrap and put aside to rest. To make the stuffing, blanch the chard leaves until they begin to wilt, then drain and refresh in cold water. Press out excess water. Mince the chard and put in a bowl. Soak the bread crumbs in the milk, squeeze out excess milk, and add to the chard with all the other stuffing ingredients. Mix thoroughly. Roll out the pasta dough until paper thin, and cut out disks about 2 $^3/4$ inches in diameter, preferably using a fluted cutter. Place 1 teaspoon of the filling in the center of each disk, brush the edges with egg white, and fold over to form half-moons, pressing the edges firmly together to seal. Cook the pasta in boiling salted water until *al dente*, 5 to 7 minutes. Drain and arrange immediately on pre-warmed plates. Drizzle with the melted butter and sprinkle with Parmesan shavings and parsley.

PANSOTI WITH WALNUT SAUCE

Pansoti (also spelled pansotti), which means "chubby," is a dish from Liguria. The pasta triangles are stuffed with herbs and cheese, and served with a walnut sauce. This recipe will make about 80 pansoti.

$^3/_4$ recipe fresh pasta dough no. 3 (see page 40)
For the herb stuffing:
3 cups mixed fresh herb leaves
3 cups fresh basil leaves
1 $^1/_3$ cups fresh borage leaves (or use another herb)
1 small egg, 1 garlic clove, minced
$^1/_4$ cup ricotta cheese
$^1/_4$ cup freshly grated Parmesan cheese
salt and freshly ground pepper
For the walnut sauce:
$^1/_2$ cup white bread crumbs
1 tablespoon water, 1 cup walnut pieces
3 tablespoons olive oil, $^1/_4$ cup cream, salt
For serving:
1 cup freshly grated Parmesan cheese

To make the stuffing, briefly blanch all the herb leaves, refresh in cold water, and dry thoroughly in paper towels. Mince the herbs, and purée with the other ingredients in a food processor. Set aside. Roll out the pasta dough thinly and cut out 2-inch squares. Put 1 teaspoon of the stuffing on each square, brush the edges with water, and fold over into triangles, pressing the edges together firmly to seal. To make the sauce, moisten the bread crumbs with the water. Continue as shown in the picture sequence. Cook the pansoti in boiling salted water about 10 minutes, then drain, serve with the suce and Parmesan.

Making the walnut sauce:

Using a mortar and pestle, pound the walnuts to a paste, or grind them in a blender or food processor with the crumbs.

Mix in the oil and cream alternately, then season with salt. Stir until the sauce has a smooth consistency.

Delicious meat stuffings

The shape of the pasta does not matter too much here: what it contains is the important thing

TORTELLI WITH OXTAIL STUFFING

Making *pasta ripiena*, or stuffed pasta, takes a lot of time. For this recipe, you'll have to allow even more time, to cook the meat for the stuffing. But your labors will be rewarded with a truly wonderful dish, ideal either as a first course or an entrée. The following recipe is sufficient for 8 servings.

1 recipe fresh pasta dough no. 3 (page 40)
egg white lightly whisked with a fork
For the stuffing:
3 1/2 pounds oxtail
1 teaspoon salt, freshly ground pepper
1/4 cup vegetable oil
1 garlic clove, unpeeled but bruised
1 cup diced carrot
1 1/4 cups thinly sliced celery
1 1/2 cups thinly sliced leeks
1/4 cup diced parsley root (optional)
5 juniper berries, 1 bay leaf
5 fresh sage leaves, 2 tablespoons tomato paste
2 cups red wine (Merlot), 1 tablespoon flour
1 tablespoon chopped fresh herbs: parsley, lovage or celery leaves

Preparing the oxtail stuffing:

Locate the joints in the oxtail by pressing with your thumbs, then cut across in sections (or ask your butcher to do this).

Season the oxtail. Heat the oil in a roasting pan and brown the oxtail. Add the garlic and all the prepared vegetables.

Cook about 10 minutes, stirring well. Add the juniper berries, bay leaf, sage, and tomato paste, and pour in the red wine.

Take out the pieces of oxtail, remove as much of the meat from the bones as possible, and mince it.

Strain the sauce, pressing on the vegetables and seasonings with a ladle so that some of the vegetables are forced through into the sauce.

Distribute the meat stuffing, evenly spaced, on one sheet of dough. Brush a little egg white on the dough around each portion of stuffing.

Lay the second sheet of dough over the top. Cut out tortelli using a fluted 2 1/4-inch round cutter.

1 egg yolk

To finish:

1 pound fresh chanterelles, 3 tablespoons butter

salt, 2 tablespoons chopped fresh parsley

Prepare the oxtail as shown in the first three steps of the picture sequence. Cover the roasting pan and braise in the oven preheated to 350°F for about 2 hours; stir occasionally. After 1 hour, dust the meat with the flour. Continue as shown in the next two steps of the picture sequence. Mix the minced meat with the chopped herbs and egg yolk; add a few spoonfuls of the sauce to moisten the stuffing. Allow the stuffing to cool. Roll out the dough in two thin sheets. Stuff and cut the tortelli as shown in the last two steps of the picture sequence. Let the pasta dry a little. In the meantime, clean the chanterelles very carefully; if they are large, cut them in smaller pieces. Boil the sauce to reduce it a little. Cook the tortelli in boiling salted water until they rise to the surface; lift out with a slotted spoon and arrange in pre-warmed dishes. Heat the butter in a large pan, add the chanterelles, and season with salt and chopped parsley. Sauté for a few minutes over high heat. Mix with the sauce and pour over the tortelli.

AGNOLOTTI
WITH RABBIT STUFFING

"*Agnolotti*" is the term for ravioli in Piedmont, and they can be either round or square. There is a particular type of square agnolotti described as "*dal plin*," which means "with a pleat." These may contain various stuffings, although they are usually made with meat.

1 recipe fresh pasta dough no. 3 (see page 40)
For the stuffing:
3/4 pound boneless rabbit meat from the leg
1/2 pound lean boneless pork
3 to 4 tablespoons vegetable oil, 1 garlic clove, minced
2 tablespoons chopped shallots, 3/4 cup diced carrot
2/3 cup diced celery
1 teaspoon chopped fresh thyme
some chopped fresh rosemary
1 teaspoon salt, freshly ground pepper
about 2 cups veal stock, 1 pound spinach
3/4 cup freshly grated Parmesan cheese, 2 eggs
To finish:
a handful of fresh sage leaves, 4 tablespoons butter

Carefully trim the rabbit and pork and cut in even-sized pieces. Heat the oil in a suitably sized pan and quickly brown the meat. Add the garlic, shallots, carrot, celery, and herbs, and season lightly with salt and pepper. Fry over a fairly high heat for about 15 minutes, stirring so that the ingredients brown evenly. Pour on 1 cup of the veal stock and simmer until the meat is cooked, about 1 hour longer. Drain the meat in a strainer set in a bowl; reserve the liquid. Let the meat cool, then put through a meat grinder or chop in a food processor. Wash the spinach thoroughly, remove the stems, and blanch briefly in boiling salted water. Drain, press dry, and mince. Add to the meat together with the grated Parmesan and eggs, and stir to form a thick paste. In the meantime, mix the cooking liquid from the meat with the rest of the veal stock and boil to reduce until only 2 to 3 tablespoons remain. Mix this reduced liquid into the stuffing, and check the seasoning. Roll out the pasta dough as thinly as possible and make the agnolotti as shown in the picture sequence. A "pleat" can be pinched or pressed into each square. Let dry at least 2 to 3 hours, then cook in boiling salted water until they rise to the surface, about 3 minutes. Remove with a slotted spoon and arrange on pre-warmed plates.

A delicious variation on this dish is to serve the agnolotti with jellied meat juices. And during the truffle season in Piedmont, agnolotti are topped with paper-thin slivers of white truffle. They also taste superb served with nothing more than butter.

Preparing agnolotti:

Mark out rectangles, 1 1/2 x 2 1/4 inches, on the thinly rolled sheet of dough. Put a small ball of stuffing on half of each rectangle.

Cut out the rectangles using a fluted pastry wheel. Brush the edges of each rectangle with water to moisten.

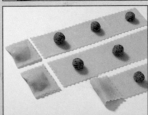

Fold the dough over to enclose the stuffing and press the edges together firmly to seal.

Agnolotti are splendid served with sage butter. Simply toss the sage leaves in hot melted butter and pour over the pasta.

RAVIOLINI WITH MEAT STUFFING

The lightly spiced stuffing here is made from beef and pork, plus generous quantities of spinach and mushrooms. It can be used to stuff many other shapes of pasta – from cannelloni to tortellini – as well as the small ravioli called raviolini. It is worth making a little more of the stuffing than required (the following recipe is sufficient for 8 servings), since the remainder can be frozen.

1 recipe fresh pasta dough no. 3 (see page 40)
For the meat stuffing:
1 garlic clove, ^{1}/4 cup vegetable oil
^{1}/3 cup minced onion, ^{3}/4 cup diced celery
^{1}/3 cup diced carrot
^{1}/2 pound each boneless pork and beef, freshly ground
1 teaspoon salt, ^{1}/4 teaspoon freshly ground pepper
2 teaspoons paprika, 2 teaspoons tomato paste
^{1}/2 pound spinach, washed
2 cups beef stock (see page 82)
2 cups diced mushrooms
2 tablespoons chopped fresh parsley, 2 egg yolks
For serving:
tomato sauce (see page 70)
freshly pared Parmesan cheese, 4 tablespoons butter, melted

The meat stuffing should be worked in a food processor until coarse-fine but not puréed. Use the pulse button so the stuffing remains quite coarse in texture.

Peel and mince the garlic. Heat the oil and sauté the onion and garlic until translucent, then add the celery and carrot and sauté a few minutes more. Add the ground meats to the vegetable mixture and brown over high heat, stirring to break up any lumps. Season with the salt, pepper, and paprika, and stir in the tomato paste. Coarsely chop the spinach and add to the meat mixture. Remove from the heat immediately and let cool. Over a low heat, boil the stock until reduced to 4 to 5 tablespoons; stir into the stuffing. Chop the stuffing, in batches, in a food processor to make it a little smoother but not enough to turn it into a paste. Add the mushrooms, chopped parsley, and egg yolks and mix well. Roll out the pasta dough in two sheets and lay one over a well-floured raviolini mold; trim off excess dough. Spoon the stuffing into a pastry bag fitted with a plain tip and pipe a small quantity in each hollow (or you can spoon in the stuffing). Lay the second sheet of dough on top and roll lightly with a rolling pan to seal and cut out the raviolini. Tap the raviolini from the mold. Cook in boiling salted water until they rise to the surface; remove with a slotted spoon and arrange on pre-warmed plates. Spoon a little tomato sauce over each serving, sprinkle with Parmesan shavings, and drizzle on the melted butter.

TURKISH PASTA TRIANGLES WITH BEEF STUFFING

"*Manti*" is the Turkish name for these small triangles of stuffed pasta.

1 recipe fresh cornmeal pasta dough (see page 43)
For the beef stuffing:
1 garlic clove, 5 tablespoons olive oil
^{1}/4 cup minced onion, ^{2}/3 cup minced scallions
^{1}/2 cup diced carrot, ^{1}/3 cup diced parsley root (optional)
^{3}/4 pound beef chuck or round, freshly ground
1 small hot chili pepper, 1 tablespoon chopped fresh parsley
1 tablespoon chopped fresh mint
^{1}/2 tablespoon salt, freshly ground pepper
For the sauce:
2 garlic cloves, 1 cup plain yogurt, ^{1}/2 teaspoon salt
To finish:
6 tablespoons butter, 1 tablespoon paprika

Let the cornmeal pasta dough rest at least 1 hour. Peel and mince the garlic. Heat half of the oil in a suitably sized pan and sauté the onion and garlic until translucent. Add the scallions, carrot, and parsley root (if using) and cook until the vegetables are soft. Heat the remaining oil in a second pan and brown the meat over high heat, stirring to break up lumps. Add the sautéed vegetables. Cut the chili in half lengthwise, remove the core and seeds, and mince. Add to the meat mixture with the parsley and mint, and season with salt and pepper. Mix everything together thoroughly. Roll out the pasta dough as thinly as possible. Cut out 1 ^{1}/4-inch squares. (To prevent the dough from drying out, keep the squares covered with a slightly damp cloth.) Place a small ball of stuffing on each square, fold the squares over into triangles, and press the edges together firmly to seal. If necessary, dampen the edges slightly with water so that they stick together. To make the sauce, peel and mince the garlic cloves; mix with the yogurt, and season to taste with salt. Cook the pasta parcels in boiling salted water until they rise to the surface. Remove with a slotted spoon and arrange on 4 pre-warmed plates. Spoon the yogurt sauce over the pasta. Melt the butter with the paprika until it foams, and pour over the top.

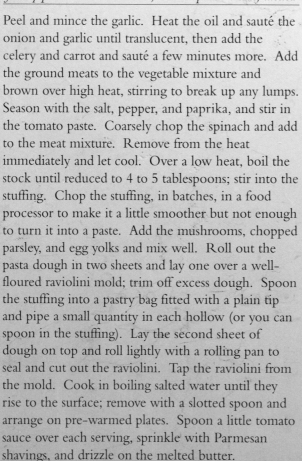

MAULTASCHEN

This is a southern German version of ravioli, which is usually stuffed with a mixture of meat and spinach. The recipe will make about 24 squares.

For the dough:
$2^{1}/3$ cups all-purpose flour, 3 eggs, 1 teaspoon salt
1 tablespoon oil
1 egg white, lightly whisked with a fork
For the stuffing:
3 cups stale bread cubes, $^{1}/2$ cup lukewarm milk
3 ounces Canadian bacon
3 tablespoons butter, $^{1}/3$ cup chopped onion
$^{1}/2$ cup chopped scallions
$^{1}/2$ pound bratwurst, removed from casing
$^{1}/2$ pound spinach, 2 eggs
$^{1}/2$ teaspoon salt, freshly ground white pepper
1 tablespoon dried marjoram
1 tablespoon minced fresh parsley
To finish:
1 quart meat stock
4 tablespoons butter, $^{2}/3$ cup chopped onion
1 tablespoon chopped fresh chives

Sift the flour onto a work surface and make a well in the middle. Break the eggs into the hollow, and add the salt and oil. Mix the ingredients together with a fork and knead into a pliable dough. Shape into a ball, cover with a cloth, and let rest 15 minutes. Soak the bread cubes in the lukewarm milk, and squeeze dry. Cut the bacon in small squares. Heat the butter and sauté the onion and scallions until translucent; add the sausage and cook, stirring. Continue as shown in the picture sequence left. Roll out the pasta dough thinly on a floured work surface. Using a ruler and pastry wheel, cut out rectangles about 2 $^{1}/2$ x 5 inches. Continue as shown in the picture sequence below. Heat the butter and lightly brown the onion. Arrange the cooked pasta squares on plates and pour a little of the stock over them. Garnish with the browned onion and chives.

For the stuffing, blanch the spinach, refresh in cold water, squeeze dry, and mince. Combine the spinach, soaked bread, sautéed onions, Canadian bacon, and the remaining stuffing ingredients and mix well together.

Put a small spoonful of stuffing on one half of each pasta rectangle. Brush the edges with egg white, then fold the rectangles over into squares and press to seal.

Bring the stock to a boil in a large pan, add the stuffed pasta, and cook until they rise to the surface.

SCHLUTZKRAPFEN

This specialty from the southern Tyrol, with its delicate spinach stuffing, is very similar to ravioli. The dough contains rye flour, which gives these pasta parcels from Italy's northernmost province a robust flavor. The recipe will make about 45.

For the dough:
1 cup + 3 tablespoons all-purpose flour
1 cup rye flour
$^1/2$ teaspoon salt
1 egg, 1 to 2 tablespoons olive oil
about 5 tablespoons water
1 egg white, lightly whisked with a fork
For the spinach stuffing:
$^3/4$ pound spinach
1 tablespoon chopped fresh parsley
$^1/2$ tablespoon chopped fresh lovage or celery leaves
1 tablespoon butter
2 tablespoons minced onion
4 teaspoons flour, $^1/2$ cup hot milk
salt and freshly ground pepper
freshly grated nutmeg
3 tablespoons freshly grated Parmesan cheese
For serving:
$^1/2$ cup freshly grated Parmesan cheese
4 tablespoons butter, melted

Mix together the two kinds of flour and pour onto a work surface. Form a well in the middle and add the salt, egg, oil, and 4 tablespoons of the water. Mix the ingredients together with a fork, working from the middle outward, and knead into a pliable dough. Add more water if necessary. Wrap in plastic wrap and let rest. Blanch the spinach in boiling salted water until it wilts. Refresh in cold water, squeeze dry, and mince. Mix with the herbs. Heat the butter in a saucepan and sauté the onion until translucent. Sprinkle on the flour, stir well, and cook 1 minute. Stir in the milk, bring to a boil, and simmer gently until thickened. Stir in the spinach mixture, salt, pepper, nutmeg, and, finally, the Parmesan. Put to one side. Roll out the pasta dough very thinly and cut out disks 3 inches in diameter. Place $^1/2$ tablespoon of stuffing in the middle of each disk, brush the edge with egg white, and fold over into a half-moon shape. Press the edges together with a fork to seal. (The rolling out and stuffing must be done as fast as possible, because the rye flour in the dough makes it dry out quickly.) Cook the pasta in boiling salted water about 10 minutes; remove with a slotted spoon and arrange on plates. Sprinkle with the cheese and pour the melted butter over the top.

Polish pierogi

Pierogi, Polish stuffed pasta, have their origins in ancient Slav cuisine

The name of these stuffed pasta shapes has its roots in "*pir*," meaning banquet or feast, but where they may once have been a delicacy, pierogi have become an everyday dish. They can be made with a wide range of substantial stuffings, depending on individual taste and the season of the year. Russian *pirozhki* are similar, but are based on a yeast dough. The recipes here will make about 30 pierogi.

PASTA DOUGH FOR PIEROGI

2$^{1}/_{3}$ cups all-purpose flour, 1 egg
$^{1}/_{2}$ teaspoon salt, $^{1}/_{2}$ cup water
In addition:
1 egg white, lightly whisked with a fork

Make the pasta dough as directed on page 41. While it is resting, prepare the stuffing (see recipes on this and the facing page). Roll out the dough thinly and cut out disks 2 $^{3}/_{4}$ inches in diameter. Brush the edges with egg white. Put about $^{1}/_{2}$ tablespoon of stuffing in the middle of each disk, fold over into a half-moon shape, and press the edges together firmly to seal. Cook in batches in boiling salted water. When the pierogi have risen to the surface, cook 5 minutes longer, then remove with a slotted spoon.

MUSHROOM PIEROGI WITH FOIE GRAS

For the mushroom stuffing:
1 onion, $^{1}/_{2}$ tablespoon oil, 1 $^{1}/_{2}$ cups diced mushrooms
salt and freshly ground pepper
freshly grated nutmeg, 1 egg
To finish:
$^{1}/_{2}$ pound foie gras, thinly sliced, 1 $^{1}/_{2}$ tablespoons butter
salt and freshly ground pepper
2 tablespoons minced shallots
2 tablespoons veal stock, fresh flat-leaf parsley

Slice the onion. Heat the oil and sauté the onion until translucent. Add the mushrooms and cook 10 minutes longer. Season with salt, pepper, and nutmeg. Remove from the heat, stir in the egg and let cool. Stuff the pierogi and cook as directed. In the meantime, briefly brown the foie gras in the hot butter. Season with salt and pepper and remove from the pan. Sauté the shallots in the butter until translucent. Add the stock and stir to form a sauce. Arrange the pierogi on plates with the slices of foie gras, pour the sauce over, and garnish with parsley.

PIEROGI WITH SAUERKRAUT AND BACON

For the sauerkraut stuffing:
1¹/4 cups sauerkraut
1 onion
2 tablespoons oil
salt and freshly ground pepper
To finish:
1 tablespoon butter
¹/2 cup minced bacon
¹/4 cup minced onion
1 tablespoon chopped fresh parsley

Cook the sauerkraut in a little water for 15 to 20 minutes; let cool slightly, then squeeze dry and mince. Transfer to a bowl. Cut the onion in thin slices and brown lightly in the oil. Mix with the sauerkraut, season to taste and let cool. Stuff the pierogi and cook them as directed. Heat the butter until it foams and sauté the bacon briefly. Add the onion and cook until it has browned slightly. Stir in the parsley. Arrange the pierogi on plates and pour the bacon and onion mixture over.

MEAT PIEROGI WITH TOMATOES

For the meat stuffing:
1 heaping cup stale bread cubes, 1 tablespoon water
1 onion, 1 tablespoon oil
³/4 cup mixed ground meats: beef, pork, veal
1 tablespoon stock
salt and freshly ground pepper
To finish:
2 tablespoons butter
2 shallots, minced
3 tomatoes, peeled, seeded, and chopped
1 tablespoon shredded fresh basil for garnish

Moisten the bread cubes with the water. Mince the onion. Heat the oil and sauté the onion until translucent. Add the ground meats and fry, stirring to break up lumps. Add the moistened bread and stock and stir until the liquid has evaporated. Season with salt and pepper and let cool. Stuff the pierogi and cook as directed. Heat the butter and sauté the shallots until translucent. Add the tomatoes and cook briefly. Arrange the pierogi on plates, pour the tomato mixture over, and garnish with basil.

Sauerkraut and meat are typical stuffings for pierogi. There are also sweet stuffings in Polish cooking, for example blueberries mixed with sugar and white bread crumbs.

Sophisticated stuffings

Definitely not everyday recipes: unusual stuffings for pasta

TORTELLINI WITH SEAFOOD AND TWO SWEET PEPPER SAUCES

Green pasta stuffed with fish and shrimp, and served with red and yellow pepper sauces, is a combination as original as it is delicious. If you prefer a meat stuffing, use that for the raviolini on page 188.

1 recipe fresh green pasta dough (see page 46)
For the stuffing:
3/4 pound sole or turbot fillet, 1/2 cup cream
1/2 pound shrimp, minced
salt and freshly ground pepper
1 tablespoon chopped fresh dill
For the sweet pepper sauces:
1 pound each yellow and red bell peppers
3 tablespoons butter, 2 shallots, diced
1 garlic clove, chopped
salt and freshly ground pepper
2 sprigs of fresh thyme, 2 bay leaves
1/3 cup Sauternes, 1 1/4 cups veal stock
For serving:
3/4 cup freshly grated pecorino cheese

Cut the fish in cubes and purée in a blender or food processor, then press through a strainer. Mix to a smooth paste with the cream. Stir in the minced shrimp, season, and add the dill. Cover and refrigerate. Make the red and yellow pepper sauces separately, using half of the ingredients for each one. Remove the core and seeds from the peppers and dice them. Heat the butter and sauté the shallots and garlic until soft. Add the diced peppers, season with salt and pepper, and add the thyme and bay leaf. Pour on the wine and stock and simmer until the peppers are soft and the liquid has almost all evaporated. Pound with a potato masher, and press through a strainer (or a vegetable mill). Roll out the pasta dough thinly and cut out 1 1/2-inch squares with a pastry wheel. Place a ball of filling the size of a hazelnut in the middle of each square, and shape the tortellini as shown on page 179. Cook the tortellini in boiling salted water until they rise to the surface. In the meantime, heat the pepper sauces. Remove the tortellini with a slotted spoon and arrange on plates. Spoon over the red and yellow pepper sauces and sprinkle with pecorino.

PUMPKIN RAVIOLI

This stuffing derives its interesting flavor from the contrast between the pumpkin, candied fruits, and amaretti cookies on the one hand, and the cheese and seasonings on the other. This combination of tastes is extremely popular in Italy, and is well worth trying. A glass of *vin santo* from Tuscany is the perfect accompaniment.

1 recipe fresh pasta dough no. 3 (see page 40)
1 egg white, lightly whisked with a fork
For the stuffing:
1 small pumpkin, weighing about 1 ^{1}/2 pounds
3 amaretti cookies
^{2}/3 cup minced candied fruit
^{2}/3 cup freshly grated Parmesan cheese
salt and freshly ground pepper
freshly grated nutmeg
To finish:
^{1}/2 cup (1 stick) butter
a handful of fresh sage leaves
1 cup freshly grated Parmesan cheese

Bake the pumpkin, whole, in the oven preheated to 400°F for about 50 minutes or until the flesh is tender; let cool. Break the amaretti in small pieces – the best way is to put them in a plastic bag and crush them with a rolling pin. Cut the pumpkin in half, remove the seeds, and scoop out and mince the flesh. Put into a bowl with the candied fruit, the amaretti, and the Parmesan and mix well. Season with salt, pepper, and nutmeg. Roll out the pasta dough thinly and cut out disks about 2 inches in diameter, preferably using a fluted cutter. Put a small ball of stuffing on half of the disks, brush the edges with egg white, and cover with the remaining disks. Press the edges together firmly to seal. Cook the ravioli in boiling salted water until they rise to the surface. In the meantime, heat the butter until it browns slightly, and add the sage leaves. Remove the ravioli with a slotted spoon, arrange on plates, pour the sage butter over, and sprinkle with Parmesan.

Egg rolls

These Chinese appetizers are simple to make

CRISPY EGG ROLLS

Egg rolls have their origins in southern Chinese cooking, but many other Asian countries, from Vietnam to the Philippines, have their own variations. Egg-roll skins can be found in most supermarkets, and in Asian markets, where you can also get fresh pork belly.

For the stuffing:
3 tablespoons oil
$^1/_2$ pound firm tofu, cut in $^3/_4$-inch strips
1 or 2 garlic cloves, cut in thin strips
1 tablespoon fermented black beans, crushed
2 teaspoons water
1 pound canned bamboo shoots, cut in thin strips
$^3/_4$ pound white radish (daikon), cut in thin strips
$^3/_4$ pound boiled fresh pork belly, with its cooking liquid
$^1/_2$ teaspoon sugar, 1 teaspoon dark soy sauce
$^3/_4$ pound small shrimp, peeled and deveined
salt and freshly ground pepper
3 cups bean sprouts
3 tablespoons chopped fresh cilantro
For the egg rolls:
40 egg-roll skins, $8^1/_2$-inches square
1 tablespoon flour, mixed with $1^1/_2$ teaspoons water
oil for frying

For the chili pepper and garlic sauce:
4 garlic cloves
2 hot red chili peppers
1 teaspoon sugar, 2 teaspoons rice vinegar
1 teaspoon salt

Heat 2 tablespoons of oil in a wok and brown the tofu lightly over very high heat, stirring constantly. Put to one side. Pour the remaining oil into the wok and brown the garlic lightly over low heat. Add the fermented black beans and stir-fry until lightly browned, then mix in the water. Add the bamboo shoots and daikon and stir-fry 2 minutes. Stir in a little of the pork cooking liquid, the sugar, soy sauce, shrimp, and pork, cut in strips. Stir-fry until everything is cooked. Season with salt and pepper. Put the tofu back into the wok and simmer gently until the liquid has almost all evaporated. Let the stuffing cool, then use to make the egg rolls as shown in the picture sequence right. Before rolling up the egg-roll skins, sprinkle the bean sprouts and cilantro evenly over the stuffing. Seal the ends with the flour and water paste. Heat oil in the wok until it is almost smoking, and fry the egg rolls until golden brown all over. Serve with the chili pepper and garlic sauce or sweet soy sauce. To make the chili pepper and garlic sauce, pound the garlic and chilies to a paste in a mortar and pestle, then mix in the sugar, rice vinegar, and salt.

LUMPIA

These are the Filipino version of egg rolls. Only half the size of the Chinese variety, they can be steamed as well as deep-fried.

For the stuffing:
1 hot red chili pepper, 2 garlic cloves
1/4 cup peanut oil
1 cup minced cooked pork
1 cup minced cooked chicken breast

Making egg rolls:

Stir-fry the ingredients for the stuffing, adding them in the order specified so that they cook quickly and evenly.

Vegetables in the stuffing should remain a little crunchy. Remove the stuffing from the wok and let cool.

Lay out the egg-roll skins on a work surface and put about 1 heaping tablespoon of the stuffing in the middle of each one.

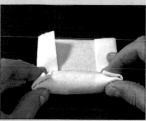

Fold the bottom edge of the egg-roll skin over the stuffing. Brush all the edges with egg white, or use a flour and water paste to seal.

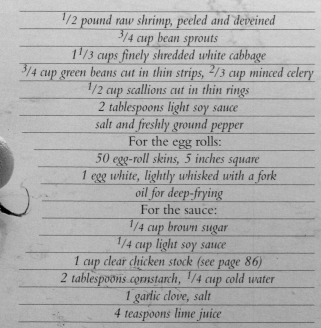

Fold the sides in and then roll up neatly. Press all the edges firmly to seal.

1/2 pound raw shrimp, peeled and deveined
3/4 cup bean sprouts
1 1/3 cups finely shredded white cabbage
3/4 cup green beans cut in thin strips, 2/3 cup minced celery
1/2 cup scallions cut in thin rings
2 tablespoons light soy sauce
salt and freshly ground pepper
For the egg rolls:
50 egg-roll skins, 5 inches square
1 egg white, lightly whisked with a fork
oil for deep-frying
For the sauce:
1/4 cup brown sugar
1/4 cup light soy sauce
1 cup clear chicken stock (see page 86)
2 tablespoons cornstarch, 1/4 cup cold water
1 garlic clove, salt
4 teaspoons lime juice

Cut the chili pepper in half, remove seeds, and mince. Peel and mince the garlic. Heat the oil in a wok and fry the garlic briefly. Add the pork, chicken, and shrimp – in that order – and stir-fry about 2 minutes. Add the bean sprouts, cabbage, beans, celery, scallions, and chili and stir-fry 3 minutes longer. The vegetables should remain crunchy. Add the soy sauce, season, and drain off any excess liquid. Let the stuffing cool. Put 1 tablespoon of stuffing on each egg-roll skin, brush the edges with egg white, and roll up as shown in the picture sequence. Heat a deep pan of oil to 350°F and fry the lumpia until golden and crisp, about 4 minutes. Drain on paper towels and serve hot, with the sauce for dipping. To make the sauce, combine the sugar, soy sauce, and stock in a pan and bring to a boil. Mix the cornstarch with the cold water and add to the sauce; simmer gently, stirring, until the sauce thickens. Mince the garlic and add to the sauce with a little salt and the lime juice.

Baked pasta dishes

Baked pasta dishes are very popular, both as a separate course, the *primo*, as in Italy, and as one-dish meals, needing only salad and, perhaps, bread as accompaniments. Whether you are using fresh or dried pasta, it must be cooked before going into the oven, as must all the other components of the dish, since the baking serves only to heat everything through or just crisps the surface. This crisping can also be achieved simply by placing the dish under the broiler.

Dishes such as noodles baked with ham and cream sauce or macaroni and cheese are common all over North America and Europe. However, the real classics come from Italy, with pride of place going to lasagne in all its variations. Cannelloni and other stuffed pasta are also often browned in the oven or under the broiler. Cheese always plays an important role here, whether it is the mild-flavored mozzarella or the stronger-tasting Parmesan, or other cheeses that melt easily.

Pasta by itself would turn brittle in the heat of the oven, so it needs to be in a liquid, such as a tomato sauce or a little cream, often mixed with cheese. The béchamel sauce in lasagne serves this purpose. When cooking pasta for a baked dish, it is important that the pasta be almost but not quite *al dente*, since it always absorbs a little sauce during the baking, which of course softens it a little. This is why it is preferable not to use very thin pasta for baked dishes.

One unusual specialty from the Po Valley is pasta "*in sarcofago*" – a stuffed pasta, such as tortellini, packed into a sort of pie crust. At the Restaurant Fini in Modena, short pastry is used for the crust, although puff pastry could also be used. The pastry is cut open at the table, so that guests can enjoy the wonderful aroma of mushrooms and herbs that rises from the filling.

With vegetables or ham

Whether made with vegetables or with meat, baked pasta dishes with an egg and cream sauce always taste splendid

PASTA AND VEGETABLES AU GRATIN

This is just one example of the many dishes that a creative cook can produce from a combination of pasta and vegetables. Other good examples are cauliflower or broccoli with tomatoes, or fennel and eggplant seasoned with anchovies and topped with blue cheese. The quantities given here will produce 4 to 6 servings.

3/4 pound elicoidali or rigatoni
butter for greasing the baking dish
4 tablespoons butter, melted
For the vegetables:
1/2 pound eggplant, 1/2 pound zucchini
2 celery stalks, 1 garlic clove
3/4 pound ripe tomatoes
1/4 cup olive oil, 1/4 cup minced onion
1 tablespoon chopped fresh thyme
1/2 tablespoon salt, freshly ground black pepper
1/2 cup dry red wine
For the cheese sauce:
1 cup freshly grated pecorino romano cheese
1 cup cream, 3 egg yolks
1 tablespoon chopped mixed fresh herbs: parsley, lovage or celery leaves, savory, rosemary
salt and freshly ground pepper
freshly grated nutmeg

Remove the stem end from the eggplant, and cut into 3/8-inch cubes. Slice the zucchini and celery thinly. Peel and mince the garlic. Blanch the tomatoes, peel them, cut in half, remove the seeds, and dice. Heat the oil in a large pan and sauté the onion and garlic until translucent. Add the eggplant, zucchini, and celery and fry over high heat for 4 to 5 minutes, stirring. Add the tomatoes and thyme, season with salt and pepper, and pour in the red wine. Cook uncovered over high heat until the vegetables are soft and the red wine has reduced by half. Cook the pasta in boiling salted water until almost *al dente*, drain, and mix with the vegetables. Transfer the mixture to a buttered baking dish. To make the sauce, whisk the pecorino with the cream and egg yolks, add the chopped herbs, and season with salt, pepper, and nutmeg. Pour the sauce over the pasta and vegetables. Bake in the oven preheated to 400°F for 20 to 25 minutes, moistening the top occasionally with the melted butter. For a particularly crisp topping, mix equal quantities of fine white bread crumbs and freshly grated Parmesan cheese and sprinkle over the top of the dish halfway through the baking time.

HAM AND PASTA BAKE AUSTRIAN-STYLE

This dish uses homemade pasta squares (*quadrucci*). The quantities given here will make enough for 4 to 6 servings.

For the pasta dough:
2^1/$_3$ cups all-purpose flour
3 eggs, 1 teaspoon salt, 1 tablespoon vegetable oil
For the ham:
2 ounces prosciutto, ^{1}/$_2$ pound cooked ham
^{1}/$_3$ cup minced onion, 2 tablespoons butter
For the sauce:
3 eggs, ^{1}/$_2$ cup sour cream, ^{1}/$_2$ cup milk
1 teaspoon salt, freshly ground pepper
In addition:
butter for greasing the baking dish
4 tablespoons butter, melted
1 tablespoon chopped fresh chives

Make the pasta dough as directed on page 41 and let rest, then roll out and cut quadrucci (see page 54). Cut the prosciutto and ham in small cubes. Sauté the onion in the butter until translucent. Cook the pasta squares in boiling salted water until almost *al dente*, drain, and rinse briefly with cold water so that they do not stick together. Continue as shown in the picture sequence. Bake in the middle of the oven preheated to 400°F until the top is crisp and golden brown, 30 to 40 minutes. Brush occasionally with melted butter, so that the top does not dry out. Sprinkle with chopped chives before serving.

The Austrians like this dish to have a good, hearty flavor, which is why both prosciutto and cooked ham are used. For an even richer flavor, cook the pasta in ham or chicken stock.

Preparing the ham and pasta bake:

Put the cooked pasta squares in a bowl, add the prosciutto and ham and the sautéed onion, and mix together.

Butter a baking dish, and pour in the pasta and ham mixture. Smooth the surface.

Whisk together the eggs, sour cream, and milk, and season. Pour this mixture evenly over the pasta.

Macaroni bakes

These are some of the most popular pasta dishes outside Italy

WITH EGGPLANT AND RABBIT

Macaroni and other tubular pasta, such as the thinner bucatini or the fatter ziti, could have been created especially for baked dishes. They lend themselves readily to layering, and the finished dish is easily cut for serving. The following recipe is similar to the Greek dish *pastitsio*, although it uses rabbit instead of lamb, and the pasta is cooked in veal stock. The quantities given are sufficient for 6 to 8 servings.

For the eggplant:
1 eggplant, weighing 3/4 to 1 pound
1 garlic clove
1/2 teaspoon salt, freshly ground pepper
1/2 cup vegetable oil
For the macaroni:
3/4 pound long macaroni
1 1/2 quarts veal stock
For the rabbit stuffing:
1/2 to 3/4 pound boneless rabbit, from the leg
1/2 teaspoon salt, freshly ground pepper
1 small hot chili pepper
1 pound ripe tomatoes
2 tablespoons vegetable oil
2/3 cup minced bacon
1/4 cup minced onion, 1/3 cup minced carrot
1/2 cup minced leek
2 tablespoons chopped fresh herbs: thyme, parsley, lovage or celery leaves
For the cheese sauce:
1 1/2 tablespoons butter, 2 tablespoons flour
1 cup milk
salt and freshly ground pepper
1/2 cup grated Swiss Gruyère or Emmental cheese
In addition:
butter to grease the baking dish

Cut the eggplant in 1/4-inch slices. Peel and mince the garlic. Marinate the sliced eggplant as shown in step one of the picture sequence. Cook the macaroni in the boiling veal stock until almost *al dente*; drain, reserving the stock. Cover the macaroni and put to one side. Dice the rabbit, put in a bowl, and season with salt and pepper. Cut the chili pepper in half, remove the seeds, and mince; add to the meat. Blanch the tomatoes, peel them, cut in half, remove the seeds, and dice. Heat the oil in a suitably sized pan and sauté the bacon, onion, carrot,

Preparing the macaroni bake:

Layer the sliced eggplant in a shallow dish, seasoning each layer with garlic, salt, and pepper. Pour the oil over, cover, and let marinate.

Cover the bottom of a buttered baking dish with a layer of macaroni, and spoon half of the meat stuffing on top.

Make another layer of macaroni on top of the meat stuffing, and arrange the eggplant slices on top, overlapping them slightly.

Cover the eggplant with another layer of macaroni, then spoon on the rest of the meat stuffing.

Add a final layer of pasta on top of the meat. Pour the cheese sauce over the surface and spread out evenly.

Depending on the size of the portions, baked pasta dishes can be served either as a first course or as a filling entrée. A crisp salad is an excellent accompaniment.

and leek over high heat. Add the rabbit and brown for a few minutes, stirring constantly. Stir in the tomatoes and simmer 5 to 10 minutes. Pour in the reserved veal stock, add the chopped herbs, and cook slowly, uncovered, until the liquid has almost all evaporated. To make the sauce, melt the butter in a small pan, sprinkle on the flour, and cook, stirring, 1 to 2 minutes; do not brown. Pour in the milk and mix to a smooth consistency, then season and cook gently about 20 minutes, stirring from time to time. Add the cheese and stir until melted. Butter a $2^1/2$-quart baking dish and layer the prepared ingredients in it as shown in the picture sequence. Bake in an oven preheated to 400°F for 30 to 40 minutes.

With beef – a popular variation. Cook $1/2$ pound long macaroni until almost *al dente*, drain, and let cool. Heat 2 tablespoons oil in a large pan and brown 2 cups sliced fresh mushrooms; remove the mushrooms from the pan. Brown $1/3$ cup chopped smoked bacon in the same pan. Pour off excess fat, then add $3/4$ cup chopped onion and 2 minced garlic cloves and fry until soft. Add $1/2$ pound ground beef and fry over high heat 2 to 3 minutes, stirring to break up lumps. Season with 1 teaspoon salt, some pepper, 1 tablespoon paprika, and $1/2$ tablespoon chopped fresh marjoram. Add 2 tablespoons tomato paste and 2 cups diced tomatoes and simmer 5 minutes. Pour in $1/2$ cup robust red wine and $1/2$ cup meat stock and simmer 15 minutes longer. Drain the meat mixture, reserving the liquid. Add $1/2$ teaspoon sugar to the liquid, and boil to reduce by about half. Make a layer of macaroni in a buttered baking dish. Arrange the meat and tomato mixture and the sliced mushrooms on top, and cover with the remaining macaroni. Pour the reduced cooking liquid over the top and sprinkle with 1 cup grated Emmental or Swiss cheese. Bake in the oven preheated to 425°F for 15 to 20 minutes.

Stuffed and baked

Large pasta shapes are ideal for stuffing and baking

STUFFED PASTA ON A BED OF SWEET PEPPERS

Mezze maniche rigate, a short, thick, tubular pasta, is just perfect for stuffing. Here a delicious combination of venison and sweet peppers is used.

3/4 pound mezze maniche rigate or similar
For the stuffing:
1 pound boneless shoulder of venison, 1/2 pound slab bacon
1 teaspoon salt, freshly ground pepper
2 juniper berries, crushed
a pinch of ground allspice
1 teaspoon paprika
grated zest of 1/2 orange
1 cup cream
For the peppers:
3 tablespoons oil, 1/3 cup minced onion
1 red, 1 green, and 1 yellow bell pepper, seeded, cored, and cut into 3/8-inch dice
1/2 garlic clove, 1/2 teaspoon salt
freshly ground pepper
In addition:
1/4 pound gorgonzola cheese, diced
3/4 cup cream, 2 egg yolks
2 tablespoons chopped mixed fresh herbs: thyme, parsley, rosemary
salt and freshly ground pepper
1/3 cup freshly grated Parmesan cheese

Cook the pasta in boiling salted water until almost *al dente*, drain, and rinse with cold water. To make the stuffing, trim the venison and cut in cubes. Cut the bacon in cubes. Sprinkle with all the seasonings, cover, and let marinate 1 to 2 hours. Finely chop the meat with some of the cream, in batches if necessary, in a food processor. Mix in the rest of the cream. Press the stuffing through a very fine strainer, then put it into a pastry bag fitted with a small round tip. Use to stuff the pasta. To prepare the peppers, heat the oil in a pan and sauté the onion until translucent. Add the diced peppers and minced garlic, season with salt and pepper, and cook over medium heat for 5 to 6 minutes. Layer the prepared ingredients in the baking dish as shown in the picture sequence. Bake in the oven preheated to 400°F for 40 minutes. After 20 minutes, sprinkle with the grated Parmesan. Serve hot.

Filling the baking dish:

Cover the bottom of the dish with the pepper mixture. Lay the stuffed pasta on top.

Scatter the diced gorgonzola over the pasta. Mix the cream with the egg yolks, herbs, and seasoning, and pour over the top.

PIPE RIGATE
WITH VEAL STUFFING

The alternative name for this shape of pasta is
lumaconi or *lumache* (snails). Baked in a creamy sauce,
the pasta is deliciously moist and the cheese topping
turns beautifully brown.

20 pipe rigate
For the stuffing:
1/2 pound ripe tomatoes
3 tablespoons vegetable oil, 1/4 cup minced shallots
1/2 cup minced scallions, 1/2 cup minced celery
2 tablespoons chopped mixed fresh herbs: parsley, oregano, basil, thyme
salt and freshly ground pepper
3/4 pound boneless veal
In addition:
butter for greasing the dish, 1/2 cup cream
1/3 cup freshly grated Parmesan cheese
2 tablespoons butter, cut in small pieces
1 tablespoon butter, fresh sage leaves

Blanch the tomatoes, peel them, cut in half, remove
the seeds, and chop. Heat the oil and sauté the
shallots and scallions until translucent. Add the
celery and fry briefly. Add the tomatoes and herbs,
season with salt and pepper, and cook 5 minutes
longer. Remove from the heat and let cool. In the
meantime, chop the veal in cubes. Finely chop the
cooled vegetables with the veal, in batches, in a food
processor. Cook the pasta in boiling salted water
until almost *al dente*, drain, and rinse with cold water.
Put the stuffing in a pastry bag fitted with a small
round tip and use to stuff the pasta. Place the stuffed
pasta in a buttered baking dish. Season the cream
with salt and pepper and pour over the stuffed pasta,
ensuring that it is distributed evenly. Sprinkle with
the grated Parmesan. Bake in the oven preheated to
375°F for about 15 minutes. Dot with the pieces of
butter and bake 5 minutes longer. In the meantime,
heat the tablespoon of butter in a small pan and toss
the sage leaves in it. Pour over the baked pasta and
serve immediately.

KRAUTKRAPFEN

In this traditional dish from Bavaria, the pasta rolls look like pieces of strudel standing upright. The dish can be cooked on the stovetop or in the oven.

For the pasta dough:
1²/3 cups all-purpose flour, 2 eggs
1 teaspoon oil, salt, 1 tablespoon water
For the sauerkraut stuffing:
1/2 pound onions
2 tablespoons clarified butter
2/3 cup minced bacon
scant 2 pounds sauerkraut (about 3 cups), rinsed
1/2 teaspoon salt, freshly ground pepper
a pinch of sugar, 6 juniper berries
2 bay leaves, 2/3 cup white wine (Riesling)
In addition:
1/2 egg white, lightly whisked with a fork
10 tablespoons (1 1/4 sticks) butter
1 to 2 tablespoons chopped fresh chives

Make the pasta dough as directed on page 41. For the stuffing, peel and slice the onions. Heat the clarified butter in a pan and cook the bacon. Add the sliced onions and sauté until translucent. Add the sauerkraut and mix well. Season with salt, pepper, and sugar. Add the juniper berries and bay

The sauerkraut for krautkrapfen must be well drained. Put it in a strainer and press with a wooden spoon until all the liquid has been squeezed out.

Place the sauerkraut stuffing on the rolled-out dough and distribute evenly with a fork, working from the center outward.

Brush the edge of one long side of the sheet of dough with egg white so that the edges stick well when the sheet is rolled up.

Starting from the opposite long side, carefully roll up the sheet of dough tightly, and press the edges firmly together.

Holding the roll of dough loosely between the fingers, cut with a sharp knife into 1 1/4-inch pieces.

leaves, pour in the wine, and simmer 15 minutes, stirring occasionally. Let cool and remove the bay leaves and juniper berries. Roll out the pasta dough thinly into a sheet 18 x 24 inches. Continue as shown in the picture sequence. Arrange the pieces of pasta upright in a buttered pan. Do not pack the pan too tightly. Melt the butter and pour half of it over the pasta. Bake in the oven preheated to 400°F for 20 minutes. Pour on the rest of the butter and bake 20 minutes longer. Sprinkle with the chopped chives and serve.

With ham and cheese Replace the bacon with 1/2 pound of chopped ham, preferably real Bavarian smoked ham or Westphalian ham; add the ham to the softened onions and brown lightly. Shortly before the end of the cooking time, sprinkle the pasta rolls with 1 cup grated Emmental or Swiss cheese and continue to cook until the cheese has melted and browned lightly.

PASTA ROLLS WITH A PORK AND SPINACH STUFFING

This is a recipe from Emilia Romagna. The quantities given will make 24 pasta rolls.

1 recipe fresh pasta dough no. 3 (see page 40)
For the stuffing:
¹/3 cup minced onion
2 garlic cloves, minced, 4 tablespoons butter
³/4 pound lean ground pork
5 ounces pork or lamb liver, minced
1 pound fresh spinach, stemmed and washed
2 cups roughly chopped mushrooms
salt and freshly ground pepper
In addition:
1 egg white, whisked lightly with a fork
3 tablespoons butter, 2 tablespoons chopped scallions
2 tablespoons each minced carrot and celery
¹/2 cup melted butter, 2 tablespoons white bread crumbs
2 tablespoons freshly grated Parmesan cheese

For the stuffing, soften the onion and garlic in the butter. Add the ground pork and fry until it changes color, stirring to break up lumps. Add the liver, spinach, and mushrooms and fry briefly to wilt the spinach. Season and set aside. Roll out the pasta dough thinly and cut out 4 sheets, each 6 x 8 inches. Cook in boiling salted water for 2 minutes, then remove with a slotted spatula to a damp dish towel and blot dry. Spread the stuffing on the sheets of pasta, leaving the edge of one long side clear; brush this with egg white. Roll up each sheet from the other long side and press the edges firmly to seal. Heat the butter and briefly sauté the scallions, carrot, and celery until nearly tender. Spread over the bottom of a dish. Cut each pasta roll across into 6 pieces and arrange upright in the baking dish. Pour half of the butter over the rolls and bake in the oven preheated to 400°F for 15 minutes. Sprinkle with crumbs and Parmesan, drizzle with the remaining melted butter, and bake 10 minutes longer.

Cannelloni

Pasta tubes with endless possibilities

Cannelloni can be filled with a huge variety of stuffings. The recipe here calls for a meat stuffing, in fact the one given for raviolini on page 188. However, cannelloni can also be stuffed with vegetables, cheese, poultry, and seafood. They can be covered with various sauces, such as a béchamel, or just with cheese, and then baked or browned under the broiler. Making cannelloni from scratch is a long process, but you can save time by using dried cannelloni (8 tubes are required for this recipe).

CANNELLONI WITH MEAT STUFFING

This might be regarded as a basic recipe for the creative cook, as it can be varied in every respect. For example, the tomato sauce, which keeps the cannelloni moist, can be replaced by a delicate vegetable and tomato *brunoise*.

1 recipe fresh pasta dough no. 3 (see page 40)
1 quantity of meat stuffing (see the recipe for raviolini on page 188)
$^1/_2$ cup cream, $^1/_2$ cup freshly grated Parmesan cheese
4 tablespoons butter, cut in small pieces
For the tomato sauce:
4 tablespoons butter, 1 tablespoon minced onion
$^3/_4$ pound ripe tomatoes, peeled and diced
20 fresh basil leaves
$^1/_2$ teaspoon salt, freshly ground pepper

First make the sauce: heat the butter and soften the onion. Add the diced tomatoes and cook gently until thick – they should not disintegrate completely. Add the basil, and season with salt and pepper. Pour the tomato sauce into a baking dish. Roll out the dough thinly and cut out rectangles 3 x 5 inches. Cook for 2 minutes in boiling water, then remove with a slotted spatula. Continue as shown in the picture sequence. Dot with the small pieces of butter and bake in the oven preheated to 400°F until lightly browned on top, about 20 minutes.

Preparing cannelloni:

Lay the rectangles of dough on a damp cloth. Spoon some of the stuffing along a short side of each rectangle, and roll it up.

Arrange the cannelloni in the baking dish on top of the tomato sauce. The dish should be big enough to hold the cannelloni in one layer.

Mix the cream with the Parmesan, and spoon evenly over the cannelloni.

CANNELLONI WITH SEAFOOD STUFFING

1/2 recipe fresh green pasta dough (see page 46)
For the stuffing:
1 pound sea trout or weakfish fillets, well chilled
1/2 cup cream, well chilled
salt and freshly ground pepper
8 scampi (Dublin Bay prawns) or large shrimp
For the béchamel sauce:
2 tablespoons butter, 3 tablespoons flour
2 cups milk, 1/2 teaspoon salt
freshly ground pepper
a pinch of freshly grated nutmeg
1 egg yolk, 1/2 cup cream
In addition:
3 tablespoons freshly grated Parmesan cheese

Increase the quantity of spinach pulp when making the dough, to give it a particularly vivid green color. Cut the fish fillets in cubes and purée, in batches if necessary, in a blender or food processor. Transfer to a bowl and refrigerate as soon as each batch is puréed. Press the purée through a strainer, stir in the cream, season, and refrigerate again. Peel and devein the scampi or shrimp, and refrigerate. To make the béchamel sauce, melt the butter, add the flour, and cook, stirring, 1 to 2 minutes; do not brown. Pour in the milk, stirring to remove lumps. Season with salt, pepper, and nutmeg, and cook 20 minutes, stirring frequently. Whisk the egg yolk and cream with 2 tablespoons of the sauce. Remove the sauce from the heat, thicken with the egg-yolk mixture, and strain into a clean pan. Keep warm over low heat. Roll out the pasta dough thinly and cut 8 rectangles, 2 3/4 x 3 1/4 inches. Cook in boiling salted water for 2 minutes, then remove with a slotted spatula, spread out on a damp dish towel and blot dry. Put some of the fish purée on each rectangle, leaving a border clear on all sides. Lay 1 scampi in the middle of each rectangle and roll up, pressing the end firmly to seal. Lay the rolls in a buttered baking dish. Pour the béchamel sauce over and sprinkle with cheese. Bake in the oven preheated to 400°F for about 9 minutes, then turn on the broiler and quickly brown the top.

LASAGNE NEAPOLITAN-STYLE

In this vegetarian version, two kinds of mild cheese – ricotta and mozzarella – make the dish pleasantly light. The quantities given below are sufficient for 8 to 10 portions.

1 recipe fresh pasta dough no. 3 (see page 40)
For the tomato sauce:
2 pounds ripe plum tomatoes or 1 28-ounce can tomatoes
2 garlic cloves, $^{1}/4$ cup olive oil
salt, freshly ground black pepper
For the ricotta stuffing:
1 pound (2 cups) ricotta cheese
$^{1}/3$ cup freshly grated Parmesan cheese
a pinch of freshly grated nutmeg
In addition:
butter to grease the dish
$^{1}/2$ cup fresh basil leaves, $^{1}/2$ pound mozzarella cheese

Roll out the pasta dough thinly and cut sheets from it to fit the chosen baking dish (a 10 x 6-inch dish was used here). For the tomato sauce, wash and quarter the fresh tomatoes or drain canned ones.

Peel and mince the garlic. Heat the oil in a heavy pan and sauté the garlic until it colors slightly. Add the tomatoes, season, and stir. Cover the pan and simmer 30 minutes. Press the sauce through a strainer or food mill and set aside. Mix the ingredients for the ricotta stuffing in a bowl and season. Cook the sheets of dough, one or two at a time, in boiling salted water for 2 minutes. Remove with a slotted spoon, lay out flat on damp cloths, and cover with another damp cloth. Arrange two of the pasta sheets in a buttered baking dish so that they overlap each other and hang over the long sides of the dish by 3/4 inch. Pour one-fourth of the tomato sauce over the pasta and scatter one-fourth of the basil leaves on top. Cover with another sheet of pasta, laid lengthwise, and spread with a third of the ricotta stuffing. Put another sheet of pasta on top and cover with a third of the sliced mozzarella. Repeat these layers twice. Cover the last layer of mozzarella with a sheet of pasta, and fold the overhanging pasta over the top. Add the remaining tomato sauce and basil and bake in the oven preheated to 425°F for about 20 minutes.

LASAGNE VERDI BOLOGNESE-STYLE

One of the classic recipes from Bologna, the pasta stronghold. Cooks in this area are not only especially skilled at making exquisite pasta, they also produce the best meat sauces. It is precisely this combination that is required for a good lasagne. The quantities listed here are sufficient for 8 to 10 servings.

1 recipe fresh green pasta dough (see page 46)
For the bolognese sauce:
3 tablespoons olive oil
1/2 pound each freshly ground beef round and lean pork
1/4 cup minced onion
1/2 cup each finely diced carrot and celery
3 tablespoons tomato paste
salt and freshly ground black pepper
2 cups meat stock
1 tablespoon minced fresh parsley
For the béchamel sauce:
2 tablespoons butter
3 tablespoons flour, 2 cups milk
salt and freshly ground white pepper
a pinch of freshly grated nutmeg
In addition:
butter to grease the dish
3/4 cup freshly grated Parmesan cheese

Roll the pasta dough out thinly and cut squares that are slightly smaller than the width of the chosen baking dish. Here an 11 x 6 1/4 inch dish was used, so the pasta was cut in 6-inch squares. For the bolognese sauce, heat the oil in a heavy pan and fry the meat over fairly high heat until browned, stirring to break up lumps. Add the onion, carrot, and celery, and stir in the tomato paste. Fry briefly with the meat. Season with salt and pepper, pour in the stock, and add the parsley. Let simmer 30 minutes. To make the béchamel sauce, melt the butter, stir in the flour, and cook 1 to 2 minutes without

Preparing the lasagne:

Cook the pasta squares, one at a time, in boiling salted water for 2 minutes. Remove with a slotted spoon and lay out flat on a cloth to drain.

Butter the baking dish. Arrange two pasta squares in the dish to cover the bottom, overlapping them slightly in the center.

Spoon in half of the bolognese sauce and spread it out evenly to cover the pasta.

Arrange another two pasta squares on top, overlapping them slightly in the center as before.

browning. Pour on the milk, stirring to remove any lumps, and bring to a boil. Season with salt, pepper, and nutmeg, and simmer over low heat for 20 minutes, stirring frequently. Strain the sauce. Continue as shown in the picture sequence.

Cover the pasta layer with half of the béchamel sauce. Repeat the layers of pasta, bolognese sauce, pasta, and béchamel sauce.

Sprinkle the last layer of béchamel sauce with the Parmesan. Bake in the oven preheated to 425°F for 20 minutes

Sweet pasta dishes

Pasta for dessert? Why not? Stuffed pasta, in particular, opens up a wide range of possibilities. Ricotta cheese, which is neutral in taste, can be seasoned with salt or with sugar, as can quark, an unripened soft cheese popular in Germany and Austria, and both are ideal for stuffing pasta. A sauce flavored with vanilla or orange would be delicious as a partner. Other sweet stuffings could be based on cake or bread crumbs or crushed cookies. Soft fruit is not such a good choice for stuffing pasta – the juice from raspberries or strawberries, for example, would turn the pasta mushy in seconds.

Pasta doughs containing unsweetened cocoa powder look appetizing and taste great. The same idea can be applied to make what might be called "chocolate pasta." Even a standard egg pasta dough can be used for sweet dishes, as long as the accompanying sauce is carefully chosen. Vanilla, cinnamon, poppy seeds, and finely grated lemon or orange zest are particularly good flavorings. A somewhat curious but certainly original dish is sweet lasagne, where the pasta sheets are layered with apples, raisins, and vanilla sauce. This looks most attractive when baked in small individual molds. And at the other end of the spectrum is a delicious treat for children – pasta simply tossed in butter and sprinkled with cinnamon and sugar.

Deep-fried pasta is excellent served as a sweet dish. In China there are several recipes that use honey as a sweetener. Less familiar are the deep-fried pasta recipes from Italy, which have a long history. For these, the dough, flavored with a little white wine or vermouth, is cut into broad strips, sometimes braided, and then deep-fried. When cooked, they are sprinkled with confectioners' sugar. They make a wonderfully crunchy treat, for which a glass of *vin santo* is the perfect accompaniment.

Poppy seeds are a popular flavoring for desserts throughout central and eastern Europe.

BUCATINI WITH POPPY SEEDS, CREAM, AND PLUM PRESERVES

Any shape of pasta can be used for this dish, including tagliatelle or spaghetti. However, chunky shapes such as bucatini or elbow macaroni go particularly well with this combination of flavors.

3/4 pound bucatini
5 tablespoons butter
1/2 cup ground poppy seeds
For serving:
1 cup heavy cream, 2 tablespoons plum preserves
1 tablespoon lemon zest cut in thin shreds
a few fresh lemon balm or mint leaves

Cook the bucatini in lightly salted boiling water until *al dente*. Drain thoroughly. Heat the butter in a pan until it begins to foam, add the ground poppy seeds, and stir well; keep warm. Whip the cream until thick. Add the pasta to the poppy-seed butter, stir to coat evenly, and transfer to 4 plates. Arrange a portion of whipped cream and plum jam on each plate. Garnish with the lemon zest and herb leaves and serve immediately.

POTATO NOODLES WITH POPPY-SEED BUTTER

The potato dough does not necessarily have to be shaped into noodles. It can also be used to make small dumplings or be cut in strips.

1 to 11/4 pounds baking potatoes
1 cup + 3 tablespoons all-purpose flour
1 egg, salt and freshly ground pepper
5 tablespoons butter, 2/3 cup ground poppy seeds
To finish:
1/4 cup confectioners' sugar

Bake the potatoes as directed on page 223, and put them through a potato ricer while still warm. Add the flour, egg, and seasoning and mix to a smooth dough. Use your palms to roll into noodles about 1 1/2 inches long with tapering ends. Cook in lightly salted boiling water about 6 minutes. In the meantime, melt the butter and add the ground poppy seeds. Remove the noodles from the water with a slotted spoon and drain thoroughly. Arrange on 4 plates, pour over the poppy-seed butter, and sprinkle with confectioners' sugar.

CHOCOLATE PASTA

Children are not the only ones who will love this pasta with its wonderful chocolate flavor.

For the chocolate pasta dough:
2 cups all-purpose flour
1 cup + 2 tablespoons unsweetened cocoa powder
1/4 cup confectioners' sugar, 4 eggs
1 teaspoon vanilla extract

Sift the flour and cocoa powder onto a work surface. Add the confectioners' sugar, eggs, and vanilla and knead to a smooth dough. Wrap in plastic wrap and let rest before cutting out the desired pasta shape.

CHOCOLATE TRENETTE WITH VANILLA SAUCE

1 recipe chocolate pasta dough (see above)
For the vanilla sauce:
3 egg yolks, 1/4 cup sugar
1 cup milk, 1/4 vanilla bean
For garnish:
1/4 cup chopped pistachio nuts

Roll out the pasta dough thinly and cut out trenette, which are slightly narrower than tagliatelle (see pages 52 and 53). Beat the egg yolks with the sugar until pale and creamy. Pour the milk into a pan, add the vanilla bean, split lengthwise in half, and heat until scalding hot. Gradually pour the hot milk into the egg-yolk mixture, stirring constantly, then pour the mixture back into the pan. Cook over low heat, stirring, until the custard sauce thickens enough to coat a wooden spoon. Remove the vanilla bean. Cook the trenette in lightly salted boiling water until *al dente*, drain, and arrange in deep plates. Pour the vanilla sauce over and sprinkle with the chopped pistachios.

CHOCOLATE NOODLES WITH A CRUNCHY HAZELNUT AND CREAM SAUCE

1 recipe chocolate pasta dough (see left)
For the sauce:
1/2 cup sugar
3/4 cup roughly chopped hazelnuts, 1/2 cup heavy cream

Roll out the pasta dough thinly and cut the thinnest possible noodles (capelli d'angelo). This is difficult with a knife, but most pasta machines have a very thin cutting roller. To make the hazelnut crunch, melt the sugar in a heavy pan and cook until the sugar syrup turns light brown. Add the hazelnuts, stir in quickly, and remove immediately from the heat. Pour the hot mixture onto an oiled marble slab, roll out into a sheet using an oiled rolling pin, and let cool. When set, crush coarsely with a paperweight or meat pounder. Whip the cream until thick and stir in two-thirds of the hazelnut crunch. Cook the noodles in lightly salted boiling water until *al dente*, drain, and arrange in deep plates. Pour the sauce over and garnish with the remaining hazelnut crunch.

Sweet pasta dishes baked in the oven

Baked in puddings, pasta is beautifully tender and tastes wonderful

BAKED NOODLE PUDDING
WITH CHESTNUTS

Peeled chestnuts are available in cans and also vacuum-packed, and are very convenient to use, but fresh chestnuts have a much better flavor.

1 pound fresh chestnuts, 3/4 pound tagliatelle
4 tablespoons butter, 1 1/4 cups confectioners' sugar
3 egg yolks, 1 teaspoon vanilla extract
1/4 cup cream, 2 egg whites, 1/4 cup sugar
In addition:
2 tablespoons butter for greasing the baking dish
confectioners' sugar for sprinkling

Using a small, sharp knife, cut a cross in the top of each chestnut. Arrange them in a shallow baking pan and bake in the oven preheated to 425°F until the shells split open and can be peeled off with a knife. Peeling is most easily done while the chestnuts are still warm, so remove them from the oven in batches. Peel off the bitter inner skin, too. Roughly chop the peeled chestnuts.

Cook the tagliatelle in boiling salted water until *al dente*, drain and rinse briefly in cold running water, and then drain again well. Continue as shown in the picture sequence. Bake the pudding in the oven preheated to 425°F until the top is browned, 20 minutes. Sprinkle with confectioners' sugar.

Cherry compote, spiced with cloves and cinnamon, makes a splendid accompaniment for the noodle pudding with chestnuts. Pitted fresh cherries, or well-drained canned ones, can also be mixed into the pudding before baking.

Making the baked noodle pudding:

Brown the chopped chestnuts in the butter; gradually sprinkle on the confectioners' sugar and continue to cook until the chestnuts are caramelized.

Mix the chestnuts with the cooked noodles. Whisk the egg yolks with the vanilla until foamy, and whisk in the cream. Add to the chestnut mixture.

Beat the egg whites with the sugar until stiff, then fold into the noodle mixture. Transfer to a buttered baking dish.

VIENNESE NOODLE PUDDING WITH HAZELNUTS

1/2 recipe fresh pasta dough no. 4 (see page 40)

6 tablespoons butter, 3/4 cup confectioners' sugar

4 eggs, separated

1 cup ground toasted hazelnuts

1/4 cup white bread crumbs, 1/2 teaspoon ground cinnamon
grated zest of 1/2 lemon

butter and fine bread crumbs for the dish

confectioners' sugar for sprinkling

Roll out the pasta dough thinly and cut out trenette, which are slightly narrower than tagliatelle (see pages 52 and 53). Cook in boiling salted water until *al dente*, drain, and rinse briefly in cold water to prevent them sticking together. Beat the butter with half of the confectioners' sugar and the egg yolks until the mixture is thick and pale. Beat the egg whites with the remaining confectioners' sugar until stiff, and fold into the egg-yolk mixture. Mix the hazelnuts with the bread crumbs, cinnamon, and lemon zest. Add to the egg mixture with the noodles and fold everything together gently. Pour into a baking dish that has been buttered and coated with bread crumbs. Smooth the surface. Bake in the oven preheated to 400°F until set and lightly browned, 25 to 30 minutes. Sprinkle with confectioners' sugar, and serve with stewed fruit and whipped cream.

BAKED NOODLE PUDDING WITH CRANBERRIES

(not illustrated)

1/2 recipe fresh pasta dough no. 4 (see page 40)

4 tablespoons butter, 3/4 cup confectioners' sugar

4 eggs, separated, 3 tablespoons amaretto liqueur

1 1/4 cups ground toasted almonds

1/4 cup white bread crumbs

butter and fine bread crumbs for the baking dish

1 cup stewed cranberries, confectioners' sugar

Roll out the pasta dough thinly and cut out tagliatelle or trenette, which are slightly narrower than tagliatelle (see pages 52 and 53). Cook in boiling salted water until *al dente*, drain, and set aside. Prepare the egg mixture as in the preceding recipe, add the amaretto, and fold in the noodles, almonds, and bread crumbs. Butter a baking dish and coat with bread crumbs. Pour in half of the pudding mixture and smooth the surface. Arrange the stewed cranberries in small piles on top and cover with the remaining pudding mixture. Bake in the oven preheated to 400°F until the top is lightly browned, 30 to 35 minutes. Sprinkle with confectioners' sugar.

QUARK DUMPLINGS WITH CRANBERRIES AND SABAYON

Quark is a soft unripened cheese that tastes like mild sour cream. For these dumplings, it should be as dry and firm as possible, so drain it in a fine-mesh strainer first if necessary.

For the dumplings:
5 ounces (about 2/3 cup) quark
4 cups white bread cubes
2 tablespoons sugar, 1/2 teaspoon salt
4 tablespoons butter, melted, 1/4 cup sour cream
2 eggs, 6 tablespoons flour
1 tablespoon white bread crumbs
For the cranberry compote:
1 cup water, 3/4 cup sugar
3/4-inch cinnamon stick, 2 cloves
juice of 1 orange, 4 cups cranberries
For the buttered crumbs:
1/2 cup (1 stick) butter
1/2 cup white bread crumbs
For the sabayon:
3 egg yolks, 1/2 cup sugar, 1/2 cup dry white wine

To finish:
confectioners' sugar

Mix together all the ingredients for the dumplings and work into a smooth dough. Let rest 30 minutes. Shape the dough into 12 round dumplings and place in a pan of boiling salted water. Remove from the heat and let stand until the dumplings are cooked, about 10 minutes. To make the cranberry compote, combine the water, sugar, cinnamon, and cloves in a saucepan and bring to a boil, stirring to dissolve the sugar. Boil 3 to 4 minutes, then strain and return to the pan. Add the orange juice and cranberries and cook until the cranberries begin to pop. Melt the butter in another pan, add the bread crumbs, and fry until golden, stirring occasionally. To make the sabayon, beat the egg yolks with the sugar in a heatproof bowl until frothy, then set in a *bain-marie* (or use a double boiler). Pour in the wine and beat until the mixture thickens. Remove the dumplings from the water with a slotted spoon and arrange on plates with the cranberry compote and the sabayon. Sprinkle with the buttered crumbs and a little confectioners' sugar.

SEMOLINA DUMPLINGS WITH FIGS AND RED WINE SAUCE

2 fresh figs
For the dumplings:
2 cups stale bread cubes
2 tablespoons lukewarm milk
4 tablespoons butter, 1 egg
$^1\!/\!2$ cup semolina
salt, freshly grated nutmeg
For the sauce:
1 cup red wine, 2 tablespoons sugar
a pinch of ground cinnamon
juice of $^1\!/\!2$ orange
1 teaspoon pared orange zest cut in fine shreds
1 teaspoon cornstarch
In addition:
$^1\!/\!2$ cup heavy cream
fine shreds of orange zest

Moisten the bread cubes with the milk. Beat the butter in a bowl, add the egg, and beat until creamy. Add the semolina and the softened bread, and season with salt and nutmeg. Mix thoroughly. Scoop out spoonfuls and shape into oval dumplings (*quenelles*). Put in a pan of boiling salted water, remove from the heat, and let stand until cooked through, about 15 minutes. To make the sauce, combine the red wine, sugar, cinnamon, and orange juice in a pan, bring to a boil, and reduce to a third of the original volume. Add the shreds of orange zest. Mix the cornstarch with a little cold water and use to thicken the sauce. Peel the figs, slice, and add to the sauce, letting them soften slightly. Whip the cream until stiff. Drain the dumplings and arrange on plates with the figs in their sauce and whipped cream. Garnish with orange zest and serve immediately.

Semolina dumplings in soup: Beat 4 tablespoons butter until pale and creamy. Lightly beat 1 extra-large egg. Measure $^3\!/\!4$ cup semolina. Add the egg and semolina to the butter in 2 or 3 batches and mix to a smooth paste. Season with salt and nutmeg, and let rest 30 minutes. Scoop out small spoonfuls, shape into oval dumplings, and place in a pan of boiling-hot broth. Let stand until cooked through. Ladle into soup cups and serve.

Dumplings and gnocchi

Dumplings may well have originated as a form of food for those who ate with their fingers, a habit that persisted, even in Europe, until well into the 17th century. According to old recipes, dumplings were seldom "meatless" but contained "minced meat" of all kinds, that could then be consumed without any cutlery or carving skills being required. Evidence for this goes back as far as the writings of Apicius, whose collection of recipes appeared in the time of the Roman emperor Tiberius. This includes a number of recipes for dumplings containing the meat of hare and other animals. Further evidence is to be found in medieval paintings depicting devout ladies and gentlemen consuming all manner of food shaped into small balls – which must surely be dumplings.

The characteristic that dumplings share with pasta is that eggs are used to bind the dough together; the flour is of secondary importance. The skill in making dumplings lies mainly in producing a dough or paste with a firm yet light consistency. The potato, which became a popular food in the second half of the 18th century, was welcomed because it could be used to make feather-light dumplings with a good texture.

Dumplings without meat – the way we usually prepare them nowadays – may have begun in times of famine, as a way of making the most of scraps of bread, but today's dumplings can be gourmet fare. *Semmelknödel* and *Serviettenknödel*, from Germany, are two kinds of bread dumplings served as a side-dish. In Austria, a wide range of dumplings are made, both sweet and savory. Quark or apricots are popular stuffings for sweet dumplings, and smaller dumplings, known as *Nockerln*, are added to broths, just as elegant *quenelles* are served in consommé in France. In Italy, the small dumplings called *gnocchi* may be made with flour, potatoes, semolina, cornmeal, or ricotta cheese, and are usually served as a first course. There are also sweet gnocchi, and tiny ones for soup. Small dumplings of all kinds, sometimes steamed, sometimes deep-fried, are also a basic part of everyday Asian cooking.

Homemade potato doughs

Gnocchi di patate and potato dumplings

Gnocchi have been part of Italian cooking for almost as long as pasta: one has only to think of *malloreddus*, the small Sardinian gnocchi made from flour and water, or those made from semolina or polenta. And they have long played a particularly important role in the culinary tradition of Verona, where it remains the custom even today to distribute enormous quantities of gnocchi on the last Friday of carnival to passers-by in front of the Basilica of San Zeno.

In earlier centuries, gnocchi were made solely of flour and water, for it was not until the beginning of the last century that the Austrians, who had long been familiar with such starchy foods in the form of potato noodles, introduced potatoes into Italy. Cooks in virtually all parts of the Austro-Hungarian Empire made a cheap dough, with a lot of potatoes and just a little flour, that could be used in a variety of different ways: to make flat crackers, long noodles, or small dumplings similar to Italian gnocchi.

Whether the potato dough is shaped into gnocchi, dumplings, or noodles, it must be freshly made, and prepared as quickly as possible, because otherwise it becomes too soft and sticky to work with. And potato gnocchi and noodles boiled in water must be served immediately after they are cooked if their texture and flavor are to be at their best.

The quality of the potatoes is also of vital importance. Only really floury varieties are suitable, and to ensure that they remain as dry and floury as possible, they should be neither steamed nor boiled but baked in the oven. Wrapping them in foil makes them easier to peel afterward, but it produces moisture, so before they are put through the potato ricer they should be dried thoroughly. Alternatively, they can simply be baked in their skins, cut open, and the flesh scooped out.

Basic potato dough: Bake $1^{1}/4$ to $1^{1}/2$ pounds of floury baking potatoes. Peel, or scoop out the flesh with a spoon; there should be about 1 pound of cooked potato. Put the potatoes through a ricer or food mill. Mix $1^{2}/3$ cups all-purpose flour with 1 cup freshly grated Parmesan cheese, and season with salt, freshly ground pepper, and freshly grated nutmeg. Add the potatoes and 2 eggs. Mix to a smooth dough. If making sweet dumplings, the Parmesan can, of course, be omitted. Potato dumplings combine splendidly with brown butter, tomato sauce, bolognese sauce, and, above all, mushroom and game stews.

Gnocchi can be made from the potato dough described on these pages. The dough is rolled by hand into long, thin ropes and then cut in small, even-sized pieces. These are pressed against a grater to imprint a lattice-work pattern on them.

1 *Wrap each scrubbed potato in foil, or put directly onto the oven rack. Bake in the oven preheated to 400°F for about 1 hour. If wrapped in foil, peel the baked potatoes; otherwise, cut them in half and scoop out the flesh. Pour the flour onto a work surface, form a well in the middle, and add the Parmesan, salt, and other seasonings. Press the peeled potatoes through a ricer, distributing them evenly over the flour.*

2 *Add the eggs to the well, and heap flour and potatoes from the outside over the top. Working from the center outward, mix the ingredients together with your fingers. Working as quickly as possible, knead to a smooth dough by pressing and squeezing with both hands. Do not work the dough for longer than is necessary. Let it rest briefly, then shape into two long rolls 1 to 1 1/2 inches in diameter. Sprinkle with flour.*

3 *For noodles: using a sharp knife, cut each roll of dough into pieces about 3/4 inch wide. The pressure of cutting the dough partially shapes the fat noodles. Complete the process by rolling each piece on the work surface so that it tapers at both ends. Dust with flour to prevent the noodles sticking. Cook the noodles in boiling salted water until they rise to the surface. Remove with a slotted spoon. Arrange on plates, and finish with brown butter, freshly grated Parmesan, and chopped fresh herbs.*

Gnocchi with pumpkin and mushrooms

Two exquisite gnocchi recipes – a Tuscan dish with a mushroom sauce and a Piedmontese dish with pumpkin

PUMPKIN GNOCCHI WITH SPINACH

For the gnocchi:
1 small pumpkin, weighing about 1 1/2 pounds
1 egg
6 tablespoons all-purpose flour
1/2 cup freshly grated Parmesan cheese
salt and freshly ground pepper
For the spinach sauce:
1/2 pound spinach
2 tablespoons minced onion
1 1/2 tablespoons butter
1/4 cup white wine
1/2 cup meat stock
1 tablespoon cream
salt and freshly ground pepper
freshly grated nutmeg
To finish:
1/2 cup freshly grated Parmesan cheese
6 tablespoons (3/4 stick) butter, melted and lightly browned (beurre noisette)

The sauces are interchangeable – tomato sauce also goes well with pumpkin gnocchi, just as spinach sauce does with potato gnocchi.

Cooking the pumpkin:

Place the pumpkin on a baking sheet and bake in the oven until a sharp knife can be inserted easily, about 1 1/2 hours.

Let cool a little, then cut the pumpkin in half and remove the seeds and fibers from the center.

Scoop out the flesh with a large spoon. You will need 1/2 pound of pumpkin flesh (about 1 packed cup) for the gnocchi.

Preheat the oven to 400°F and bake the pumpkin, whole, as shown in the picture sequence. Purée the pumpkin flesh in a food processor. Work the pumpkin purée with the egg, flour, Parmesan, salt, and pepper to a smooth dough. Shape it into gnocchi as directed on page 222. Trim and wash the spinach. Soften the minced onion in half of the butter, add the spinach, and cook until wilted. Purée it. Combine the white wine and meat stock in a pan, bring to a boil, and reduce a little. Add the spinach purée and bring back to a boil. Add the remaining butter and the cream, and season with salt, pepper, and nutmeg. Mix thoroughly and keep warm. Cook the gnocchi in boiling salted water for 5 minutes; remove with a slotted spoon and arrange on plates with the spinach sauce. Sprinkle with the Parmesan and drizzle the brown butter over.

POTATO GNOCCHI WITH TOMATO AND MUSHROOM SAUCE

A Tuscan recipe for autumn, when fresh wild mushrooms are plentiful.

For the gnocchi:

1 ¹/4 to 1 ¹/2 pounds baking potatoes

¹/4 cup ricotta cheese, 1 egg yolk

³/4 cup freshly grated Parmesan cheese

2 tablespoons flour

salt and freshly ground pepper

freshly grated nutmeg

For the tomato and mushroom sauce:

³/4 pound ripe tomatoes, 2 shallots

1 garlic clove, ¹/4 cup olive oil

salt and freshly ground pepper

³/4 pound fresh porcini (cèpes), 1 tablespoon butter

1 tablespoon chopped fresh parsley

Bake the potatoes as directed on page 223. While still hot, peel them, or scoop out the flesh, and put through a ricer or food mill into a bowl. You need 1 pound of potato. Let cool a little, then add the ricotta, egg yolk, Parmesan, flour, salt, pepper, and nutmeg and work to a smooth dough. Shape into gnocchi (see page 222). Blanch the tomatoes, peel them, remove seeds, and dice. Peel and mince the shallots and garlic. Heat the oil in a pan and sauté the shallots and garlic until translucent. Add the tomatoes, season, and simmer gently for 15 minutes. In the meantime, clean and slice the porcini. Heat the butter in a pan and sauté the porcini; sprinkle with the chopped parsley and season with salt and pepper. Add the tomato sauce to the porcini and stir to mix. Add the gnocchi to a pan of boiling salted water, reduce the heat, and simmer until cooked through, about 3 minutes. Remove with a slotted spoon, arrange on plates, and pour the sauce over.

Semolina and polenta gnocchi

These can be rolled into oval shapes or cut from a block with a pastry cutter

POLENTA GNOCCHI WITH BACON AND GORGONZOLA

$^1/4$ pound slab bacon
For the polenta:
5 cups water, 1 teaspoon salt
3 cups polenta (coarsely ground yellow cornmeal)
In addition:
butter for greasing the baking dish
6 ounces gorgonzola cheese
$^1/2$ cup freshly grated Parmesan cheese, $^2/3$ cup cream
4 tablespoons butter, melted
1 heaping tablespoon fresh basil cut in strips

Chop the bacon in small cubes and cook in a frying pan until the fat is rendered. Drain on paper towels. Bring the water and salt for the polenta to a boil in a large pot. Pour in the polenta in a thin stream, stirring constantly and ensuring that the water is boiling all the time; this will prevent lumps from

Making polenta gnocchi:

Stir the bacon into the polenta, mixing thoroughly.

Using a wet spoon, scoop out portions of the polenta and bacon mixture and shape into smooth ovals in your wet hands.

Arrange the gnocchi in a buttered baking dish, slightly overlapping and leaning against each other at an angle.

Cut the gorgonzola in cubes and scatter evenly over the gnocchi.

Sprinkle with the Parmesan, then spoon on the cream, covering all the gnocchi evenly. Drizzle with a little of the melted butter.

forming. Keep stirring, in the same direction as much as possible. When the mixture begins to thicken into a smooth mass, the task becomes more arduous, since it will take about 20 minutes for the polenta to cook. It is done when the polenta comes away from the side of the pot. Then continue as shown in the picture sequence. Put the baking dish in the oven preheated to 400°F and bake 25 to 30 minutes, basting the gnocchi frequently with melted butter. Garnish with basil and serve hot.

GNOCCHI ALLA ROMANA

For the polenta:
2 cups water, 1/2 teaspoon salt
1 1/4 cups polenta (coarsely ground yellow cornmeal)
For the herb butter:
1/2 cup (1 stick) butter, 1 garlic clove, minced
2 tablespoons chopped fresh herbs: parsley, oregano, rosemary
In addition:
1/3 cup freshly grated Parmesan cheese

Prepare the polenta as described on page 226. Pour onto a moistened baking sheet, smooth it out into a sheet about 3/8 inch thick, and let cool. When the polenta has set, continue as shown in the picture sequence. To make the herb butter, melt the butter in a pan, briefly soften the garlic, and stir in the herbs. Place the baking dish in the oven preheated to 425°F and bake 11 minutes. Brown under the broiler.

Preparing gnocchi alla romana:

Using a 2 1/2-inch round pastry cutter, cut out ovals from the polenta.

Layer the ovals in a buttered baking dish so that they overlap like roof tiles. Sprinkle with the Parmesan.

Spoon the herb butter evenly over the gnocchi, ensuring that all of them are moistened.

Gnocchi alla romana *are traditionally made with semolina, which can be substituted for the polenta. The quantities given here are sufficient for 4 portions as a first course or for 2 portions as an entrée.*

Serviettenknödel – a classic German dish

These light dumplings usually accompany pot roasts. They need plenty of sauce

Chef Karl Eschelböck *is a perfectionist – baking his own bread for featherlight dumplings.*

Although most often served as a side-dish, *serviettenknödel* can be enjoyed on their own, freshly sliced and moistened with a little brown butter (*beurre noisette*) and, perhaps, with some grated cheese sprinkled on top. They really come into their own,

though, when accompanying meat dishes with plenty of sauce or gravy, and simpler dishes such as cèpes, chanterelles or other mushrooms in cream sauce. The name comes from the way the dumpling is cooked: wrapped in a cloth (*serviette*). The elongated shape of the serviettenknödel ensures that it cooks evenly, and makes it easy to cut in slices of equal thickness for serving. There are many variations to the basic dumpling dough, such as adding chopped fresh herbs, or a vegetable *brunoise* or sautéed minced mushrooms, or finely diced smoked ham.

Making serviettenknödel:

Put the cubes of bread in a large bowl and pour on the cold milk. Let soak until the bread is soft.

Add the onion and herb mixture, and the egg yolk and butter mixture, and mix well together.

Beat the egg whites until stiff. Fold into the bread mixture a few spoonfuls at a time.

With a spoon or wet hands, shape the mixture into an elongated sausage shape on the cloth. The dumpling should be of even thickness.

Roll up the dumpling in the cloth – loosely because it expands on cooking. Tie the cloth at both ends with string or twine.

Immerse in boiling salted water and partially cover the pan. Cook 45 minutes, turning the dumpling over halfway through.

SERVIETTENKNÖDEL WITH HERBS

The quantities given here are sufficient for 8 portions.

8 slightly stale small white rolls
1 onion, 9 tablespoons (1 stick + 1 tablespoon) butter
1/4 cup minced fresh parsley
1 tablespoon minced fresh basil
6 eggs, separated
1 teaspoon salt, a pinch of grated nutmeg
1 cup cold milk
In addition:
1 damp cloth or napkin, about 32 inches square
string or twine

Remove the crusts from the rolls and cut them in small cubes. Peel and mince the onion and soften in 1 1/2 tablespoons of butter. Mix in the herbs. Beat the remaining butter with the egg yolks until pale

and creamy, and season with salt and nutmeg. Continue as shown in the picture sequence. When cooked, remove the dumpling from the cloth and slice for serving.

SERVIETTENKNÖDEL

This is a particularly light dumpling, perfect as a side-dish with pot roasts and mushrooms. The quantities given are sufficient for 4 portions.

Roasts with gravy are perfect partners for this light bread dumpling.

$^{1}/_{2}$ *pound sliced white bread (about 10 thin slices), crusts removed*

4 tablespoons butter, 2 tablespoons minced onion

$^{3}/_{4}$ *cup cold milk, 2 eggs, 2 egg yolks*

salt and freshly ground pepper

freshly grated nutmeg

Cut the bread in small, even-sized cubes and place in a bowl. Melt the butter in a pan and soften the onion. Mix the onion with the bread and pour on the milk. Mix the eggs and egg yolks together, and season with salt, pepper, and nutmeg. Pour over the bread mixture and mix to a paste. Let rest at least 15 minutes. Shape the paste into an elongated dumpling. Put a large sheet of plastic wrap on a large piece of foil and place the dumpling on top. Fold the plastic and foil around the dumpling to make a neat package and seal well. The package should not be wrapped too tightly, since the dumpling expands slightly during the cooking process. Immerse the dumpling in a pan of boiling water and simmer 25 to 30 minutes.

A neat presentation is assured if your dumpling is of even thickness.

With cheese – hearty and delicious

Dumplings enriched with strong-flavored cheese are very popular

CHEESE DUMPLINGS

Tyrolean Graukäse
has a very strong flavor when well aged. If you cannot find Graukäse, you can use Emmental instead.

These tasty dumplings, called *kasnocken*, come from the southern Tyrol, where they are made with local cheeses such as Graukäse or Bergkäse. Emmental or a sharp Swiss cheese can also be used. The quantities listed here will make about 16 dumplings.

$^{1}/_{2}$ pound stale white bread (about 10 thin slices)
$^{7}/_{8}$ cup lukewarm milk, 1 small onion
$^{1}/_{2}$ pound Bergkäse or Emmental cheese
2 teaspoons butter, 2 tablespoons flour, 2 eggs, 1 egg yolk
2 tablespoons chopped fresh herbs: parsley, chives
salt and freshly ground white pepper
a pinch of freshly grated nutmeg
For serving:
6 tablespoons ($^{3}/_{4}$ stick) butter
$^{1}/_{2}$ cup freshly grated Parmesan cheese

Cut the bread in cubes, place in a small bowl, pour over the lukewarm milk, and let soak until soft. Peel and mince the onion. Cut the cheese in small cubes. Melt the butter in a small pan and sauté the onion until soft and golden. Mix with the bread and milk mixture, and add the cheese, flour, eggs, and egg yolk. Mix thoroughly. Add the herbs, and season with salt, pepper, and nutmeg. Moisten your hands with water. Take a tablespoon of the dough and shape into an egg-shaped dumpling. When all the dumplings have been shaped, put them in a pan of boiling salted water, reduce the heat, and let simmer gently until cooked through, 12 to 15 minutes. Remove carefully with a slotted spoon and drain on paper towels or a cloth. Heat the butter in a pan until it foams and begins to turn brown. Arrange the dumplings on pre-warmed plates, sprinkle with Parmesan, and drizzle the melted butter over. A green salad makes a welcome accompaniment.

BUCKWHEAT DUMPLINGS
WITH CHEESE

These delicious dumplings are hearty enough to be served as an entrée, with vegetables to accompany. The Tyrolean cheese, Graukäse, is the traditional one to use, but you can substitute Emmental. If coarsely ground buckwheat flour is not available, then use a food processor to grind the buckwheat yourself.

4 slices of stale white bread

3 slices of stale rye bread

^{2}/3 cup lukewarm milk

1 garlic clove, minced

1/4 cup minced onion

^{1}/2 cup leek cut in strips

1 ^{1}/2 tablespoons butter

2 tablespoons chopped fresh herbs: parsley, chives, lovage or celery leaves

^{1}/2 teaspoon salt, a pinch of freshly grated nutmeg

freshly ground white pepper, 2 eggs

^{2}/3 cup buckwheat flour

6 ounces aged Graukäse or Emmental

For serving:

6 to 8 tablespoons (^{3}/4 to 1 stick) butter

Crumble the bread into a bowl, pour the lukewarm milk over, and let soften at least 15 minutes. Sauté the garlic, onion, and leek in the hot butter until translucent; mix with the soaked bread. Add the chopped herbs, seasonings, eggs, and flour and mix to a light paste. Let rest 15 minutes. Cut the cheese in small cubes and knead into the paste. Shape into 12 small, round dumplings. Put the dumplings in a pan of boiling salted water, reduce the heat immediately, and simmer gently until the dumplings are cooked through, about 12 minutes. Remove from the water with a slotted spoon, drain, and arrange on plates. Pour plenty of foaming brown butter over, or serve with freshly cooked vegetables.

Buckwheat *has triangular seeds, which are ground to make buckwheat flour. Buckwheat groats are the hulled, crushed kernels, and when roasted are called kasha.*

Bread dumplings

Made with ham or fresh mushrooms, these are much too good to be a mere side-dish

BREAD DUMPLINGS WITH FRESH CÈPES

A treat for the autumn mushroom season. To make the most of their wonderful flavor, the dumplings must be served straight from the pan. The quantities given below will make about 12 dumplings.

8 slices of stale white bread, crusts removed
$^{1}/_{4}$ cup cream
$^{1}/_{2}$ cup milk
4 tablespoons butter, melted
3 eggs
$^{1}/_{2}$ teaspoon salt
freshly ground pepper
freshly grated nutmeg
1 pound fresh cèpes (porcini)
3 tablespoons minced shallots
1 garlic clove, minced
4 tablespoons butter
1 tablespoon chopped fresh parsley
1 teaspoon chopped fresh oregano
5 tablespoons flour

Cut the bread in very small cubes and place in a bowl. Pour the cream, milk, and melted butter over, add the eggs, and season with salt, pepper, and nutmeg. Clean the cèpes and cut in small cubes. Continue as shown in the picture sequence.

Preparing dumplings with cèpes:

Soften the shallots and garlic in the hot butter. Add the cèpes and sauté briefly, then sprinkle the herbs over.

Let the cèpe mixture cool before adding it to the bread and milk mixture. Add the flour and mix together to make malleable dough.

Divide the dough into 12 pieces and shape each into a round dumpling, moistening your hands to prevent sticking.

Put the dumplings in boiling salted water, reduce the heat, and cook until they float to the surface, about 12 minutes.

Foaming melted butter is the best sauce, together with some freshly grated Parmesan. With a crisp green salad, dumplings with cèpes make a splendid first course as well as an entrée.

The quality of the ham *is particularly important for this recipe. Westphalian or Bavarian smoked ham would be ideal.*

DUMPLINGS WITH HAM

Serve these with salad or with a vegetable such as asparagus for a light meal.

10 slices of stale white bread, crusts removed
3/4 cup lukewarm milk
1/2 teaspoon salt
freshly ground white pepper
freshly grated nutmeg
2 eggs
3 egg yolks
1/2 cup (1 stick) butter
2 tablespoons minced onion
1 1/2 cups diced mushrooms
3 cups diced lean cooked ham
3 tablespoons flour

Cut the white bread in small, even-sized cubes, put into a bowl, and pour the milk over. Season with salt, pepper, and nutmeg. Mix the eggs and egg yolks together, pour over the bread, and let soften. Melt half of the butter in a suitably sized pan and soften the onion, making sure it does not brown. Add the mushrooms and sauté briefly; let cool. Add the mushroom mixture, ham, and flour to the bread mixture and mix to a soft paste. Moisten your hands with water. Divide the paste into small pieces and shape each piece into a round dumpling. Place in a pan of boiling salted water, reduce the heat immediately, and simmer the dumplings until cooked through, about 12 minutes. Remove the dumplings with a slotted spoon and arrange on plates. Melt the remaining butter and drizzle over the dumplings.

A delicious variation can be made by adding some extra mushrooms. Clean 1/2 pound of any flavorful mushrooms and mince. Melt 1 1/2 tablespoons of butter in a pan and soften 1 tablespoon minced shallots. Add the mushrooms and sauté for a few minutes. Season with salt and pepper. After forming the dumplings, open them slightly and stuff the sautéed mushrooms into the center. Reshape the dumplings and cook as directed above.

Subject index

Recipes and culinary techniques